Teaching
Secondary Science

Second Edition

Related titles of interest:

Active Assessment Stuart Naylor and Brenda Keogh (1-84312-145-X)

Using Science to Develop Thinking Skills at Key Stage 3 Pat O'Brien (1-84312-037-2)

Problem-solving in Science and Technology: Extending Good Classroom Practice Mike Watts (1-85346-270-5)

Teaching
Secondary Science

Second Edition

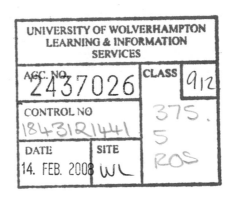
Keith Ross • Liz Lakin • Peter Callaghan

David Fulton Publishers

David Fulton Publishers
2 Park Square, Milton Park, Abingdon, Oxon OX14 4RN

270 Madison Avenue, New York, NY 10016

First published in Great Britain in 2000 by David Fulton Publishers
Transferred to digital printing

David Fulton Publishers is an imprint of the Taylor & Francis Group, an informa business

British Library Cataloguing in Publication Data
A catalogue record for this book is available from the British Library.

ISBN 1 84312 144 1

Typeset by FiSH Books, London

Contents

Preface

Our approach to teaching secondary science is based on a constructivist approach to learning where we expose children's existing ideas, so they can be challenged or built on to enable them to understand their environment and build a sustainable future. The book takes account of the following documents:

- The DfEE document *Qualifying to Teach*.
  1   Professional Values and Practice.
  2   Knowledge and Understanding.
  3.1 Teaching: Planning, Expectations and targets.
  3.2 Monitoring and Assessment.
  3.3 Teaching and Classroom Management.
- National Curriculum for England 2000.
- The Key Stage (KS) 3 National Strategy for Science.
- The QCA Schemes of Work for science at KS 3 and citizenship at KS 3 and 4.

The five parts of this book are linked to the three standards above for gaining Qualified Teacher Status:

- *Professional values and practice.* We need to know what science is all about and we need to justify its place in the curriculum (Parts I and V of this book).
- *Knowledge and understanding.* We need to understand what ideas pupils bring with them, and how best to introduce new (and sometimes strange) scientific ideas to them (Part III).
- *Teaching: planning, assessment, teaching and classroom management.* Our planning must take account of individual needs, our teaching must allow time for pupils to make sense of the new ideas and experiences we offer and our management needs to be sensitive and effective (Parts II and IV).

The Association for Science Education (ASE) website now has downloadable support material for tutors in science education, including many links to other useful websites (visit www.ase.org.uk/sci-tutors).

We have written a CD-ROM, *Science Issues and the National Curriculum* (Ross et al. 2002), which covers most of the topics in the science National Curriculum. It uses a constructivist approach to developing an understanding in science, and sets the science in everyday or environmental contexts, an approach that we put forward in this book (details at www.glos.ac.uk/science-issues).

Science and Why We Teach It

Introduction

Science deals with ideas about our environment. These scientific ideas must be tested against our sense experiences. Progress in science happens when our existing ideas are challenged and we have to invent new theories that deal with the anomalies better. Thus germ theory deals with transmission of diseases better than traditional beliefs, yet BSE in cows seems to be transmitted by a prion vector whose mechanism is not yet accepted. Newton's ideas about gravity have been superseded by Einstein's theory of relativity, but there are still inconsistencies between relativity and quantum mechanics. Scientific ideas are never complete or absolutely true.

In the same way, children build up pictures of the world in their minds, simple pictures that help them make sense of the data they receive from their senses. Babies soon recognise 'down-ness' as they look for their dropped rattle on the floor – they don't look for it on the ceiling! But these naive ideas get replaced as children need to make their mental models more widely applicable, as 'down-ness' transforms to notions of 'gravity'.

As science teachers we must understand some of these naive ideas and help children to develop alternative, more powerful, scientific ways of interpreting their environment that can go alongside their 'everyday' beliefs. Children need time to reconstruct their ideas to take account of the scientific theories that we presently hold, and to appreciate that they will change over time. They also need to appreciate that the process by which the ideas came into being, the very process of being scientific, forms an important part of their scientific education, encapsulated in the National Curriculum Orders for England (DfEE 1999): Science One, *Scientific Enquiry*.

However, in order to help children to understand their world in this scientific way they must be in a safe learning environment. A single teacher deals with approximately 30 pupils, many of whom need to be convinced that their time in school is worthwhile. As science teachers we must also understand how to create a pleasant working atmosphere in our classes, where children feel safe, and where we can expect them to do their best.

These two facets – *teaching science* and *teaching pupils* – are at the heart of being a successful science teacher, allowing the pupils in our charge to come to enjoy, understand and use the scientific way of viewing their world.

The aim of the first part of this book (Chapters 1–3) is to look at the way scientific ideas have developed over time and to compare this with the task our pupils have in coming to understand those ideas themselves. We cannot expect pupils to do this unaided, but we do need to start with their existing ideas, and we need to give them time to test out, practically and verbally, these new and often strange ideas that are part of our present-day scientific understanding.

We begin in the laboratory (Chapters 1 and 2), but then move out into the real world of our pupils: their environment and their future. As science teachers we need to provide an understanding of the need to make this a *sustainable* future (Chapter 3).

Practical work in science

As science teachers we need to start by thinking about what science is and does. In this chapter we develop a model of how science works, and later use this to show the enormous task science teachers have to achieve. Where humanity has taken centuries to develop an understanding of how our world works, our pupils must do the same in only a few years. Because the path humanity has taken is validated by experiment, we start this book by examining the role practical work has to play in school.

The National Curriculum for England (DfEE 1999) has now merged ideas about the nature of science and investigation methods into the programme of study called *Scientific Enquiry*, assessed through Attainment Target 1. This chapter examines three issues that relate to Scientific Enquiry (see Chapter 27 for further discussion):

- developing a model of what it means to be scientific;
- carrying out scientific investigations in school;
- examining the purposes of practical work in school science.

Being scientific

As science teachers we need to reflect on our own learning in science and consider what people think science to be. Consider these two questions:

1   What do scientists do?

2   What does it mean *to be scientific*?

To help you, try sorting these words into a concept map or flow diagram to show how they are linked – add extra words or omit some as needed.

Experiment	Communicate	Notice things
Predict	Discover	Hypothesise
Observe	Search for the truth	Have ideas
Make theories	Test ideas	Investigate

Now consider questions 3 and 4, first for science and then for technology:

3   What is the product of science/technology?
4   What is the purpose of science/technology?

Being scientific: discussion of questions 1 and 2

Until the middle of the twentieth century philosophers of science thought that science was the quest for absolute truth, and that the 'laws of nature' could be *induced* from the observations we made. Karl Popper (1959), Thomas Kuhn (1970) and philosophers since then have shown that scientific ideas are simply that – ideas, created in our minds to try to explain what we perceive. To be scientific an idea must be testable using our senses (or extensions of them through measuring equipment) in experiments and observations. A fuller picture is developed in Chapter 27.

A simple picture of how science starts may look like that shown in Figure 1.1a. This diagram shows how we all try to make sense of our everyday world – our ideas are expressed as the words of our everyday conversations. Science questions these everyday experiences we take for granted. Scientists realise that our naive ideas do not tell the whole picture, so they modify the ideas or create new ones. These ideas must be tested against our experiences, through controlled experiments or observations. When they are happy that the ideas and experiences seem to match they will publish their findings. Figure 1.1b is a continuation of Figure 1.1a to show the way scientific ideas develop. We cannot expect pupils to make this scientific leap of imagination from naive science, so our job as teachers is to share these scientific insights with our pupils and allow them to test and try the ideas out. We explore this teaching role in Chapter 6.

Science and technology: discussion of questions 3 and 4

Science and technology are intimately entwined, but they can easily be distinguished by thinking about what each produces:

■   the products of science are ideas and theories, communicated through publications and by word of mouth;

■   the products of technology, in contrast, are artefacts and processes – things and procedures we want or need.

The purpose of science is to try to make sense of our environment, whereas technology's purpose is to satisfy our needs (and wants) through making things (such as sliced bread) or developing processes (such as keyhole surgery). Nowadays they are so interdependent that it is not easy to see this essential difference.

The scientific investigation in school

Investigations are needed after you have noticed something interesting, and had an idea of what might be going on. Ideas come from the creative side of science (*guesswork*), but they must be investigated carefully, which is part of the logical (*checkwork*) side (Medawar 1969). It is this *checkwork* that people usually think of as 'the scientific method', and they forget about the ovals in Figure 1.1a and b – the creative side of science. We explore this further in Chapter 27.

To illustrate this, here is an investigation you might do with a Key Stage 3 class.

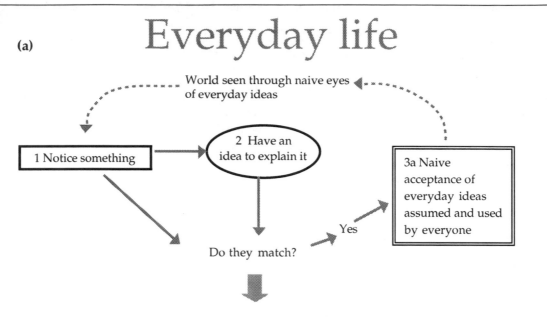

(a)

Everyday life

World seen through naive eyes of everyday ideas

1 Notice something

2 Have an idea to explain it

3a Naive acceptance of everyday ideas assumed and used by everyone

Do they match?

Yes

Science starts when we begin to question and test our naive ideas

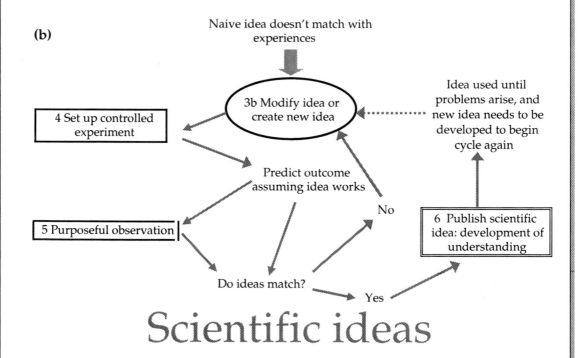

(b)

Naive idea doesn't match with experiences

4 Set up controlled experiment

3b Modify idea or create new idea

Idea used until problems arise, and new idea needs to be developed to begin cycle again

Predict outcome assuming idea works

5 Purposeful observation

No

6 Publish scientific idea: development of understanding

Do ideas match?

Yes

Scientific ideas

FIGURE 1.1 (a) A simplified picture of how we develop our everyday ideas. (b) The scientific method: ideas are generated and tested.

Electricity from metals in a lemon

You notice that when a copper and a zinc strip are pushed into a lemon, a voltage is generated between the two metal plates. What is going on?

In order to get a satisfactory answer, we need to work through the following stages. They are based on a series of planning boards providing support for primary teachers (Goldsworthy and Feasey 1999; KS 3 Strategy 2003). They use a very clear system for helping pupils with investigations that keeps a careful and separate track of input and output variables. This is linked with the *Scientific Enquiry* requirements of KS 3 (numbers in parentheses after each bullet point are from the National Curriculum: DfEE 1999: 28).

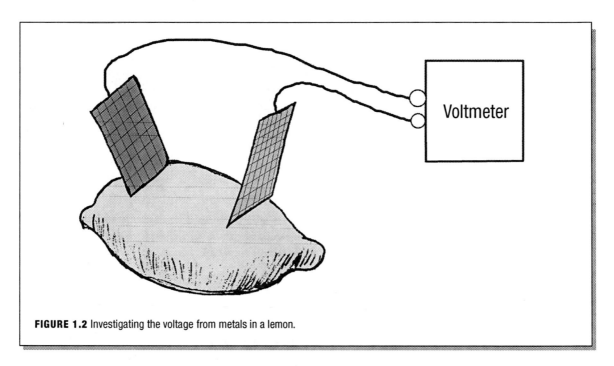

FIGURE 1.2 Investigating the voltage from metals in a lemon.

- *Reframe question.* This turns ideas into a form you can actually investigate. 'Since electrical energy is available, perhaps it is caused by a reaction between the metal and the lemon juice? We need to see what factors affect the voltage' (2a).

- *Brainstorm.* This identifies the input, or independent, variables: things we could change that might affect the voltage (type of metals, size of plates, distance apart, type of fruit juice etc.). We identified the output or dependent variable as the voltage. Although we have decided to measure the voltage, we could look for other outcomes, e.g. signs of chemical reaction (2d).

- *Deciding what to do.* Here we identify which variable we will change. All the others must therefore be kept constant (controlled variables), a process we call *fair testing*. We also need to identify those that we will measure or observe as a result of the change we make (our output or dependent variable). We may have to do preliminary work to help to set controlled variables at a sensible value (for example, if we decide to change the metals, we need first of all to see whether the size and distance apart might affect the voltage, so we can set these at a suitable constant value) (2c).

- *Asking a question.* Here we identify the question we are examining. 'If we start with both metals the same, when I exchange one of the metals with a different metal, what happens to the voltage?'
- *What I think may happen.* Here we make a prediction of what we think might happen, with a justification. 'As the metals become increasingly different in their reactivity I expect a more vigorous reaction, and so a higher voltage' (1b).
- *Safety.* Check that our experiments are safe (2f).
- *What happened.* Set up a table to record our results (2g).
- *Carry out the investigation.* Recording as we go (2h).
- *Graph of results.* Display our results, using a graph or bar chart if possible (2i and j).
- *What we found out.* Do our results agree with our idea? What have we learnt? (2k, l and m).

Preliminary or trial runs allow us to make decisions about what value we will fix for the variables we keep constant (controlled). Trial runs also give us an idea of the limits of accuracy that we can hope to work within. In school we usually do these in advance for our pupils – though occasionally we need to let the pupils 'flounder'.

Types of variables and their names

Figure 1.3 is a directed activity related to text (a 'DART', see Chapter 9) that aims to help to sort out types of variable. Investigations become more complex as discrete variables (far apart/close together) become continuous (distance apart in centimetres), and as you attempt to investigate more than one input variable at a time. Table 1.1 suggests what is appropriate at different levels of attainment (National Curriculum, p. 74, on levels of attainment in Science One).

TABLE 1.1 Variables and level of attainment

| Type and number of input variables | | Level of attainment | Appropriate mode of display |
Categoric	Continuous		
1		4	Bar chart
	1	5	Line graph
2		6	Bar + bar
	2	7	Line + line

At Level 4 pupils might have asked whether the voltage changes when we pushed the metals in deep, compared with shallow, whereas at Level 7 pupils could investigate separation distance *and* depth of metals, both measured in millimetres.

We return to investigations in Chapter 19, particularly how they are assessed as coursework for GCSE. While they represent the main focus for practical work by practising scientists, practical work in school has a number of other purposes, which we discuss next.

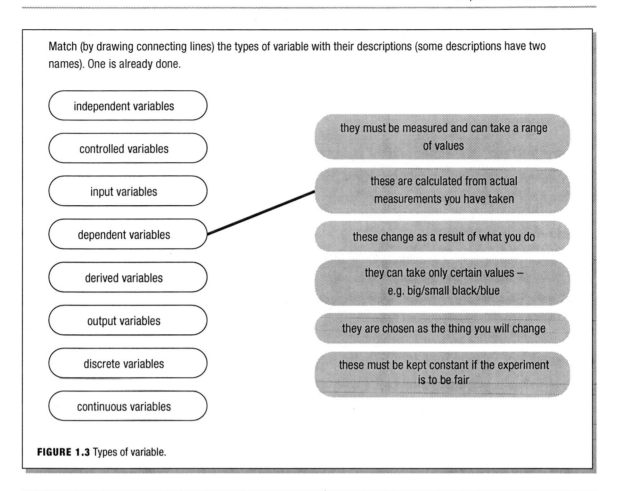

Match (by drawing connecting lines) the types of variable with their descriptions (some descriptions have two names). One is already done.

- independent variables
- controlled variables
- input variables
- dependent variables
- derived variables
- output variables
- discrete variables
- continuous variables

- they must be measured and can take a range of values
- these are calculated from actual measurements you have taken
- these change as a result of what you do
- they can take only certain values – e.g. big/small black/blue
- they are chosen as the thing you will change
- these must be kept constant if the experiment is to be fair

FIGURE 1.3 Types of variable.

The purposes of practical work

Science teaching in the UK is dominated by practical work. We must ensure that we can justify the time we devote to it. Eight activities are described below involving the process of rusting. They are designed to help us to focus on the role played by practical work in science lessons, but note that not all of them are practical work in the strict sense.

■ Which of these are best in helping pupils to *understand* what happens during rusting? (They may, for example, think that the iron 'rots' like wood – an idea we need to challenge.)

■ Which give a good picture of the *process* of being scientific? (Following the stages in Figure 1.1b.)

■ Which are unhelpful in both respects? (Perhaps because they are too complex, or don't allow the pupils to think.)

1 'Nail tubes': iron nails left in four test tubes

This is the traditional experiment where pupils place clean iron nails in four tests tubes:

(a) Anhydrous calcium chloride at the bottom, covered by cotton wool, then the nail, and closed with a bung (a).

(b) Nail completely covered with freshly boiled water. This is covered with a layer of oil (b).

(c) Cover half the nail with water and leave it in the tube exposed to the air (c).

(d) Cover half the nail with salty water and leave it in the tube exposed to the air (d).

Leave the four tubes for a week and comment on your findings. Result: only the nails in tubes (c) and (d) have rusted.

2 'Water and air': are water and air both needed for rusting?

Begin the lesson by acknowledging that most people agree that water is needed for iron to rust. Talk about the way some iron objects have been preserved in boggy or muddy conditions (Roman nails, *Mary Rose* cannon) where the air cannot reach. We might conclude that air and water are both needed for rusting to be successful.

- When the discussion is over ask each group of pupils to design an experiment to test the idea *that air and water are both needed for rusting*.
- Make sure they say (predict) what they think might happen before carrying out the experiment, and explain why they think that.

3 'Damp fibre': damp iron 'wool' (better called 'fibre') left in a tube over water

This is another experiment often performed in school.

- Place some damp iron fibre at the bottom of a boiling tube.
- Invert the tube, with the damp iron and air in it, over a beaker of water, and clamp it so that most of the tube is above the water line.
- Leave it for two hours and then look at the water level inside the tube, and observe the iron for rust.

Can you explain why the water has risen up into the tube and the iron has gone rusty?

4 'Air is used': someone suggested that *air is used up* when iron rusts

Start with a similar discussion to 2 above. If air is involved perhaps it is actually used up when iron rusts. Get pupils to design a way to test this idea.

- 'Say what you think will happen if air really is used up when iron rusts.'
- 'Say what you think will happen if rusting does not use up air.'
- 'Finally, record what actually happened, and comment on the results.'

5 'Weight': weight changes on rusting

Tell this story to your pupils:

Two iron nails, both weighing the same, were left to go completely rusty – no iron metal was left, there was simply a pile of rust. If you could collect all the rust up from one of the nails and weigh it, would the pile of rust weigh more, the same or less than the original nail? If you did the same with the second nail, would the result be about the same as the first, or could it be completely different?

This question addresses many misconceptions people have about rusting:

- some think it has been eaten away, so gets lighter;
- some think a mould has grown on it, so it may get heavier, but the two nails would not behave in exactly the same way.

When they have recorded their answer say: 'Each nail had a mass of 10 g. The pile of rust from each nail had a mass of nearly 15 g. So, on weighing, we found both the iron nails got heavier.' The pupils can now discuss this result in their groups. If necessary they need to change the reason they gave originally. They could think up another experiment they could do to see if their (new) idea was right.

6 'Protecting': protecting iron from rusting

Get your pupils to think of all the ways we protect iron from going rusty (bikes, buses, bridges, boats etc.). For each method see if they can think how it works. You could provide reference books for them.

7 'Other metals': do all metals rust?

Get your pupils to put small samples of a range of metals on damp cotton wool. They can predict which will 'rust'. *Result*: only the iron will rust (go rust coloured) but many of the others will corrode, usually forming whitish coatings.

8 'At Home': nails left at home

Ask them to take two clean bright nails home and leave one in a place that they think will make it go rusty, and the other in a place where it will stay shiny. They bring them in a week later, mounted on card to say where they were placed and whether they thought they would rust or not. Arrange them along a bench or wall display from most to least rusty (Driver *et al.* 1994: 11 and 12). We will undoubtedly find that many nails left in very wet places have not rusted as much as the pupils thought they would.

Those kept dry will have remained shiny. The lesson can now explore the ideas children have about rusting, and could lead to investigations (such as 2 and 4 above) to test out new ideas to explain why rusting did not happen as much as they thought.

Discussion

In this discussion of these eight activities, they are referred to by their number and short name.

We need to be very clear what *purpose* practical work serves, especially when it can appear to be 'recipe-following'. 1 'Nail tubes' and 3 'Damp fibre' can both be undertaken with very little (mental) involvement by the pupils. In 1 'Nail tubes' the use of strange words and substances, such as *anhydrous*, only helps to make the investigation more obscure. The inclusion of salt, although useful when we come to an electrolytic explanation of rusting, is unhelpful at this preliminary stage when we are trying to show the part air plays. These same two investigations would arise from the discussions in 2 'Water and air' and 4 'Air is used', but this time pupils would have had a far greater sense of ownership of the investigation, and would have *predicted* possible outcomes.

The role of air in rusting

Pupils will not normally think about the role of air, which is shown by the first four investigations. However, by getting the pupils to participate in the *design* of the investigation, we immediately allow them to see its purpose. The discussion arising from 8 'At home', where they bring their own nails in, illustrates an ideal situation that mirrors the process of the scientific method from Figure 1.1a and b: we notice water causes rusting, so we test this idea, but our nails don't rust much. Perhaps air is needed as well.

This would lead children to plan an investigation, 4 'Air is used'. They will see that the water level does rise so they will begin to believe that air (or a part of it) has joined the iron. This may lead them to predict that it will increase in weight. 5 'Weight' is a very slow experiment to do but the faster process of igniting and blowing on 10 g of iron fibre while it is resting on ceramic paper on a top pan balance (hazard: wear eye protection) involves combustion rather than rusting and may not be seen by pupils as analogous. However, we can *give* results to pupils – a case where we can still learn from the experiment without actually performing it.

6 'Protecting' is an extension of this approach. Practical experiments are not the only, or necessarily the best, way for pupils to understand scientific ideas. 7 'Other metals' is an important investigation for pupils to do practically, not so much to learn about ways of investigating, though we need to keep all the metals in similar conditions; in this case the practical work gives experiences that pupils will not normally get from their everyday lives.

Between them, these eight activities introduce pupils to ideas about rusting and the process of being scientific. Some focus more on the *process* (2 'Water and air' and 4 'Air is used') and others more on *ideas* about rusting (5–8). A couple, 1 'Nail tubes' and 3 'Damp fibre', are *recipes*, discussed in the next subsection.

Meaningless recipes

Unless we are very careful about setting them up, 1 'Nail tubes' and 3 'Damp fibre' are in danger of being undertaken as a recipe with no purpose and from which pupils will learn little. This can be especially true of the traditional approach of 1 'Nail tubes', if the expressions *anhydrous calcium chloride* and *freshly boiled water* are not fully explored. Until pupils understand what function these strangely named materials play they will follow the instructions, but without meaning. 'Stuff to make the air dry' and 'water which has had all the dissolved air removed' would be better terms to use at KS 3. Both of these assume that pupils realise that air can contain water (vapour) and water can contain (dissolved) air. These are important ideas that need to be explored before undertaking this rusting investigation; they can be linked to the formation of dew and clouds (damp air) and the fact that water-dwelling animals, such as fish and water fleas, use dissolved air for respiration. Our aim must be to give purpose to all practical work, a point we discuss next.

Analysis of practical work

Sutton (1992: 2) recognises three kinds of practical work:

- experiencing a phenomenon;
- exercising a measurement skill or some other useful procedure from the craftsmanship of science;
- investigating in the sense of carrying out a small enquiry in the scientific tradition.

He makes a strong case for giving pupils time each side of any practical work to enable them to think:

the national curriculum specifies an entitlement to be involved in planning as well as doing investigations. This goes some way towards ensuring that the practical activities will be adequately embedded in a process of grappling with scientific ideas, but more generally there remains a problem of connecting practical work with the discussion and appreciation of ideas [approached through] WORD WORK as the core of a science lesson.

(Sutton 1992: 2)

Time for *word work* has now been recognised by the KS 3 strategy, in the importance it places on plenaries in lessons where your pupils can reflect on what the lesson is all about.

Practical work has many uses in science – it is important that we identify the purpose every time we plan practical activities with children. We finish this section on practical work by drawing together Sutton's classification (see above) and his plea for time to grapple with ideas, with the rusting examples we have used. Below are some of the most important reasons why we do practical work:

Gaining experiences

Before children can begin to think about why something happens they must have experienced it. An important part of our work at KS 3 will be in this category, e.g. 7 'Other metals' or an opportunity to experience (safely!) the 50 cycles per second of AC mains electricity (see Box 1.1).

- Describing, sorting, classifying (similarities and differences);
- A starting point for investigations, questions, predictions, hypotheses.

Hold a very strong small magnet in your clenched fist, and hold it near a transformer working off the mains (e.g. a lab pack). When you switch the transformer on you feel the 50 cycles per second vibration as the cycling magnetic field from the mains drags the magnet to and fro.

BOX 1.1 Experiencing 50 hertz mains

Illustrations

When you have challenged children's ideas about why something happens you may want them to test out this new idea you are giving them in a controlled environment, e.g. 1 'Nail tubes' and 3 'Damp fibre', or asking them to feel their heart beat after exercise to suggest a link between blood flow and supplying food and air to the muscles.

- giving instructions of what to do;
- illustrating concept or process for discussion.

Making observations

Observations cannot be naive. What we observe is always a combination of the ideas stored in our brains and the sense data we receive. Each child will observe only what they are able to make sense of. Asking children to 'observe' carefully is a good way of finding out what ideas they do have in their minds, e.g. 2 'Water and air', 4 'Air is used' and 8 'At home'. Few children will arrive at the rusting lesson thinking that rust is an oxide. See Chapter 2 for a further discussion of observation.

■ Opportunity for making use of knowledge and understanding.

Basic skills

Sometimes it is important to teach children how to use a particular technique or piece of equipment. It is much better to embed such introductions into an investigation, but the newness of the task means that you want the investigation to be simple, e.g. 1 'Nail tubes' and 3 'Damp fibre', or learning to use a microscope by examining bits and pieces they find around the room.

■ selecting or using equipment;

■ display skills (e.g. graphs);

■ techniques (e.g. measuring force, temperature etc.).

Motivation

Practical work is said to motivate children, and we sometimes threaten withdrawal of practical work as a way of encouraging good behaviour, in the knowledge that pupils usually enjoy *doing*. However, practical work that lacks purpose and focus cannot provide that motivation – it will be just another recipe for the pupils to work through.

■ There are many ways to motivate pupils. The main thing is to convince them that what they are doing is important and useful, e.g. 8 'At home'.

Investigations

This could be described as the ultimate aim of children's practical work in school. 2 'Water and air', 4 'Air is used', 7 'Other metals' and 8 'At home' are whole investigations, but 5 'Weight' is very much an investigation too, though pupils only do a *part* of it. The investigation of the voltage from metals in a lemon is another example.

■ Investigations arise from observations, discussions and ideas that need testing.

■ Investigations encourage pupils to think, plan, carry out and interpret.

■ Pupils don't have to do whole investigations – see Chapter 19 for a discussion of *partial* investigations at GCSE.

We need to re-examine all the practical activities we ask pupils to do in school. We shouldn't give them to the class simply to do 'because this experiment has always been done this way'. We need to consider if there are better ways to use the time.

Summary

In this chapter we explored the nature of science, and the need to clarify the purpose of practical work in schools. Chapter 2 looks at this scientific process from the starting point of the pupils. They come with naive ideas about their world that we need to become aware of as teachers. Only then can we help them to see the wonder and power of scientific explanations that have been developed over the ages. We have only a few years to do what has taken humanity centuries, but we must be successful in this if they are to leave school with an understanding of how their planet works – an understanding that should help them to look after it (Chapter 3).

2

Observation always has purpose

This chapter shows that no observation is theory-free. To illustrate this we use what, to many pupils, is a 'silly' idea: that matter is made up of unchanging particles. Pupils would not spontaneously take on this counter-intuitive point of view. Water, for example, may form droplets, but they soon join up to form the liquid again.

We examine the huge problem we set our pupils in asking them to take on this revolutionary idea over the space of a few years, during their tender teens. At the same time, we can examine the process of observation. Our aim as science teachers is to bring pupils from their naive acceptance of phenomena towards a greater use of scientific models to explain them.

We only see what our brains allow us to see

Ask a fashion designer, a doctor, an architect, a parent and a motor mechanic to walk along the high street and then ask them to describe what they saw – all will give a different picture. Ask them to walk through the rain forest of an Amazonian Amerindian and they will see none of the complex detail that the tribal people take for granted. In your home town you feel at ease, you know where everything is and what each noise means; but a stranger, receiving exactly the same sensory data, can become bewildered and lost.

This section will show that naive observation is not possible. The myth of objective scientists, able to collect data without putting any of their own ideas into what is collected, has long been put to rest.

The scientific method could be summarised by the words: 'purposeful observation'. Observation is a product of the interaction of sensory data and the prior concepts that are stored in our memories. These mental concepts influence what we look for, and thus what we perceive. Those who are blind from birth and have their sight restored take weeks or months to learn what the light inputs to their eyes mean. Those setting foot in a land whose language they do not understand receive the same sounds as the natives but make no sense of them. Only later do they begin to make sense of what they hear.

To most people the clear circles on Alexander Fleming's agar plates meant nothing, but Fleming, a microbiologist, saw moulds killing bacteria. Darwin had seen selective breeding among pigeons at home, and saw the same thing with Galapagos finches. Others would have taken no notice. Mendel, a trained mathematician, saw huge significance in his 3:1 ratio of tall to short peas, but his results failed to impress his peers.

You may feel uncomfortable that we are saying that scientists are biased in their observations: aren't they supposed to be objective? The answer is that objective observation is meaningless, it cannot be done. When we observe, our minds are trying to make sense by comparing our existing ideas with our sense data. Consider this scenario, acted out in a GCSE science lesson on photosynthesis where leaves (left in the dark and the light) are tested for starch:

> As teachers we make sense of the scientific words written on the worksheet and of the iodine going black on one leaf but not on the other, which was kept in the dark. We connect this all together with our picture of the process we call photosynthesis.
>
> Many pupils, however, see strange words on bottles and go through a complex series of processes with a couple of leaves, one of which goes black. They dutifully write, 'This shows that photosynthesis requires light'. Without the complex set of ideas held by the teacher, pupils make little sense of this wonderful 'experiment'.

The creative side to science

Theories can be useful but they can only ever be an approximation to the truth. As we saw in Chapter 1, they are created in our minds, but they must be tested against reality – this provides a clear distinction between the creativity of Newton (Laws of Motion) and of Shakespeare (*Macbeth*).

This approach to scientific creativity is illustrated in this chapter by consideration of the idea that matter is made of indestructible particles in motion: the *kinetic theory of matter*. Many children find this model unhelpful. Water is clearly not made of little bits, unless it is rain, and then the drops join up again. Many children find the idea that particles (atoms) persist through evaporation and burning very hard to conceptualise: *their* particles are bits of real matter that 'evaporate to nothing' or get 'burnt up'.

To show how difficult it is to relinquish the idea that matter is continuous, look at Figure 2.1, where an undergraduate, with A-level science, has illustrated an adventure story of a water molecule. The water molecules, HOH, are in the mouth, with salt particles (shown as separate ions, but labelled *atoms*). But what is this watery solution in which the particles swim? The idea that matter is nothing *but* these particles is difficult for this student to grasp. How much harder is it for pupils at KS 3? We explore this idea further in the next section.

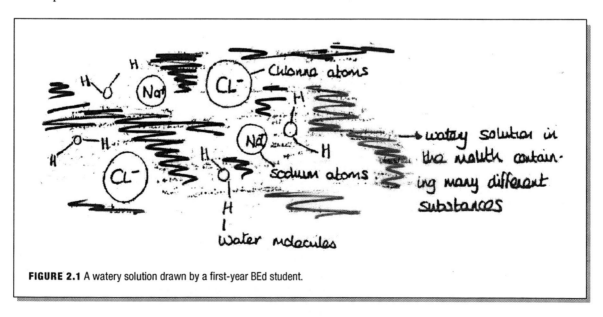

FIGURE 2.1 A watery solution drawn by a first-year BEd student.

Matter is made of indestructible particles called atoms

We, as science graduates, already have the idea of atoms in our minds, so when we observe phenomena related to matter and materials, we see things differently from those who do not possess this idea. Our ideas influence the way we see things. As teachers we need to help pupils to see the power of the atomic view of our world – without it they will understand few of the environmental pressures we are placing on the planet. For them petrol will burn away in cars, aerosols will disappear into thin air, rubbish will rot away to nothing.

It took decades of careful measurement of combining weights before Dalton worked out what it could all mean. His revolutionary atomic theory took several more decades to be accepted following its publication in 1810, but by 1869 Mendeleev had published his ideas about the periodic table, which we accept today. Two thousand years before all this the Greeks and, one thousand years later, the Islamic scientists both used notions of matter being made of atoms, but their atoms were not well defined and their ideas were difficult to test (Butt 1991). The National Key Stage 3 Strategy for science has recognised *particles* as one of five *key ideas* that pupils need to gain a scientific understanding of the world.

Consider a china cup, half full of water and half full of air. Figure 2.2 shows possible *models* for the arrangement of particles in a solid (china), a liquid (water) and a gas (air), all at room temperature. As a simplification we will consider the particles making them up as being spheres of equal size. Which of these represents the particles in the solid, the liquid and the gas?

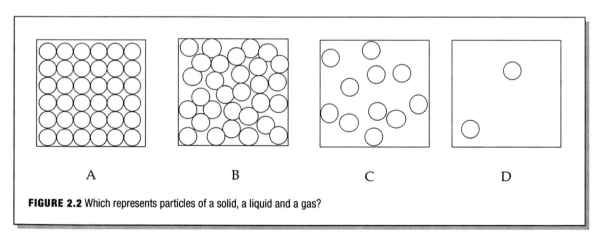

FIGURE 2.2 Which represents particles of a solid, a liquid and a gas?

There is no problem in choosing A for the solid. Many textbooks, however, suggest that particles in a liquid are spaced out, relative to the solid, so you may have chosen C for the liquid. But liquids are virtually incompressible and have densities of the same order as solids. The particles must therefore still be in contact, but now randomly distributed and able to slide past each other. In contrast, gases are about 1000 times less dense than solids and liquids, so even D has particles too close for a gas at atmospheric pressure.

Now consider how energetic the particles are. *Kinetic* theory suggests movement but the idea that particles of a solid are vibrating is not easy for pupils to accept. If we accept that the particles of the solid china are moving, are the particles of the water moving with less, the same or with more energy? What about the particles of gas? Remember they are all at the same temperature.

Because most textbooks show ice turning to water then to steam, we have grown to believe that particles of a gas move with more energy than those of a solid at the same temperature. But the energy of a particle depends only on temperature. At absolute zero they are essentially at rest. Substances at equal temperature do not exchange heat energy (this is how equal temperature is defined). That implies that their particles must also have the same average energy – otherwise the more energetic particles will knock the less energetic ones, transferring energy from one substance to the other. If particles of a gas do not move with extra energy why does diffusion take place more quickly in gases? And what makes some substances stay as a gas at room temperature when others, with the same energy per particle, remain solid? Although the energy of movement is the same, the freedom to move is not: particles of a gas move from place to place, whereas in the condensed state movement is mostly vibrational. The state of a substance depends on the strength of the forces between its particles. Materials that are gases at room temperature have small forces; those that are solids have larger forces between the particles. Let us consider these misconceptions one by one.

Review of particle misconceptions and ideas for challenging them

Misconception 1: atoms burn

Children often assume that our particles are bits of ordinary matter that melt, boil, burn and expand. But our particles are different and very strange. They can be used to explain what happens when substances melt, expand, get hot or get dirty, but nothing happens to the actual particles themselves. Matter is conserved at an atomic level (except in radioactive processes). This conservation of matter (mass) during physical and, especially, chemical change can only be fully appreciated if we consider matter as being made up of *indestructible*, unchanging particles that simply reorganise or rearrange themselves when real materials change (e.g. burning). It is helpful to recall that the Greek word that gave us *atom* means *indivisible*.

Idea for teaching

■ Think of a toy car made of Lego bricks. When you make it into a different model, e.g. a person, the car goes and the person appears (like bulk matter changes), but the actual bricks are unchanged, just rearranged (like the atoms).

Misconception 2: half-way liquids

Many pupils show the arrangement of particles of liquids as being 'half way' between a solid and a gas (Figure 2.2 C rather than B).

Ideas for teaching

■ Fill a 50 ml syringe with air and another with water. Try compressing them and you will find that it is impossible to compress the water. Indeed, try suggesting that after your glass of pop is filled you could squash it down and put more in – your pupils will ridicule you. But no one will complain if you attempt to pump more air into a football that is 'full'.

■ Use a hairdrier to blow air gently through a bed of tiny polystyrene balls (fluidised bed *model* of liquids). The whole solid mass of balls gets no larger in volume, but behaves like a liquid if you shake the tube.

Misconception 3: fast gases

Many people (and textbooks) assume that particles of a gas must be moving with more energy than those of a liquid or solid. This is only true if the gas is at a higher temperature than the solid or liquid. Where the particle masses are different (as in the demonstration in Figure 2.3) the more massive particles will move at a lower speed, keeping their kinetic energy the same.

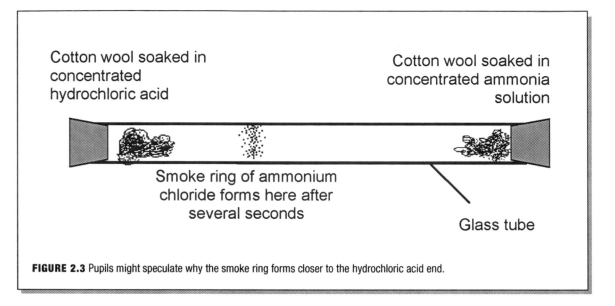

Cotton wool soaked in concentrated hydrochloric acid

Cotton wool soaked in concentrated ammonia solution

Smoke ring of ammonium chloride forms here after several seconds

Glass tube

FIGURE 2.3 Pupils might speculate why the smoke ring forms closer to the hydrochloric acid end.

Ideas for teaching

- Brownian motion. This is best viewed by the whole class using a flexicam attached to a TV or LCD projector. Individual observations of smoke under a microscope by pupils is notoriously difficult to achieve (Driver 1983). There is a video clip of Brownian motion on the CD that accompanies the Intel Play digital microscope primary schools received during science year, and putting 'Brownian motion' into *Google* will give you a web version.

- We can show diffusion in solids (a drop of food colouring placed on agar gel spreads out over a number of days), liquids (a drop of food colouring in hot water spreads over several minutes and faster than in cold water) and gases (set up the ammonia and hydrochloric acid demonstration (Figure 2.3), but note COSHH regulations).

- Pupils can act out being particles. Use one pace per second (back and forth for solid; keeping in contact but making some headway for liquids; and moving in straight lines until you hit something for gases).

All these give evidence of particles in motion. However, the reason why diffusion in solids is slow is not because the particles have less energy, but because they vibrate essentially in one place, and these diffusion experiences will reinforce this misconception unless we are careful to link it only to freedom to move. By using hot and cold water the link between faster movement and higher temperature can be seen. Solid state diffusion is achieved only because crystals have imperfections, allowing atoms to move into spaces – an important process in the heat treatment of alloys.

Other ideas for teaching about particles

For all particle work we need to distinguish a *model* (trying to explain what we observe) from a *phenomenon* (something that actually happens).

For *models*, we need to remember that scientific theories are all analogies or models: none is true, all have their faults. We need to consider the good and bad points of each model we see or use in our explanations. Where is it useful, where does it break down? Examples include:

- Comparing 'pouring' a beaker of peas with a beaker of sand to model the phenomenon of pouring water (doesn't explain why diffusion occurs, doesn't explain surface tension).
- Using the vibrator model of gas and computer models for solid, liquid and gas (doesn't explain surface tension).
- Imaginative writing (model in the mind) such as Figure 2.1.
- Creating a bubble raft model of metals, where bubbles can slip past each other while being attracted together (helps with surface tension explanation but unlike bubbles, atoms don't pop).

For *phenomena* we need to try to explain what we see using various particle models. Examples include:

- Looking at crystals. What model is needed to explain their regular shapes?
- Placing a loosely rolled 10 g ball of (degreased) fine iron fibre on ceramic paper on a top pan balance. Ignite it with a 4.5 volt battery (wear safety goggles), and blow gently to keep the iron burning. What particle model is needed to explain why it gets nearly 40 per cent heavier? (*The iron forms the blue/black magnetic oxide at this temperature, with three iron atoms (= 3 × 56) to four oxygen (= 4 × 16), so 10 g of iron becomes 13.8 g of oxide.*)
- Comparing hot gases from a hairdrier and from above a Bunsen flame by catching the 'air' in glass jars. Why does condensation only form inside one of the jars? Why does that same jar, when placed over a lighted candle, cause the candle to go out much more quickly that if you had used hot air from the other jar? (In this case we need to explain that the particles of the gas above the Bunsen burner are not the same as those in fresh (hot) air from the hairdrier. Methane and air (containing oxygen) combine in the Bunsen flame, producing new gases in which the atoms have rearranged themselves. No longer can we represent particles of the substances as round identical spheres. For chemical changes we need to represent the actual atoms: in our example, those that make up the particles of methane and air.)

It is interesting to survey science textbooks to see how many perpetuate the myths relating to particle models discussed above. Even more interesting is to survey your pupils' ideas about indestructible particles. There is more on *elicitation* in Chapter 5.

Words and how we see the world

What word do we use for these indestructible bits of the materials in our environment? The word *particle* causes immediate problems, since pupils rightly see them as little bits of real matter, which *do* melt, boil, burn etc. But using the word *atom* is also problematic. What if the substance is made from molecules or ions, rather than being a giant atomic lattice (or inert gas)? How happy would you be with the student who labelled the ions in Figure 2.1 as atoms?

It is only at the level of atoms that indestructibility really holds, as we saw with the combustion of methane in the example above; and even then some researchers think we should refer to the atomic 'cores' (atom less its valence electrons) as the 'particle' that remains unchanged during all chemical processes (Taber 2002). We pick up the problem of scientific words in the next chapter, and reconsider our approach to teaching particles in Chapter 12. In this chapter we have been using particle models to develop an understanding of observation.

Observation is not just a process of receiving information through our senses. The models and ideas we have in our brains are an intimate part of the observation process too, influencing what we observe and how we observe it. Once we have this particle model we see things differently. This is from an undergraduate student's learning log: 'but once I learnt to see everything around me as a mass of tiny spheres changing from one position to another, all chemical reactions can be seen simply and with clarity.' When scientists do want to avoid bias in their observations – for example, during the trialling of new drugs – they have to undertake experiments under what is called double-blind conditions: half the patients get a dummy drug (the placebo), but neither the doctors nor the patients know who has the real thing and who has the dummy. In this way neither can the patients 'think' themselves better, nor can the doctors 'see' improvements that are not really there.

Summary

This chapter has shown that naive observation is not possible. There are no such things as objective scientists, able to collect data without putting any of their own ideas into what is collected. The scientific method may start when we notice something, but even this process depends on ideas and processes already in our minds. Once we start investigating, we are following up an idea. Whether we continue using that idea, or whether it has to be replaced by something more detailed or even different, depends on the outcomes of our observations.

3

Science, sustainability and citizenship

For many years science has been recognised as an effective vehicle to explore the notion of environmental education. The term has shifted and evolved and is now subsumed within education for sustainability. Yet the role of science is as important as ever. How can we begin to understand the world we live in and recognise the impact we have on it without having grounding in the science that explains and supports it? How can we begin to act as responsible stewards of the planet without appreciating how it works? This chapter explores such questions and brings together ideas and examples of how science, sustainability and effective citizenship come together.

Brief history of environmental education

It is generally accepted by government and society that education about, for and through the environment is an essential requirement for the survival of humanity. We don't have to look far to hear the call for a more environmentally literate workforce and a more environmentally aware public. Yet over the past two decades environmental education has been progressively marginalised from the school curriculum: perhaps even more so during the evolution of the National Curriculum. It seems to have suffered from identity crises, which have fuelled the debate about its nature and purpose. With the advent of personal, social and health education (PSHE) and citizenship, environmental education seems to have found its niche under the term 'education for sustainable development' (ESD). This has emphasised the important development in the relationship between environmental concerns and developmental issues. The Qualifications and Curriculum Authority (QCA) recognises ESD as a whole-school curriculum and management approach, not a new subject, and recognises that its roots are in environmental and development education. It is emphasised on their website (www.nc.uk/esd) that many of the building blocks of education for sustainable development are already present in every school. The website has been designed to help teachers, curriculum coordinators, school managers and governors to develop approaches to education for sustainable development.

The website promotes ESD by engaging pupils of all ages in activities that enable them to take part in decision-making and democratic processes affecting the quality and structure of their environment. Case-study material illustrates this locally, nationally and globally. However, being able to translate the rhetoric of ESD into practice with a view to altering attitudes and behaviour requires more than exposure: it requires relevance and understanding. To achieve this pupils need to look at the underlying principles that are often seated in the roots of science.

The science of environmental issues

In order to develop a clear understanding of human impact on the environment it is essential to understand how the environment works: how the components interact and how they behave on all levels. This relates equally to the diversity of organisms that exist around us and to the particles that make them and the environment they live in. How did the components of the atmosphere get there in the first place, where do they come from and how do they behave under different conditions? These questions are fundamental if we want to understand issues such as global warming and the possible long-term effects it will have on the planet.

Gaining an understanding of the science behind environmental issues forms the underpinning philosophy supporting this book. References throughout are made to the CD-ROM *Science Issues and the National Curriculum*, which explores key environmental issues and the science behind them. Without this understanding science exists in a vacuum and science education becomes meaningless; learning in science needs to relate to everyday life.

Becoming a good citizen

Having this knowledge is one thing, but knowing what to do with it is another. Research (Kerr *et al.* 2001) indicates that there are various dimensions to becoming a good citizen:

- engagement (in something);
- knowledge (of something);
- skills (such as problem-solving);
- concepts (understanding the science behind the issues);
- attitudes (the development of positive attitudes);
- participation (taking an active role in society).

The Citizenship Scheme of Work (QCA/99/457) forms part of the wider PSHE and aims to 'give pupils the knowledge, skills and understanding they need to lead confident, healthy, independent lives and to become informed, active, responsible citizens'. The PSHE and citizenship framework is composed of four interrelated strands, designed to support children's personal and social development:

- developing confidence and responsibility and making the most of their abilities;
- preparing to play an active role as citizens;
- developing a healthy, safe lifestyle;
- developing good relationships and respecting the differences between people.

Citizenship as an examinable subject was introduced to the secondary curriculum in September 2002, having been an integral part of the primary curriculum since 2000. The scheme of work at both primary and secondary level is composed of 12 individual units (see Box 3.1).

- Taking part – developing skills of communication and participation.
- Choices.
- Animals and us.
- People who help us – the local police.
- Living in a diverse world.
- Developing our school grounds.
- Children's rights – human's rights.
- How do rules and laws affect me?
- Respect for property.
- Local democracy for young citizens.
- In the media – what's the news?
- Moving on.

BOX 3.1 PSHE and citizenship framework – the units

They have clearly defined areas of study and are highly prescriptive in their content. The Citizenship Scheme of Work (QCA 2001) advocates the use of constructivist and social constructivist approaches to teaching and learning: active learning and participation (where children are encouraged to assess evidence, negotiate, make decisions, solve problems, work independently and in groups, and learn from each other) are central to the learning process put forward. We discuss these approaches to learning in more detail in Part II of this book. During teaching opportunities should be made available for pupils to:

- take some responsibility for their own learning;
- explore and discuss topical issues;
- participate in groups of different sizes and composition;
- find information and advice;
- work with adults other than teachers;
- work outside the classroom;
- take time to reflect.

The issues associated with citizenship education can be highly controversial and provide opportunities to explore an array of teaching and learning methods, in particular debate. As with any discussion-led activity, its success in terms of teaching and learning is largely governed by the experience and expertise of the teacher and a need for the pupils to have a firm grasp of the underlying principles. Pupils need to see the big picture, make connections and have the conceptual tools to construct their own understanding. This is where science comes in. The 'hot potatoes' of the world of debate include GMOs, conservation and biodiversity, the use of drugs and global warming, all of which require good scientific understanding before the pupil can take ownership of the concept and play an active role in debate.

Activities to support teaching

Pupils need to be fully equipped to play this active role and this requires the development of certain critical thinking skills that are fundamental to our decision-making process. These skills include:

- enquiry;
- information-processing;
- problem-solving;
- creative thinking;
- reasoning or critical thinking;
- evaluation skills;
- metacognition (thinking about thinking).

These don't develop overnight; they need to be honed and nurtured, and opportunities should be offered whereby they can be practised and perfected. One activity that goes some way to support this is the process of 'diamond ranking'. Pupils are given a set of 13 prepared statements relating to the topic for debate. Working in groups, they have to arrange the statements in a diamond shape: the most and least agreeable statements at the top and bottom, with the others arranged in the middle forming the shape of a diamond.

This approach allows the pupils to externalise their own ideas and to listen to and discuss each other's. To establish the situation where this activity works effectively, the pupils have to feel unthreatened and be free to talk. This is easier to achieve in a group situation than in a whole-class debate. The pupils can then begin to respect their own and each other's thoughts and ideas. This activity can eventually progress to semi-structured and then open debate without the scaffolding of the prepared statements. For further discussion on pupil talk see Chapter 8.

Sometimes it is desirable to move away from teacher-initiated activities to benefit from the rich pickings of externally produced resources. These usually focus on a particular theme and draw on a wealth of supporting information to develop the one-off session or a whole scheme (see Box 3.2).

For years commercial organisations have been producing educational resources, which either promote or raise awareness of some aspect of the company's business. The electricity generation companies are no exception. One resource (*Energetic Maths for a Sustainable Future* by British Energy) emphasises human impact on the environment in terms of electricity wastage and explores ways of reducing that impact in a sustainable manner. This resource examines the bigger picture relating supply data to issues of demand, for example when a major event happens in a TV soap, which multiplies the ratings. This has the effect of consolidating behaviour, which invariably affects peak demand. This educational resource explains the effect of that demand and highlights the environmental impact associated with it. Personal behaviour and its impact are explored via hypothetical electricity bills and the use of an 'appliance usage' audit. From this pupils can make connections between their own demand and environmental impact and identify any unnecessary wastage. The teaching sequence culminates in group work aimed at producing a statement on sustainability in terms of personal electricity usage.

BOX 3.2 Energetic Maths for a Sustainable Future

Educational resources such as this, if used effectively, are enormously successful at getting the environmental message home, because they involve pupils in something that is of relevance to them. For example, it puts leaving the TV on 'stand-by' into context. The pupils can begin to appreciate that collectively as a population we waste the equivalent of 25 per cent of a conventional power station's output by leaving the 'little red light' on. This message is even more powerful when it is recognised that this practice is responsible for the majority of household fires.

Global citizenship

We are urged to think globally but act locally. A group of trainee students working with the global-ITE project (see http://www.global-dimension.co.uk) visited a primary school in rural India, where water was so scarce that pupils were urged to use only a drop at a time to clean their slates. In Mumbai they stayed in high-class hotel accommodation with flush loos and showers, and visited schools with networked TV in every classroom. You don't have to travel to become aware of contrasts in the conditions under which humanity lives, but in the affluent West we are shielded from such contrasts, and tend to take what we have and our lifestyles for granted. If we are to have a sustainable future the resources of the world, which are not limitless, need to be shared more evenly among humanity. By bringing global images to the UK classroom in a sensitive way, we can begin to ask UK pupils to examine their lifestyles and to question the way we treat resources as if they are limitless.

Summary

We have emphasised the need to relate learning in science to everyday life and to the issues and concerns that go with it. Pupils will develop their own viewpoints on issues of sustainability and citizenship, but they will need help, guidance and support along the way. This is an exciting yet challenging aspect of the curriculum, which is essential for the next generation to move towards a more sustainable future.

II

How Children Make Sense of Their World

Introduction

We begin by establishing, in Chapters 4 and 5, the importance of finding out how children use words and what ideas are held by them (*elicitation*). Only then can we see how to help them to develop and, where necessary, revolutionise these ideas (Chapters 6–11). We must compress an understanding that took humanity many centuries to develop into just a few years of schooling. We cannot expect children to come up with the inspired ideas of scientists through the ages (though they occasionally do), so our job as teachers is to present these ideas to the pupils ourselves (*intervention*). Scientists took time to take on new ideas; often members of the 'old school' had to die off before the new ways of thinking became 'mainstream'. As teachers we have to take children through similar revolutions in thought if they are to share the powerful scientific ways of thinking that have enabled us to begin to understand our environment (*reformulation*). This is at the heart of what is called a *constructivist* approach to teaching and learning (Chapter 6).

We need to move away from last-minute revision guides, full of *markobine gandos* (Chapter 4) that children learn by heart to put in their short-term memory and pass an exam. What point does that serve? If we are going to teach science it must be to help young people to come to understand the way the world works, and enable them to look after it (and themselves). If they *understand and use* these scientific ideas, then they *truly* know. The ideas they have met in school need to become a part of their make-up and way of life. With this deeper understanding pupils can pass an exam now, next week or next year – revision becomes a daily activity as pupils *use* their scientific ideas. Anything that has to be revised at the last minute has clearly not been useful to the learner, and after the examination will probably be forgotten. In contrast, ideas that are used become embedded in our minds. This approach to learning is developed in Chapter 6, where we draw a parallel with the way science itself advances.

Chapters 7–11 explore in some detail how we can give pupils the time to take on board the new ideas and experiences we have given them through our *intervention*. Pupils need time to construct meaning for themselves through *reformulation*. We have called these 'active learning' techniques.

Language and learning

This chapter examines the words we use in science and looks for ways to enable our pupils to come to a real understanding of them. We need to do more than ask pupils to learn a single definition of a word and instead generate a real feeling for the ways a word is used. Pupils need words to be used in context. Connections need to be made to ideas they already understand.

The role of language in learning and the value of finding the roots of meaning

Words and ideas are useful but there can never be one correct meaning or definition of each one. Despite the best efforts of scientists to keep meanings fixed and precise, the meaning of what is written and said in science (as in any aspect of human life) changes over time: public meanings change over historical time, and private understandings change over the lifetime of an individual. It is therefore important to uncover how children use words. We may accuse them of muddled thinking, when it is simply that they are using words differently from us. As teachers, we need to listen carefully to children as they use words, and watch out, especially from the context of what they say, for understanding conveyed through an underdeveloped and possibly inadequate vocabulary. There are *grains of truth* in what children say, as we see towards the end of this chapter. But first we look at the place of language in learning.

Language plays a pivotal role in learning. Imagine going into a classroom where all the scientific words have been replaced by made up words like *giky martible* (Sutton 1992) and *markobine gando* (Ross 1990). You would read or hear things like 'When an orbal of quant undual to the markobine bosal passes through a dovern mern it is deranted so as to cosat to a bart on the bosal called the markobine gando.' Nonsense, you may say, but you can still answer questions such as: 'What happens to the deranted orbal when it passes through a dovern mern?' For an acceptable answer see Box 4.3 (p. 34). We need to ensure that our science lessons and texts are not perceived this way by our pupils, leaving them to learn things by heart in order to pass examinations.

Private understandings and public knowledge

When children use one word for two separate ideas it is time to teach them a new word. For example the words *shadow* and *reflection* are often muddled up by children in primary school. When taught the word *shade*, and shown that it is the same as *shadow*, children can associate it with places where light has been blocked out. When shown that *flex*ible means bendable children might connect the word re*flect*ion with light bouncing off a surface.

Some materials let light through without much distortion – they are transparent. Primary school teachers often describe such materials as 'see-through'. There are other materials that light passes through, but you cannot see through them; they are *translucent*. This is less easy to translate into English: 'lets-light-through-but-you-can't-see-through' is cumbersome. Telling children that the scientific word for see-through is transparent, and the other is translucent, can be like using the words *markobine gando*. They have no meaning, so just have to be learnt. But children know many words with the Latin word 'trans' (meaning *through*) in them; transport, transfer, trans-Atlantic, Ford Transit van. In each case they can see that something is moving, either 'through' or 'across'. Less easy, but worth exploring, is the difference between -parent and -lucent (meaning 'see' and 'light'). What other words do they know containing these roots? Apparent, appear, to peer into the gloom are all linked with seeing; and lucid, Lucifer link with clear and light. By contrast, the Greek word for light is *photos*, which gives us words such as photograph and photosynthesis.

Many scientific words have a classical origin, and most teachers point this out for their pupils. Box 4.1 lists a few of them.

Words in Greek and Latin:
   micro = small, *scope* = look at, *tele* = far, *vision* = see, *graph* = draw,
   lysis = to break, *phone* = hear, *hydro* = water, *electron* = amber (when rubbed it becomes electrically charged)

give us these scientific words:
   microscope, telescope, television, telephone, hydrophone, hydrolysis, electrolysis, etc.
   Thus *hydro*-gen is the water generator or the *element generates water:* when hydrogen burns it forms water, H_2O.

Words for Greek and Latin numbers help us understand words like:
   *bi*cycle, *bi*nocular, *di*oxide (2); *quad*ruped, *quad*rant (4); *hexa*gon, *hex*ane (6); *octo*pus, *Octo*ber (8); *deci*mal, *deca*ne (10) and *cent*ury, *centi*pede (100).
   Note here that the -*pus*, -*ped*, -*pede*, all mean foot (as in pedestal, pedal, pedestrian), though centipedes don't actually have 100 feet, just as millipedes don't have 1000.

BOX 4.1 Some classical roots of scientific words

Origins of words

Let us consider the origin of more of the words used in science, but whose origin (etymology) is perhaps less obvious.

For each word in the list that follows, see how far you are able to uncover the root meaning:

circuit	ovary	electricity	evaporate	igneous
insulate	mammal	month	vaccination	volatile

Think of how the word came to be used in science. Look for other words with similar roots (perhaps in other languages such as French) that can help children to come to understand how they are used. Box 4.4 (pp. 34–5) shows the etymology (origin) of each word, and indicates other words that might help children uncover the meaning.

By revealing to children how words got their meaning and comparing them with other familiar but similarly derived words we can help children to understand the accepted literal meaning of new words used in science. It helps them move away from learning *markobine gando* by rote, towards building the word into their real understanding. Sutton (1992: especially Chapters 3, 5 and 8) shows the value of knowing where words came from and how they get used.

How did new scientific words come into being?

In this section we consider the problems caused when no word yet existed for the idea scientists wanted to talk about, and the choices that had to be made when inventing a new word. We still have the same problem today as scientific ideas develop, and new words are needed.

Consider the words in Table 4.1 associated with the use of fuels from two West African languages from The Gambia, and from the English language. In Mandinka one word covers steam and heat. This means that the material nature of steam, as a mixture of water vapour and condensation, could be confused with heat energy in the form of infra-red radiation – the glow you feel round a fire. In Wolof, where one word covers smoke and steam, the confusion between the solid particulates associated with smoke and the water droplets associated with visible steam cannot be as easily sorted as it could be in Mandinka and English. English-speaking children frequently use the words steam and smoke synonymously, but at least we have the words available to separate out the two ideas.

TABLE 4.1 Words associated with the use of fuels (Ross 1989)

English	smoke	steam	heat
Mandinka	sisiyo	fingjalo	
Wolof	sahar		tangor

New words for scientists

Children will hear new words being used by their teachers long before they will be confident enough to use them themselves. Children should begin to use scientific vocabulary when everyday words become inadequate and further delay would cause confusion. In a similar way, scientists will increasingly feel the need for new words to represent the new ideas that they are working on. When a new word was needed, scientists did not always invent one – sometimes they took an existing word and used it a special way. While new words suffer the problem of strangeness, and lack all meaning at first, familiar words come with a whole baggage of meaning that can be equally confusing. Both processes of word acquisition have their problems.

Consider the common words in Table 4.2 that have been used for a special meaning in science. Tick the box to show if their scientific meaning is extended, restricted or just different, compared with their everyday use. A commentary on these words is provided in Box 4.5 (p. 35).

UNIVERSITY OF WOLVERHAMPTON
Walsall Learning Centre

ITEMS ISSUED:

Customer ID: WPP61231614

Title: Explaining science in the classroom
ID: 762094862X
Due: 18/10/13 23:59

Title: Teaching secondary science
ID: 7624370266
Due: 04/10/13 23:59

Total items: 2
27/09/2013 15:29
Issued: 3
Overdue: 0

Thank you for using Self Service.
Please keep your receipt.

Overdue books are fined at 40p per day for
1 week loans, 10p per day for long loans.

TABLE 4.2 Common words with a special meaning in science

	Scientific word, compared with its everyday meaning, is:		
	Extended	Restricted	Different
Animal			
Current (electricity)			
Energy			
Force			
Fruit			
Growth (of living things)			
Plant (life)			
Power			
Table (of results)			

Scientific words: should we use existing words or invent new ones?

The question of whether invented or borrowed words make things easier is not possible to answer – there are problems with both. As science teachers we need to be acutely aware of conflicts in meanings of *borrowed* words, and give as much help as possible for *invented* words. We need to be aware that children may not be using a word in the way we might wish them to. It may be that they understand the science very well, but are using the wrong word. Equally, they may appear to be using the right words but have no real idea of what they are saying.

To end this chapter on words and language we invite you to consider the *grains of truth* in the statements in Box 4.2 made by children and adults that appear to contain misconceptions. We discuss the issue of misconceptions more fully in Chapter 5.

Grains of truth

When children use words they often mean something completely different from the accepted scientific meaning. In the ideas in Box 4.2, there is a grain of truth in what the children (and adults!) are saying, but they all represent an inappropriate use of words. Many are phrases we all have come to use in our everyday language, which set up barriers against a scientific understanding.

Burning destroys

This is a case where the Mandinka and Wolof languages come out better than English (see Table 4.3). Wolof, for example, has two words for the English word *burn*. *Laka* is similar to our char, and is used (normally) for the decomposition reaction when organic matter is heated, forming non-flammable smoke and char. This has been called char-burning (Ross 1991). *Taka* is used for the combination of air and fuel when flames are seen (flame-burning).

In the following 'grains of truth':

- explain in what way the accepted *scientific* view is contradicted by these statements;
- spot the grains of truth in them (some are very big grains);
- consider the implications for teaching.

(The *italicised* statements are discussed below. For a discussion of the others see Chapters 5 and 12–14.)

Chemistry (Chapter 12)

Burning destroys
Petrol is turned into heat in a car
Wax is fireproof
Water in a puddle disappears

Physics (Chapter 13)

Things sink because they are heavy
A ton of lead is heavier than a ton of feathers
Heavy objects fall faster than light ones
Hot air rises
Gravity operates downward
There is no gravity in space/on the moon
Moving objects need a force on them to keep them going
Energy is used up
Electric current is used up
We see when our eyes look at objects
Blankets make things warm
Wood is warmer than metal

Biology (Chapter 14)

Plant roots breathe
Food is turned into energy in our body (during digestion)
Plants feed on soil through their roots
Air keeps us alive
Animals are furry and have four legs

BOX 4.2 Grains of truth

Burning certainly destroys the *object*, whether energy has caused it to decompose (char) or oxides have built up, releasing thermal energy (flame). That is the very big grain of truth. But at an *atomic* level there is no destruction.

TABLE 4.3 Meanings of the word 'burn' (Ross 1989)

English	Burn	
	flame-burn (combustion)	char-burn (scorch, char)
Mandinka	maala	jani
Wolof	taka	laka

The implications for teaching are clear: at junior level we need to be careful to distinguish between the two types of burning (*taka* and *laka*, char and flame), both in words and in getting children to observe the contrasts. A log of wood put on the fire takes heat from the fire until it is hot and begins to give off flammable smoke; only then does it burst into flame and begin transferring energy. Later on molecular explanations can be given, and flame burning can be seen as a constructive process, where fuel and oxygen combine.

There is an exact parallel with the way we deal with food. The digestion process is equivalent to char-burning (breaking the fuel up into small bits for entry into the blood) and respiration is equivalent to flame-burning (combination of these broken bits with oxygen to build up oxides).

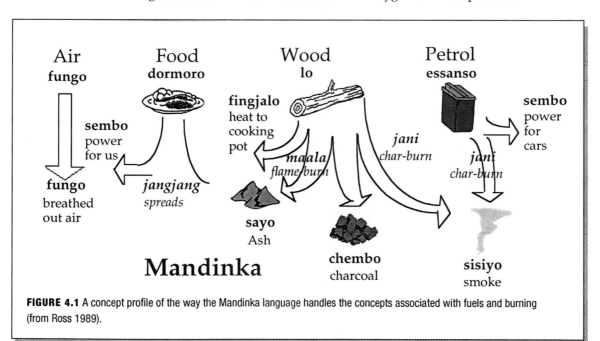

FIGURE 4.1 A concept profile of the way the Mandinka language handles the concepts associated with fuels and burning (from Ross 1989).

Things sink because they are heavy

There is a grain of truth in this if children use the word *heavy* to mean dense – as we all do: 'Wood is lighter than stone', 'Metal is a heavy substance'; 'A ton of lead is heavier than a ton of feathers'. What we need to do is to show children that the word *heavy*, in its strict scientific sense, is a measurement of the force of gravity acting on the mass of a body – a measure of its weight. So you can have a light piece of lead, and a heavy bag of feathers, but the density of the lead is still high, so it will still sink.

When children say a ton of lead is heavier than a ton of feathers, or that heavy objects sink and light ones float, they probably understand the science well enough but it is their use of the words *light* and *heavy* that we must sort out. They know that certain materials are much 'heavier' than others, meaning (in adult, scientific use of words) that the material is more dense than others. Children use the same word heavy for two different ideas: absolutely heavy (this is a heavy book, you are too heavy to lift) and high density (lead is a heavy material, so it sinks). When the same word is used for two different ideas, there is bound to be some degree of confusion (refer again to Table 4.1).

Summary

Figure 4.1 is a concept profile of the way the Mandinka language handles the concepts associated with fuels and burning (Ross 1989). It makes a useful summary for this chapter. As you read the Mandinka words on their own they have no meaning (assuming you do not speak the language). They are like the scientific words we present to children. As we explore the range of meanings and the origins of words and how they link together, children gradually build them into their own world. We also see here the way in which concepts are embedded into everyday language. Built into the language are our naive ideas about how things work. Our task, as science teachers, is to become aware of these in-built but naive ways of thinking – and that is the task of Chapter 5. Subsequent chapters in Part II explore the ways in which we can build on or challenge these ideas in our teaching.

Appendix

These boxes contain responses to questions asked in this chapter.

It cosats to a bart on the bosal called the markobine gando.

BOX 4.3 An acceptable answer to the question on page 28

Circuit: circle, bicycle, circus, all suggest going round in a circle. In the case of electricity, it is the electrical current which goes round. This carries electrical energy from the cell to the bulb. [From Latin *circum* meaning round.]

Ovary: oval, ovum, from the Latin *ovum*, an egg – hence egg-shaped and egg container.

Electricity: *electron* is the Greek word for amber, the yellow fossil resin that traps mosquitoes that once sucked dinosaur blood. When rubbed it acquires a static electric charge, and so it came to represent the new phenomenon of 'ambericity'. Interesting, but on this occasion of no help to children.

Evaporate: vapour is another word for gas, especially if it condenses easily. [From Latin *e-*, *ex-*, meaning out of.]

Igneous: ignite = set fire to, so igneous rocks are from fire. [From Greek *igni* and Sanskrit *agni*, meaning fire.)

Insulate: insular means cut off (a peninsula is half cut off, as penumbra is half a shadow) so insulate means to protect or cut off from. [From the Latin word for island.]

Mammals: have mammary glands for producing milk. The same mmm sound used by babies has come to be used as the word for their mother: mam mum mom, hence, mammal [also from Latin *mamma* meaning breast].

Month: the moon circles the Earth once in every 'moonth' [this helps with spelling too].

Vaccination: from Jenner's work on cow pox: French *vache*, a cow

Volatile: does not mean reactive and dangerous in its scientific meaning, but rather 'to fly away'. Compare with the tennis word 'volley' – literally to let fly. Volatile simply means a substance that evaporates easily, like water, wax and the odiferous component of wych hazel. [From the Latin *volare* meaning to fly, as in French *voler*, Spanish *volar*.]

BOX 4.4 Origins of words used in science (see page 29)

Animal: *extended*. In science, an animal is a multicellular consumer that relies on other living things for nutrients. In everyday life it has a meaning closer to mammal (though humans are not normally classed as animals), as in 'There are animals, birds and insects living in the forest' – in its scientific meaning birds and insects are animals. (See Chapter 14.)

Current (electricity): *different*. In science this refers to the flow of electrons or coulombs round a circuit, and is measured as charge, in coulombs, per second (amps). In everyday life it has a meaning closer to energy or power, as in 'How much current does this drill use?' (see Chapter 13.)

Energy: *different*. In science energy has two meanings: a quantity, measured in joules, that remains the same throughout a change, and a measure of the ability a system has to do useful work (properly called free energy). The everyday life meaning is closer to the free energy idea, as in 'I've had a huge energy bill this quarter because I've used so much.' Joules cannot be used, but their usefulness does go. (See Chapter 13.)

Force: *restricted*. In science it is measured in newtons and causes objects to change their state of motion, or shape. In everyday life it has a much broader meaning, as in 'She forced me to do it'. (See Chapter 13.)

Fruit: *extended*. In science a fruit develops from a fertilised flower (carple), and contains the seeds of the plant, such as pea pods, hazelnuts, rose-hips and tomatoes. In everyday life the term is restricted to fruiting bodies that are soft (sweet) and edible. (See Chapter 14.)

Growth (of living things): *extended*. In science growth is concerned with differentiation and development of specialised cells as well as increasing the number of cells. In everyday life it is usually used to indicate that something gets bigger (though this often entails more complexity too).

Plant (life): *extended*. In science plants are one of the major kingdoms of life, comprising multicellular life-forms with roots, stem and leaves, that obtain their nutrients from inorganic sources through photosynthesis. In everyday life plants tend to be kept in pots, and are different from trees, flowers and vegetables. (See Chapter 14.)

Power: *restricted*. In science power is measured in watts and is a measure of how fast energy is transferred (joules per second). In everyday life it is used very generally covering ideas of energy (What is this powered by?) and social hierarchies. The word *powerful* contains the essence of the scientific meaning, 'able to deliver energy quickly'.

Table (of results): *different*. In science, a place to write your results. In school, a place on which pupils sometimes scratch their names.

BOX 4.5 Scientific meanings of everyday words (see Table 4.2, p. 31)

Children's ideas of the world

It is difficult to teach children new ideas until we know the existing ideas they hold; these often appear to conflict with accepted scientific ideas and are described as 'misconceptions' or 'alternative frameworks of belief' (Driver *et al.* 1994). Chapter 4 showed that there are many grains of truth in these 'alternative ideas'. We extend this discussion in this chapter, in which we pay careful attention to what children say about their ideas in science.

Children's alternative ideas

Methods of teaching science which are based on the idea that pupils build up, or construct, ideas about their world are often called *constructivist* approaches. If we want pupils to understand and use scientific ideas their existing beliefs need to be challenged or extended. We cannot always replace their naive ideas, but we can encourage pupils to use the scientific ones when appropriate, and to show them the inconsistencies in many of their existing ideas. This chapter looks at ways to probe and display their ideas. In Chapters 6–11 we look at active learning approaches that allow pupils to reconstruct the scientific ideas we present to enable them to make them their own.

The sample questions that follow have all been used in schools to probe children's understanding or misunderstanding. They are very basic, indeed so simple that we might wonder how older pupils could ever answer them inappropriately. Before you read the commentary on the questions, it will be useful if you try to answer the questions yourself at your own level and then as a child may see them. Better still, try them out on small groups of pupils across the age and ability range. What alternative ideas did you predict and find? If you are trying them with children, it is best to have the materials with you – for example, use two blocks of ice and wrap one in a hand-towel for question 1.

1   *Frozen tank*. The water in the toilet tank froze. Later that day someone put a blanket round the iced-up tank. Will this make the ice in the toilet tank melt faster, more slowly, or make no difference?

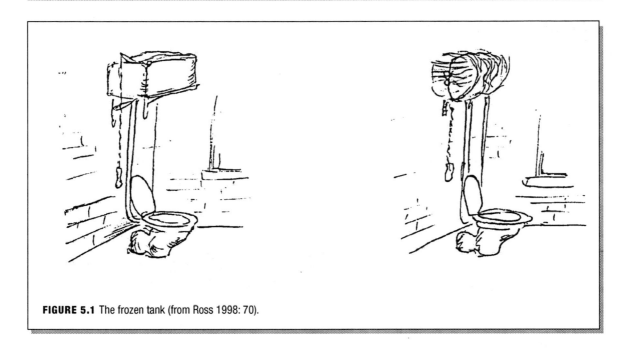

FIGURE 5.1 The frozen tank (from Ross 1998: 70).

2   *Temperature*. Predict the temperature of the water in each cup in Figure 5.2.

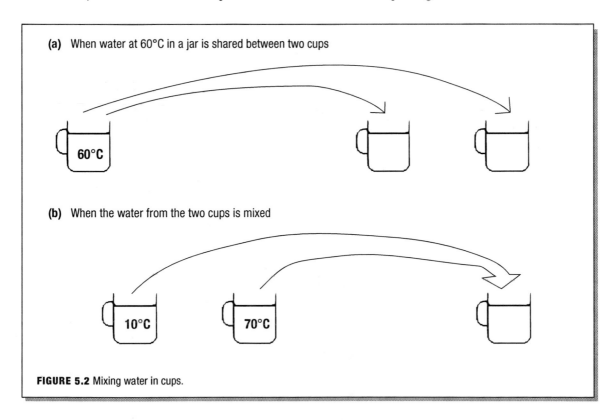

(a)   When water at 60°C in a jar is shared between two cups

60°C

(b)   When the water from the two cups is mixed

10°C   70°C

FIGURE 5.2 Mixing water in cups.

3   *Candle.* (a) The picture in Figure 5.3 shows a lighted candle. Use the possible answers on the right to answer the two questions on the left. (b) If you aim the hot air from a hairdrier into a dry jar, the jar will get hot but does not get damp. However when the same jam jar is held upside-down to collect the hot air above a candle flame, condensation collects on the inside of the jar. Where does this water come from?

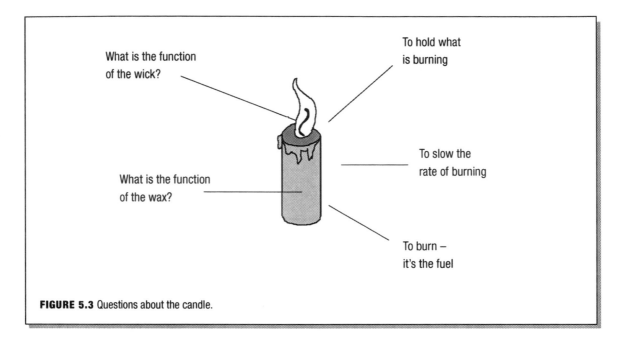

FIGURE 5.3 Questions about the candle.

4   *Weight.* Predict (and explain) any change in weight: (a) to plasticine if you flatten it out; (b) to a sugar lump if you crush it and weigh all the bits; (c) to a cup of water if you add salt to the water then stir.

5   *Football.* Multiple choice question in the form of a 'concept cartoon' after Keogh and Naylor (http://www.conceptcartoons.com) see Figure 5.4.

6   *Exhaust gas.* Suppose you collect everything that comes out of the exhaust pipe of a car on a journey (exhaust gas, fumes etc.), and somehow press it all together so you can measure its mass (e.g. by weighing). Compared to the mass (weight) of petrol that was used for the journey, the mass (weight) of exhaust will be: (a) much less (lighter); (b) about the same; (c) much more (heavier).

7   *Cell and bulb.* For this you need a 1.5 volt cell, a matching bulb and one piece of wire. Can you make the bulb light using just the cell and a single piece of wire?

8   *Living – plant – animal.* This activity is best done by making a set of cards with labelled pictures of the following: person, fire, car, cow, daffodil, tree, fish, whale, spider, bird, grass, cabbage, cat, seeds, frogspawn. Sort the cards to show those that are alive, dead, never lived. Are any left? Now sort the cards into *animals* or *not animals*. Now sort the cards into *plants* or *not plants*. (from Osborne and Freyberg 1985: 30)

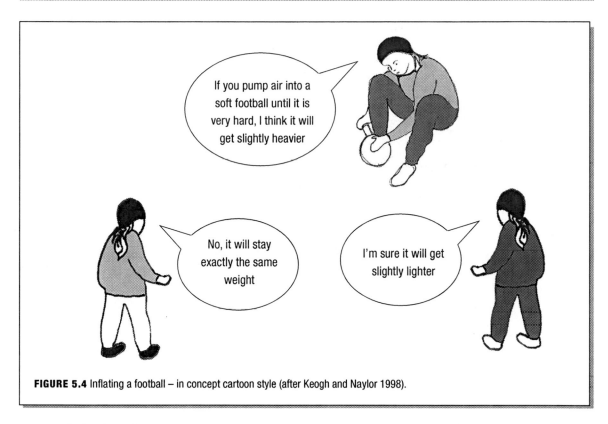

FIGURE 5.4 Inflating a football – in concept cartoon style (after Keogh and Naylor 1998).

9 *Seeing*. In order to see we need to open our eyes and we need a source of light. Draw lines to show how the light and our eyes help us see the book. Use arrow heads to show directions.

FIGURE 5.5 How do the light and our eyes help us to see (from Guesne 1985)?

10 *Gravity.* This question (see Figure 5.6) causes problems for younger children.

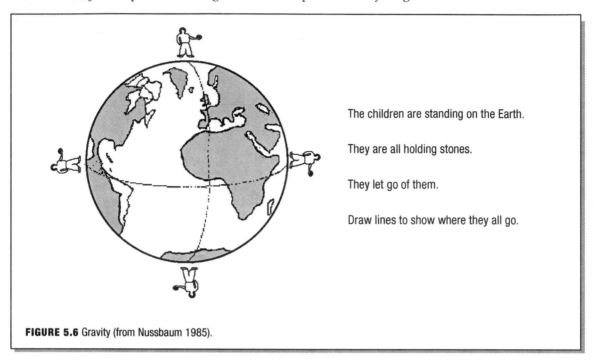

The children are standing on the Earth.

They are all holding stones.

They let go of them.

Draw lines to show where they all go.

FIGURE 5.6 Gravity (from Nussbaum 1985).

11 *Force.* A ball has been thrown up, away from the Earth. Three of the drawings in Figure 5.7 show the ball on its way up, at the top of its flight, and on its way down. Also drawn, as an example, is the ball being pushed by your hand against gravity. For the three pictures, draw arrows to indicate the size and direction of any forces that you think are acting on the ball. The longer the arrow, the larger the force. Label the force(s) as we have done on the first example. Before you rush to answer this, consider what is happening to the speed of the ball – is it getting slower, or faster?

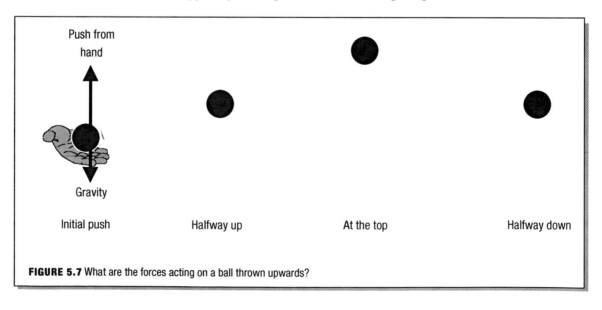

FIGURE 5.7 What are the forces acting on a ball thrown upwards?

12 *Food*. Every day we eat food (e.g. carbohydrate), which we digest and which is sent round our bodies as fuel, for energy. Choose any of the following to explain why we don't normally get heavier each day. This question is about how the *material* (the actual stuff of the carbohydrate, made of atoms) leaves our body. (a) It is all used up and only energy is left. (b) It comes out as faeces. (c) After use it is stored in our bodies. (d) We breathe a lot of it out as carbon dioxide and water vapour. (e) It comes out as energy – movement and heat.

Discussion of the questions

Children's responses to such elicitation questions show they have a range of 'alternative' ideas that may remain unaffected by teaching *unless we take them into account* when designing the activities we ask the children to do. The following commentary on the questions gives a flavour of the extent of our problem as science teachers.

1 *Frozen tank*. Many answer this by saying the blanket will make the ice melt more quickly because of their learning experiences from their own bodies, when blankets stop heat generated by our bodies from escaping. The word *insulation* in everyday life has come to mean 'keep warm' or even 'make warm', as in 'our new insulation makes our house very warm'. The blanket will, of course, slow down the rate at which heat energy can enter the tank from the surroundings and so the blanket will make the ice melt more slowly. It is for this reason that we wrap ice cream in newspaper (Newell and Ross 1996).

2 *Temperature*. Younger children tend to add (the mixture in Figure 5.2(b) is 80°) or halve (each cup in Figure 5.2(a) is 30°) the temperatures. Those who realise that 70° and 10° will not make 80° often go for 60° (if we don't add, then perhaps we subtract). The idea that temperature measures the degree of hotness is difficult because 'hot' and 'cold' are used in everyday life as if the human body was a sort of zero point. This makes the use of a single scale of hotness difficult. If the cups at 10° and 70° have equal amounts of water in them, the temperature will be halfway between them, i.e. 40°. Children need time at KS 2 and 3 to gain this sort of experience of temperature as an intensive property, by practical activity. They have no problem if the questions are asked using qualitative descriptions of temperature rather than numbers, i.e. mixing *hot* and *cold* water or sharing *hot* water into two cups (Stavey and Berkovitz 1980).

3 *Candle*. (a) Many pupils think the wax slows down the burning of the wick. No longer do we see candles made of animal fat – a solid fuel that needs a wick, just like an oil lamp, to allow the fuel to get hot and evaporate, so allowing it to burn. So it is the wick that holds the fuel and the wax that burns.
(b) Many people explain the condensation in the same way that they explain how bathroom mirrors steam up: they think the water comes from the air as hot air (from the candle) meets the cold glass jar. But why is there no condensation from a hairdrier? In fact quite the opposite happens: a damp jar will lose its condensation when heated, like damp hair or a damp rear car window. Water is, of course, the product of combustion: hydrogen in the hydrocarbon wax fuel combines with oxygen from the air to produce water. We need to stress the importance of air during burning, and to take note of the products of combustion (see number 6, *Exhaust gas*, below, and Chapter 12).

4 *Weight*. These questions get increasingly confusing for children. Only the very young will think that shape change or crushing will alter the mass (flattened plasticine looks bigger, crushed

sugar feels lighter). However, even some children in secondary school will think that the salt disappears completely, as it dissolves, so adding nothing to the weight (Driver *et al.* 1994: Chapter 8). Research shows that infants are more likely to get this right, because they have not yet experienced dissolving (Figure 5.8). The conservation of matter is not obvious from everyday experiences, and until we have a model for matter as indestructible particles (Chapter 2) it is easy to understand why these pupils have problems.

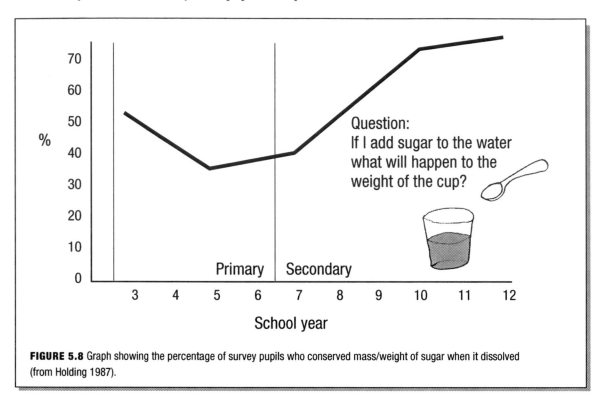

FIGURE 5.8 Graph showing the percentage of survey pupils who conserved mass/weight of sugar when it dissolved (from Holding 1987).

5   *Football.* It is not obvious that air is a *real substance*, except when it is moving (wind) or trapped as bubbles in water. The air around us cannot sink because we live in an ocean of air. But if it becomes less dense – for example, by expansion from heating – the surrounding denser air can buoy it up. Similarly, if we compress it, as we do when adding air to a football, it will be denser than the air it displaces, and so will sink, pushing ordinary air out of the way. This is well worth demonstrating to children, using a sensitive balance. Since gases are about 1000 times less dense than condensed forms of matter (solids and liquids), even if you double the pressure in a 5-litre football the mass, measured through weighing, will only increase by a few grams (Ross *et al.* 2002: Atmosphere).

6   *Exhaust gas.* (a) *Much less*: most people will say, wrongly, that the exhaust is lighter, either because they don't believe gases weigh very much if at all, or because they think some of the petrol has been used, or turned to energy to make the car go.

(b) *About the same*: here people may realise that you cannot destroy matter, so what goes in must come out, but they forget that the burning process involves combining fuel and air.

(c) *Much heavier*: these are the people who realise the importance of oxygen. Since oxygen atoms are much more massive than hydrogen, and a little more massive than carbon, the increase in mass of the exhaust gases over the original hydrocarbon fuel is significant – the exhaust gases have more than four times the mass of the petrol. Even then we have neglected the nitrogen that is mostly unchanged during the process, but forms the bulk of both the incoming air and outgoing exhaust. Once again we need to stress the importance of air in burning, and take note of the material products of combustion. See Figure 5.9 and Chapter 12 (Ross *et al.* 2002: energy).

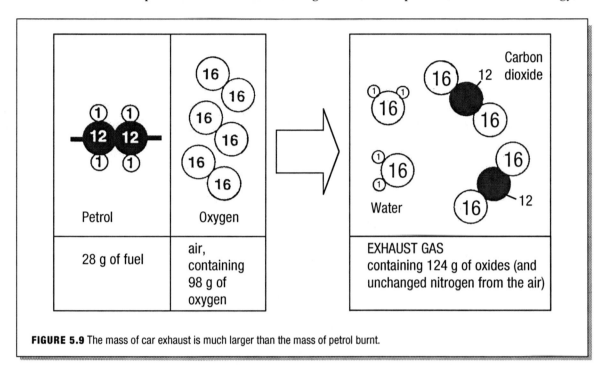

FIGURE 5.9 The mass of car exhaust is much larger than the mass of petrol burnt.

7   *Cell and bulb*. Many pupils will try to connect only one terminal on the cell to one on the bulb. Even when they use both ends of the battery they do not appreciate that the bulb, too, has two terminals. Electricity (as current) must be able to flow through all components, allowing electricity (as energy) to be delivered. Pupils are initially confused by a single mains wire going to appliances, and later when we give them bulbs in holders, they see the bulb simply sitting on the wire. All circuit work should start with naked bulbs, and the presence of two terminals on all normal electrical equipment can be pointed out (see Chapter 13) (Ross *et al.* 2002: energy and home).

8   *Living – plant – animal*. In Chapter 3 we mentioned the problem of using these everyday words in a scientific context, where their meaning becomes much broader.

Living: pupils may think fire or a car is living (is it made of cells that divide?). They may also think that seeds and spawn are dead (but they are made of cells that can divide).

Animals: pupils may select only the land mammals (cat and cow, but not whale or person). This is the everyday meaning of animal, furry with four legs. Frog spawn belongs to the *animal kingdom*, but it is difficult to argue that it is *an animal*. We need to take care how this question is asked.

Plants: pupils may have a very narrow view of plants – daffodil is a flower, tree is a tree, grass might be a plant, cabbage is a vegetable but might be a plant, seeds are seeds. If we are to use the word *plant* to represent multicellular organisms (with true roots, stem and leaves) that feed through photosynthesis, we need to make this clear to pupils in our classes.

The concept of producers and consumers is difficult to convey if pupils use the words 'plant' and 'animal' in their restricted everyday sense (Osborne and Freyburg 1985: Chapter 3).

9   *Seeing*. Many pupils even at KS 4 will unthinkingly show light coming from the eye and on to the book. The idea of sight rays is a consequence of words such as *look, notice* etc., which suggest the eye is an active seeker. Many ancient cultures (e.g. Greek and Indian) had this idea of active eyesight. Drawings that show light from the lamp scattering from the book with some rays entering the eye follow the scientific idea of the eye as a receptor. This was recognised by the Islamic school in the eighth century, who dissected the eye and realised it was a receiver of light (Butt 1991). We should, however, remember that *observation* is an active process and in order to make any sense of the light entering our eyes, we must match this input with ideas generated from our memory (Guesne 1985).

10   *Gravity*. This problem is usually solved by the time children enter KS 3, but younger children do find it difficult to imagine gravity acting towards the centre of a spherical Earth. They prefer to retain a notion of absolute up and down, allowing the stones to fall off the bottom of the page. This may also be due to their inability to see the picture as representing the land on which they are standing (Nussbaum 1985).

11   *Force*. Most people are stuck with Aristotle's view that moving objects have a force travelling with them, an idea more akin to the physicist's *momentum* (Gunstone and Watts 1985). Certainly this *seems* more sensible than Newton's idea, which says that objects moving at a steady speed in a straight line require no force. If a force does act, the object will change speed or direction, so with the introduction of the force of friction the object slows down. In our question, the hand forces the ball up with a force greater than gravity, so the ball accelerates up. However, as soon as it leaves the hand, the only force now acting (neglecting air resistance, which is very small) is gravity. This acts against the motion to slow the ball down, bringing it to rest at the top of its flight. But gravity still acts exactly as before, so the ball accelerates downwards, gradually picking up speed. You can show this in school by attaching elastic to a tennis ball and throwing it horizontally along the bench. It comes back, just like a ball thrown upwards, but now everyone can see the need for a backward (or downward) force to slow then reverse the ball's motion. The Newtonian answer will show just one downward arrow on each ball, exactly the same length as the gravity arrow on the first picture (Ross *et al.* 2002: atmosphere).

12   *Food*. This is a difficult question to ask. It requires people to make a separate account of the atoms that make up all materials (atoms), and the energy associated with them (joules).

Matter (atoms): all the carbon, hydrogen and oxygen atoms of the carbohydrate we eat have to be accounted for – they are not destroyed, as many will have us believe.

Energy (joules): energy can be stored by pulling matter apart against the attractive force of gravity; for example, when water is lifted by the sun from the oceans and stored behind a dam. In a similar way, energy can be stored by pulling matter apart against the electromagnetic force of chemical bonds; for example, when sunlight pulls oxygen away from hydrogen as water is split in photosynthesis (see Chapter 11 and Ross *et al.* 2002: energy and agriculture).

Let us consider the five alternatives of the original question, which asks about matter (atoms), not energy. Note that this question is almost identical to question 6 – for **combustion** read **respiration**.

(a) *It is all used up and only energy is left*. No, the atoms are still there.

(b) *It comes out as faeces*. No, although this is matter, it is food that has not been digested, and so has not entered the blood, and cannot be used as a fuel by us (though it can fuel other animal life, such as dung beetles).

(c) *After use it is stored in our bodies*. No, some material from food is stored, but this is before it is used as a fuel – a store implies it is yet to be used.

(d) *We breathe a lot of it out as carbon dioxide and water vapour*. Yes, this is the only acceptable response. The carbon and hydrogen atoms of the fuel rejoin with oxygen we have breathed in, forming carbon dioxide and water, transferring energy (joules) to the cell as they do so, reversing the photosynthesis reaction. The *matter* leaves as exhaust gases in our breath.

(e) *It comes out as energy – movement and heat*. No, although energy is transferred during respiration we asked only for an account of the *matter*, the atoms. Food is made of atoms, not energy.

The need to elicit children's ideas

It may be somewhat depressing to find out how many pupils reach GCSE and even A-level standard and still answer these and other **elicitation** questions in a naive way. However, experience shows that these naive ideas are built up through common experiences and they can be very persistent. We need to find out what these ideas are and devise learning techniques that will challenge or reconcile the two views: the naive and the scientific.

The remaining chapters in Part II take a closer look at how we build up ideas and concepts into our minds and devise the learning techniques that are needed. The remaining part of this chapter looks for ways in which we can uncover children's naive ideas, using elicitation techniques.

Eliciting children's ideas

It is easy to see how words mean different things to different people at different times, and how meanings and concepts develop and change over time. It is vital for a teacher to know what children mean by the words they use and the ideas that lie behind them. However, research has already shown us what many of these are likely to be (Driver *et al.* 1994), and if we spend too much time in class eliciting ideas from children we will have no time left to teach them and allow them to learn. Elicitation of ideas is important for two reasons. Teachers need to know where their pupils are, and pupils need to compare their existing ideas with the new ideas they are being taught, to enable these new concepts to be built firmly into their (new) understanding. Previous research will tell us what we might expect, but not what is actually the case in our class. So what are needed are ways to bring ideas quickly into the open, so they can be built on or challenged. Educational research may use time-consuming methods that probe more deeply, but, as teachers, we need to make use of this research, rather than repeat it. There is, however, a value in every teacher doing this probing research at least once, for one class, on one topic, because this helps the teacher to realise the existence of these strongly held naive concepts. In what follows we survey methods of probing and displaying these ideas.

Probing the cognitive structure of the whole class: talk

Question, tell each other, vote

If previous research has already uncovered possible alternative ideas, we can use this method to provide a quick picture of where the pupils are.

Present the class with a multiple-choice question, like those at the start of this chapter, in cartoon format if you wish, and give them ten seconds to make up their mind by discussing with their neighbour an explanation of their choice (preferably in a whisper). Now take a vote on each alternative. This is more powerful, and quicker, than asking them to write, because talking is so much easier than writing if you need to clarify an idea. 'Tell each other' allows the pupils to make a commitment, which is now ready to be built on or challenged. At this stage simply thank the class and say 'we'll take another vote at the end'. Assuming the class does display some misunderstandings you will need to set up discussions, videos, practical work, teacher explanations etc. to challenge them. Every now and then say 'Several of you thought...who still thinks this way?', and if necessary get other pupils to explain the problem. Take the vote in the same way at the end to enable the pupils to make a commitment to the new idea (see Chapter 8, p. 63, for further discussion of 'tell each other').

Brainstorm

This is a similar technique, but useful if you are not giving suggested alternatives. Ask the pupils a question, allow ten seconds for them to tell each other (as before) but now collect in the range of ideas. As each idea is suggested, write it on the OHP or whiteboard, and ask how many others thought that (this allows a tally to be made to find the most popular responses). The important thing is to accept every idea as of equal merit, which will encourage a full range of ideas. As the lessons progress you can show the pupils how their ideas shift (we hope!) towards the more scientifically acceptable ones.

Probing the cognitive structure of the whole class: written responses

If you want a more permanent method of eliciting the ideas of the whole class, where you can link ideas to individual pupils, one of the following written methods will need to replace the much quicker 'tell each other' or 'brainstorm' techniques above.

- *Word associations* and definitions. Get pupils to write the word/concept in an oval in the centre of a page, and write a simple definition inside the oval. Round the outside write all the words and ideas that they think are closely linked to the word. See Figure 5.10 and Sutton 1992: 61.

- *Questionnaires*. The advantage of a questionnaire is that it can be administered to a large sample but it can require considerable reading and writing skill on the behalf of the student answering the questionnaire. If multiple-choice questions are used they need to be based on interviews to generate the possible alternatives.

- *Concept mapping*. This is a very powerful technique that can be used to find out pupils' initial ideas, but can also be used by them to modify or build on them during learning, and is discussed in Chapter 10, p. 76.

- *Drawing, annotations, writing*. All the techniques we use to help pupils make sense of their learning may also reveal any remaining misconceptions. All these active learning tasks are reviewed in Chapter 10.

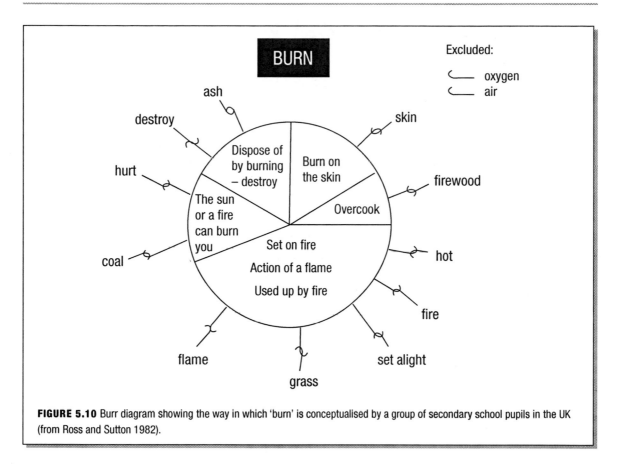

FIGURE 5.10 Burr diagram showing the way in which 'burn' is conceptualised by a group of secondary school pupils in the UK (from Ross and Sutton 1982).

- *Everyday language and idiom.* Listening to the way people talk can often uncover the 'accepted' everyday understanding typical of a culture. In everyday English we say 'it's *burnt* away', 'no *animals* allowed', '*light* as air', '*heavy* as lead'. All of these imply meanings for the italicised words that are not the same as their scientific meaning. It is almost certain that our pupils will use these words in their everyday sense (see 'Grains of truth' in Chapter 4).

Some techniques used to display cognitive structure

If we are going to pay attention to these naive ideas of our pupils we need a clear way of displaying what they think. Sometimes they can simply be described in words, as in many of the ideas presented earlier in this chapter. Here are other possibilities:

- *Burr diagrams.* A core of meaning surrounded by associated words and ideas (e.g. Figure 5.10).
- *Concept maps.* Labelling the links (Chapter 10).
- *Concept profiles.* As in Chapter 4, Figure 4.1.
- *Age profiles.* Showing changes in ideas as children get older, as in Figure 5.8.
- *Concept cartoons.* As in Figure 5.4.

Children's ideas about concepts at KS 3, for which there were research reports at the time, are displayed in Driver *et al.* (1994), a valuable record of children's ideas.

Probing the cognitive structure for research

Interviewing

The clinical interview was pioneered by Piaget's work in the 1920s and 1930s (e.g. Piaget 1929). In their account of the interview as an evaluation tool, Osborne and Freyberg (1985: Appendix A) provide a useful set of rules for potential interviewers, such as:

- Don't teach. Students should not feel that the interviewer holds all the right answers, otherwise pupils will play the game of guessing what you want them to say. Think of their answers not as right or wrong, but as interesting. Responses from the interviewer should be 'Tell me more', 'Can you explain why you think that?'

- Allow time to listen to what the student is saying – a minimum of ten seconds before you ask for more. The main point is that the student should do the talking and frequent interruptions by the interviewer do not allow students to develop their ideas.

The interview about instances technique

This uses a structured interview approach that makes analysis of students' thinking more straightforward. A series of cards depicting an instance or a non-instance of a concept. The cards shown in Figure 5.11 will help to elicit students' ideas about burning: do they distinguish between charring and combustion, and do they see respiration as a form of burning (Gilbert *et al*. 1985)?

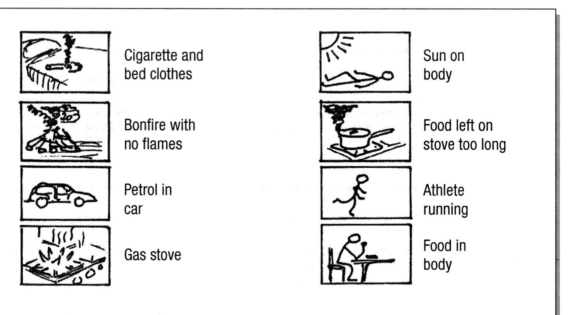

FIGURE 5.11 The interview about instances technique: example of cards used to examine the concept 'burn' (from Ross 1989).

Group or individual interviews?

The value of peer interaction, which happens when you work with a small group of pupils, cannot be overvalued, and can often help to overcome the 'I want to please teacher' or 'I'm scared of saying things to a teacher' attitude of an individual. With groups of four to six pupils some may be silent, but the others tend to argue among themselves, revealing interesting information about their scientific beliefs.

Summary

In our work with trainee science teachers we ask them to interview a small group of pupils to find out their existing beliefs, and to provide a written evaluation of the exercise. We provide feedback to the trainees by means of numbered comments, which have built up and evolved over the years. This feedback technique allows evaluative comments to be shared by the whole group, and it allows us to make detailed but very quick responses to trainees' written work. Table 5.1 shows some of the feedback comments. These comments serve as a summary of this chapter, which has shown the importance of finding out pupils' initial ideas. Only when we know the ideas held by our pupils can we start to build on or challenge them. That is the topic of the next four chapters.

TABLE 5.1 Tutor feedback comments on elicitation task for trainee teachers

---

*1 Must we *override* or *replace* children's ideas? They are sometimes too well used in everyday life to discard: 'No animals allowed in this shop.' Perhaps we need instead to make the pupils *aware* that there is conflict, and to show the limitations of both the scientific and the everyday versions.

*2 Those who question the 'taken-for-granted' make the biggest strides forward in our understanding of the world.

*3 Scientific ideas, models and metaphors are useful but not absolutely true, so it is helpful to show not only where they help our understanding of a phenomenon, but also where they break down and we need to find a more sophisticated model.

*4 It may not be necessary to make children's ideas explicit on every occasion. If teachers are aware of the range of ideas children might have, they can straight away provide appropriate learning materials – see *1.

*5 Paradigm shifts are not instantaneous: several refutations are needed, coupled with a dissatisfaction with the existing paradigm. Several of you mentioned how tenacious children's existing ideas appear to be – but see *1.

*6 The constructivist approach must not be confused with discovery learning. Evidence shows that pupils discover little by doing experiments, unless they have a clear idea of why the experiment has been set up, and what sort of outcomes are possible – in this way experiments are used to test out ideas. If pupils only hold their naive ideas, then the experiences will only serve to confirm their beliefs.

A constructivist approach to learning

There is clear evidence that children develop frameworks of belief about natural phenomena that often conflict with our accepted scientific understanding, and, just as scientists' own understandings have undergone revolutions over historical time, so children's ideas will also change. In this chapter we examine the learning process and compare it with the way scientists develop concepts.

Concept formation

Words and ideas develop and change in meaning as children get older or as science progresses over cultural or historical time. As our minds constantly try to make sense of our everyday experiences, we build up mental models that begin to fit with incoming sensory data. Consider the following example relating to gases.

Gases and vapours, to Newton, were ethereal: like light and sound and smells, they had no real substance. Such 'vapours' were classed as imponderable (meaning unweighable: *pond* is the same word as *pound*, the unit of weight). Scientists in the eighteenth century came to realise that gases were real, substantial matter, as people such as Lavoisier were trapping gases over water and mercury, and realising that they could be weighed. They were made of *stuff*, just like solids and liquids. This work led to Dalton's atomic theory in 1810, when he proposed that all matter, including gases, was made of atoms. The old idea of imponderable gases is sensible to many children and we cannot hope that they will come up with the new ideas by themselves. We shouldn't be surprised if they hold the same 'naive' ideas as scientists of old.

It is often helpful to consider children as reliving the course of history as they grapple with the task of understanding their environment. By standing on the shoulders of giants (provided, for example, through the input from teachers) they acquire an understanding unheard of 20, 50 or 100 years ago. A powerful way to help children with their misconceptions is to show them that other, quite learned, people saw the world very much as they do, and to show the children the problems with the old ideas and why new ideas were needed. Sutton (1992:80) suggests that we should show pupils scientists' initial thoughts about a revolutionary theory, and ask 'Well, Mary, what do you think these people had in mind when they put it that way?'

Not all topics lend themselves to this approach, but the principle that children need to have time and help to construct their own meanings is at the heart of constructivist approaches to teaching.

Constructivist approaches to learning

Constructivist approaches to learning are well documented (e.g. Driver *et al.* 1994; Ross 2000b). Figure 6.1 summarises the criteria that must be fulfilled if learners are to make sense of material they are trying to learn – the process of *meaningful learning*. The figure is based on the ideas of Ausubel and Bruner (see Littledyke 1998).

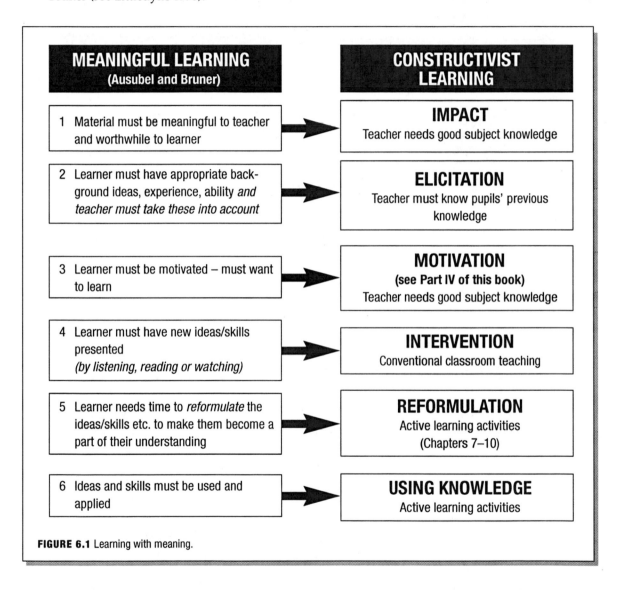

FIGURE 6.1 Learning with meaning.

The six phases of teaching need not necessarily all occur in one lesson, but even in a coherent sequence of lessons which follow through these six phases, individual lessons will still use most of them, even if the emphasis is on just one or two. To illustrate this approach, the discussion that follows uses ideas about the purpose of the wax in a candle (see also Figure 5.3 and the related discussion in the previous chapter).

Material must be meaningful to the teacher and worthwhile to the learner

The first step is to have material that is useful to the learner, and is understood by the teacher. We get pupils to take notice of something, and be curious about it.

Impact: what is going on when a candle burns?

The learner must have appropriate background ideas, experience and ability, and the teacher must take these into account

The next step is to see where the pupils are in their thinking. This was the focus of Chapter 5. We identified, through the elicitation questions, some basic ideas that children may retain right into adulthood, but that, through our awareness of what they are and of how firmly they are held, we might be able to challenge during science lessons at school.

Elicitation: perhaps wax slows the burning of the wick. After all, a fat candle with lots of wax takes longer to burn than a thin one.

These two stages, impact and elicitation, have been labelled *starter activities* by the KS 3 strategy.

The learner must be motivated, must want to learn

Without motivated pupils all our efforts are wasted. How to keep the pupils motivated and on task forms the basis of Part IV (especially Chapters 20 and 21), but teacher enthusiasm for the subject matter is also essential, and this implies that the teacher's subject knowledge is good.

The learner must have new ideas/skills presented (by listening, reading or watching)

This is where traditional teaching comes in. We cannot expect pupils to discover everything anew. We have already seen that pupils create their own naive interpretations of natural phenomena – we cannot expect them to have the same inspirations that scientists had. New experiences and new ideas need to be presented to the children, but to be effective they must be embedded in these other stages. Teachers need to *intervene* with a new idea (or clarify an idea suggested by some of the pupils).

Intervention: pupils need to realise that their initial idea doesn't work, so they are given an alternative. Since fatter candles contain the same amount of wick as thin candles, yet give out much more light, couldn't the wax be the fuel, just like the oil of an oil lamp? Pupils could blow out a candle and then try igniting the white 'smoke' coming from the wick to see the flame jump back and relight the candle. If you see wax as a fuel, this provides you with powerful evidence: wax, evaporating from the still-hot wick, recondenses as a smoke trail and ignites. But if pupils still prefer the wax-is-a-flame-retardant idea, they may only 'see' the wick relighting and decide to reject the wax-is-fuel idea: it seems sensible that fat candles burn slowly because there is so much wax to melt out of the way, slowing the burning of the wick. If we left teaching at this point pupils might 'learn' by heart that 'wax is a fuel' and get marks in teachers' tests, but 'know' in *their* reality that the 'wax is a flame retardant'. When teaching stops here pupils may remain trapped in their naive ideas, and the science they 'learn' in school would simply enable them to pass exams, then promptly be forgotten.

The learner needs time to reformulate the ideas/skills etc. to make them become a part of their understanding

If you tell something to a pupil the chances are they will forget. They need time to translate from your intervention (teaching) into ideas that belong to *them* – the idea of *ownership*. Many times we are tempted to ask a class 'Do you all understand?' and we get back the obliging chorus of 'Yes'. The 'nod of agreement' from pupils hides a chasm of misunderstanding. The best way to check if we understand an idea is to communicate it to someone else. The act of explaining is only possible if you understand it properly yourself. This is why so many teachers say, 'It was only when I started to teach that I fully understood'. We need to give pupils this same opportunity to teach new ideas to others, or themselves. How teachers can enable this to happen is the topic of the rest of Part II, Chapters 7–11.

Reformulation: in our example, pupils could be asked to make a worksheet for next year's class to compare a candle, an oil lamp and a Bunsen burner, especially the fuels each uses (wax, oil and gas), and to explain why the candle and oil lamp need a wick but the Bunsen burner doesn't.

Ideas and skills must be used and applied

However well an idea is understood, it is likely to fade in the memory if it is not used. The idea of a spiral curriculum, where topics are revisited frequently, is obviously important, but in every topic we must make links to previous topics and everyday experiences. Pupils should see topics in science not as isolated things that they have 'done' but as forming a part of a network of interconnected ideas. Concept mapping is a powerful way to encourage the making of links (see Chapter 10, p. 76).

Using ideas: wax is clearly a fuel. Candles need a wick so that the wax can evaporate and catch fire. They used to be made of tallow, animal fat, which is also used as a fuel store for the animal. So the topic links to the topic of burning and respiration, where fuel and oxygen combine, forming carbon dioxide and water, and where energy stored in the fuel–oxygen system is transferred.

Concept formation over historical time and through teaching

It is useful to compare the stages in a constructivist approach to learning and teaching with the process of being scientific we developed in Chapter 1. We need to compress the concept formation process that has taken place over many centuries by scientists into just a few years of secondary schooling.

Figure 6.2 repeats Figure 1.1, but with added help from a teacher. Instead of waiting for the inspiration of scientists through the ages to generate more universally applicable ideas, our own pupils can benefit from their teachers' knowledge. Without this help pupils are likely to remain in the first cycle of naive knowledge. Without the opportunities we give for reformulation, akin to scientists publishing their ideas, pupils may, at best, learn the new ideas by rote, long enough to pass examinations, but for them never to become a real part of their mental make-up.

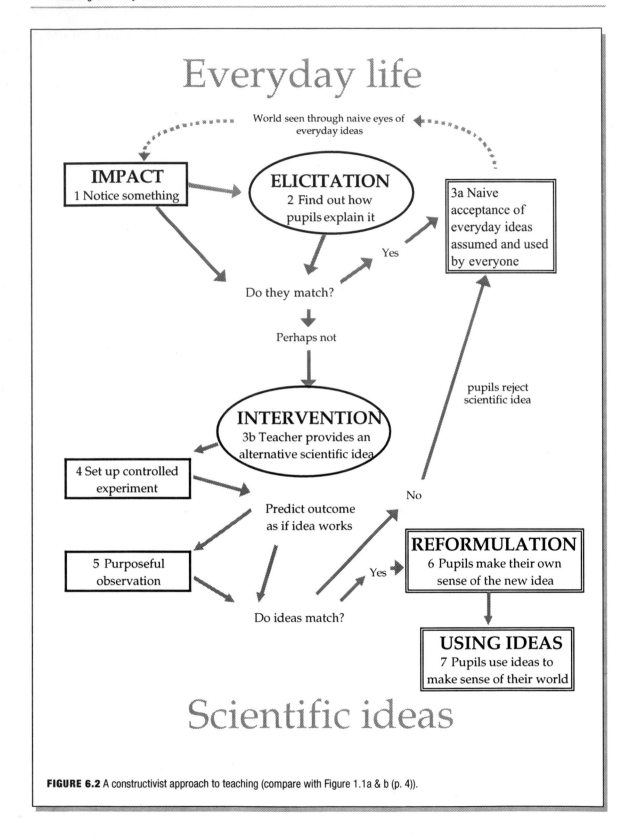

FIGURE 6.2 A constructivist approach to teaching (compare with Figure 1.1a & b (p. 4)).

Summary

We have added five of the six stages of a constructivist approach to learning (Figure 6.1) to our model of how science itself works (creating Figure 6.2). Our job, as teachers, is twofold.

- Inspired by the creativity of great scientists we need to present their revolutionary ideas to our pupils. We have almost always done that – it is called teaching. In the 1960s we thought pupils could discover everything afresh, but without this *intervention* pupils will remain trapped in the naive cycle of everyday thinking.
- We also have to give the pupils the chance to publish: to reinterpret or *reformulate* these ideas to make them their own. This stage in the teaching–learning cycle we neglect at our peril, and this is the topic of the next set of chapters.

Active learning techniques

Evidence abounds (see Chapters 4 and 5) that children retain some of their misconceptions in science despite our best endeavours to teach. What can be done? This chapter introduces techniques of active learning, where learners are given time to undertake activities allowing them to restructure their thinking to accommodate the new ideas we think we have so successfully taught. We mustn't allow ourselves to say 'the syllabus is too crowded for such luxuries'.

Far from being a luxury, the time we give children to make sense of what we have taught is essential. If pupils don't reformulate their thoughts to accommodate new ideas, they will forget everything very soon after their exams, and they will have no scientific understanding to help them understand the world they live in.

Active learning

We are now ready to respond to the range of pupils' alternative ideas by using *active learning* techniques. Our teaching has elicited the ideas held by our pupils, and there are many who hold a naive view (Chapters 4 and 5). We *intervene* by challenging this view and presenting a scientific alternative. If teaching stopped there, we might produce a picture of the world in pupils' minds with the horticultural analogy of Figure 7.1.

School science is sometimes built up as a system of separate ideas, like a carefully weeded horticultural establishment, uncontaminated by the natural ecosystems of everyday life. Children learn about heat and temperature, atoms and molecules, fair testing and Bunsen burners, but do not build them into their everyday understanding. At best they have a scientific system that is good enough to pass examinations. But after the crops have been harvested, the land is bare, the ideas are lost and everyday life is unaffected (Figure 7.2).

If school science is to be of lasting use, pupils must constantly make links, challenge their everyday ideas and see how their new ideas can be applied to understand the complex forest of experience that surrounds them every day. That is the task of active approaches to learning. We need to open the gate between school science and everyday life (Figure 7.3).

Learners need time to *reformulate* their ideas to make them become a part of their understanding. This has to be done through working with ideas and words, so-called *word-work* (Sutton 1992). Figure 7.4 is taken from the teaching sequence of Figure 6.1 and summarises the need for active learning and the techniques available to science teachers.

FIGURE 7.1 School science (from Ross 1990).

FIGURE 7.2 Harvesting school knowledge (from Ross 1990).

FIGURE 7.3 The gate of active learning (from Ross 1990).

Active learning is not pupil-centred learning

We must be careful not to equate *active learning* with *pupil-centred learning*. Active learning doesn't usually give autonomy over organisation of the learning to the learner: many active learning tasks are very directional and specific, but the main point is that they are impossible to do unless the children *think*. We cannot expect pupils to reinvent the whole of science, so their task instead is to take over the stories/ideas that scientists have used to explain the world. This may involve pupils having to modify their own ideas, to think about things they have never thought to question; or it may involve them developing ideas about phenomena they have never experienced before. In all cases they need time to *reformulate* and thus take ownership of ideas.

When we wrote this book we didn't start at the beginning and write the finished text in one go. There were discussions, drafts, redrafts and proof reading, before the final text. What we were doing was reformulating our experiences of teaching science in an attempt to make them clear to others. The process begins with talk – the easiest language medium to work with. One idea sparks off another. Everything is fluid. So it should be with teaching. Pupils need to be given the opportunity to talk things through before being asked to write. So our next chapter explores pupil talk; it also examines the power of role-play and *doing*, as a means to make sense of ideas. Reading should be easier than writing, but if the text is full of strange words, readers may make no sense of what they read. Chapter 9 explores the activities we can devise related to texts to make the reading meaningful, in Chapter 10 we look at ways to help pupils to write creatively and in Chapter 11 we introduce numbers.

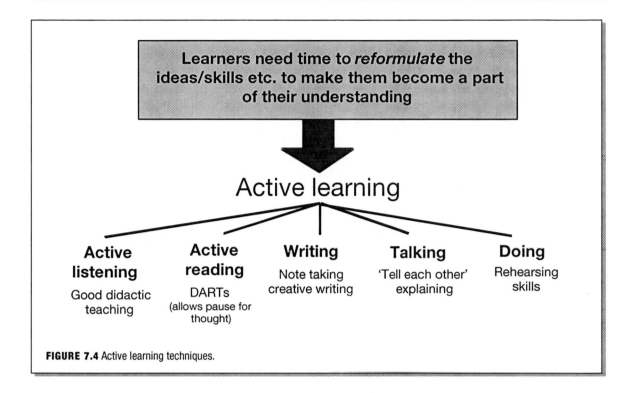

FIGURE 7.4 Active learning techniques.

A sample lesson

We can put these constructivist ideas into practice, outlined in Figure 6.2 (p. 54), by using the following structure for a typical lesson, relating to 'force, gravity and motion'.

Impact

Asking the pupils to question what is taken for granted is one of the most challenging activities, and often leads to some very constructive learning. For example, hold a ball high between your fingers and thumb and ask the pupils to watch very carefully to see what happens when you release your grip. As if by magic it moves towards the floor, with increasing speed, even though no one had pushed it. Compare this with a similarly held ball resting on a table and, later in the lesson, with a ball gripped on the bench but connected to stretched elastic that will accelerate it along the bench when released.

Elicitation

We need to allow time, at the start of a topic, to take account of pupils' ideas and to respect them. Within each lesson we need to activate children's ideas so that they can be challenged or built upon. On these occasions our elicitation needs to be brief but significant, so the lesson time can be used for intervention and reformulation activities. For the elicitation ask the pupils what forces act on the ball thrown into the air (Chapter 5, question 11 and Figure 5.7, p. 40).

Intervention

The teacher must teach by providing alternative ideas for the pupil to latch on to before any restructuring can occur. Occasionally useful ideas will have been suggested by a child, possibly from previous teaching, reading or interest, but even then they need to be clearly re-presented. Sutton (1992) suggests that we tell 'stories' to children of how scientists believe things are. Children then construct these stories into their mental map. Intervention can also allow pupils to investigate practically, gaining experiences and testing new ideas; then the reconstruction, which is to come, allows them to investigate using words.

In our example we can tell the story of Newton, who suggested that if a force acts on a ball it will change its speed or direction of motion. A ball thrown upwards begins to slow down as soon as it leaves the hand and stops, at the 'top' of its flight, before accelerating downwards. Thus we only need to show it has a single constant downward force on it: the force of gravity that acts between the ball and the planet Earth. To demonstrate the effect of gravity, throw a tennis ball sideways along the bench but with a long piece of elastic attached, which you keep hold of. Pupils can now see that for a ball to move away from your hand, slow, stop and return, a retarding force is needed (Ross *et al*. 2002: atmosphere).

Reformulation

The 'eureka' feeling when understanding suddenly bursts through the mental fog and a difficult concept is mastered is one of the joys of teaching and it is the hallmark of someone who is actively taking over meaning. It is both the excitement of learning and the reward. It is often only when you get to teach that you prove you understand, so making pupils teach each other (or themselves) must be at the heart of active learning. In our example they could explain to themselves the similarity of the two returning balls, one through gravity and one through the elastic.

Use of ideas

The last, but perhaps most important, of all of the principles of Bruner's learning strategy is that ideas must be *used*. One approach to this is to give pupils the chance to grow *pearls of wisdom*.

Pearls of wisdom

From the smallest grain of dust, oysters produce pearls. The Pearl project was developed by Gloria Coleman, a Gloucestershire primary teacher, much travelled and now retired. Her pupils found a speck of dust, an instant in time, and researched it to produce *pearls of wisdom*. It is a wonderful approach to developing subject confidence across the curriculum – a way of *using* and applying scientific ideas. Here are some grains of dust and some incidents in time that can be grown into pearls. Here is the chance to use the concept of force (or energy, particle, cell etc.) to explain everyday phenomena.

- You can see your breath on a cold day.
- A leaf 'floats down' on an autumn day.
- You hear the squeal of brakes.
- You smell toast burning.

The process will help our pupils to see the science in events we take for granted. It will enable them to integrate their active scientific knowledge and make use of it.

Summary

Pupils' understanding in science is strongly influenced by what they do, see and hear in their everyday lives. If school science is to make any impact on their understanding, it must first of all recognise the influence of their everyday lives. We must not expect that one lesson will revolutionise their thoughts. Instead we must provide plenty of opportunity for pupils to translate the new ideas presented to them into their own words and meanings, and give the pupils the opportunity to use and apply the new ideas. This will give them the chance to compare the results with their existing ideas to show that these new ideas are better. This chapter has argued that our teaching must have *reformulation* firmly embedded into it – the next chapters show how this can be done.

Children learning through talking

Only recently, and only in certain countries, has there been anything like universal literacy, yet almost everyone can use the spoken language. This chapter examines the role of talking (by teacher and pupils) and listening (by pupils and teacher) in the science classroom, especially in relation to the opportunity it gives to pupils to reformulate ideas to make them meaningful – to allow them to take ownership of knowledge. We also examine the place of role-play and other doing activities when they are expressly concerned with allowing pupils to make sense of the ideas they are being taught. Periods of silence, though useful and welcome at the right time, are less common in the science classroom than talk. The aim of this chapter is to ensure that this talk is productive.

Teacher talk

Listening to the teacher can be active learning: children in rapt attention, making sense of what you say, as you speak. University lecturers rely on this for their effectiveness. However, pupils and students still need time later to reorganise and store the new ideas. They make brief notes during the lecture, they discuss it afterwards with one another and they produce their own written record of it in the privacy of their study. Lectures may be effective for highly motivated, resourceful university students and a few pupils and sixth-form students in school. But for most of our science lessons with most pupils we can rely neither on this 'rapt attention' nor on their ability or motivation to discuss and make notes for themselves following the lesson. Listening, watching and most forms of school practical work therefore become *intervention* activities, where the teacher is telling a scientific story. *Reformulation* comes through the activities that follow. This chapter focuses on the role of talk and role-play – the easiest reformulation processes for pupils, and therefore the ones we should start with. Reading, writing and maths come later (Chapters 9–11).

Pupil talk

Pupils would talk all the time if we let them. The secret is to make this as useful as possible. Many lessons contain question and answer sessions where the pupils listen as the teacher goes round the class. Except for the child actually speaking, such an activity must be classed as *intervention*, with the rest of the pupils, it is hoped, trying to make sense of the flow of conversation, but not able to try things out themselves. A few pupils will be rehearsing answers, and putting up their hands. Many will be afraid that they will be asked and have nothing to say. A few may not care one way or another and be ready with the response 'I don't know, miss'.

This sort of questioning happens in many science classrooms all over the country: good 'Socratic' questioning, with one pupil talking and 29 listening. How can we improve this so that everyone has the chance to talk – so that everyone has the opportunity to make their own sense of what is being taught by trying to explain it to someone, but without the class becoming chaotic?

Tell each other (talk partners)

This is a very powerful technique for asking class questions that every teacher should experiment with. When you ask a question you will usually wait for hands to go up. Typically you should wait ten seconds and then ask someone (not always the ones with their hands raised). Instead, try saying: 'Tell each other what you think makes the bulb light up'. With a Year 7 or 8 class you might get away with 'Whisper to your neighbour...' and give them ten seconds of talk, not silence. Half the pupils will have an idea and tell their partner (a few may be off task altogether). You then say 'Quiet now, please: hands up those who have an idea', or simply choose people to respond. After hearing each response, you say 'Hands up those who agree. Are there any other ideas?'

In this way every child has the chance to reply. How many disappointed looks do you get when a child is 'bursting' to tell you the answer, and you choose someone else? They can now turn to their partner and nod as if to say 'I knew that, didn't I?', or else be thankful that their wrong answer remained in their small circle. The pupils who are asked to reply in open class have had the chance to rehearse their answer (verbally) to their partner, before having to speak it out in class. Far more pupils become willing to put up their hands to reply.

Many books on learning theory stress the need for 'wait-time': we tend to accept answers almost immediately, but should give pupils thinking time of about ten seconds before accepting answers. The *tell each other* technique is no slower than this wait-time class questioning, yet it involves the whole class. Its value is that it allows (nearly all) pupils to rehearse their ideas *verbally* before answering in front of the whole class. It really only works if you restrict the time to *ten seconds*. If you give more time it is better to call it group discussion, and they will be given a more structured task.

Pupil *talk* must come before they write: they must be given the chance to make their own sense of the new ideas in the lesson. *Tell each other* is the simplest and quickest way to do this. If the active talking activities involving the whole class need more than the ten-second time-span, you need to provide more structure (see below). The key to successful discussion (or any activity) is the *tight control of time*: set a series of short do-able tasks.

Structured activities using pupil talk

When you overhear your pupils arguing and discussing their science lessons outside class, struggling to make sense of ideas, excited by what they have learnt, it is a good sign that your pupils are active in their learning. There are many ways to promote this in a structured way in class:

- peer-group discussion to develop an explanation for a phenomenon (why do bulbs go dim when in series, but stay bright in parallel?);
- debating an issue, having been given resources to examine (as in many Science and Technology in Society (SATIS) activities; see Chapter 26) or the genetics debate below);

- planning a group report or poster presentation on the results of practical work or investigations;

- deciding on an explanation prior to devising further investigation (the reason why white light goes green when it hits a leaf; see box 8.1).

You need an intense very thin beam of white light that can be split by a prism into a pure spectrum. Pupils can see that coloured filters simply block some of the colours, letting only their colour through. Seal two microscope slides together with a thick band of glue from a glue gun so that you can pour into this a strong solution of chlorophyll in alcohol (made by grinding up grass with ethanol and filtering). Now the physics of light and colour can be linked with the red and blue light captured by a green leaf.

Pupil talk at the start is needed to elicit their ideas about what makes things look coloured. They are then shown the spectrum, and asked how their various ideas can be tested. Following the practical work (or teacher demonstration) with filters they can decide on which explanation (of how the filters worked) best fitted the experimental results. Finally, they can apply these ideas to the sunlight energy captured by green leaves.

BOX 8.1 What makes leaves green?

A genetics debate

Having grappled with the fundamentals of genetics and cell division, pupils are in a position to get their teeth into the major issues of today. These are displayed readily on a daily basis via the media. They were epitomised in Dolly the cloned sheep, Polly the transgenic sheep and the so-called 'Frankenstein foods', including a virus-resistant sweet potato for Kenya. There are many social, moral and ethical issues associated with these, lending themselves to group and whole-class debate. This needs to be managed effectively. To ensure that pupils can contribute to such debates they should be encouraged to collect relevant newspaper cuttings on the issues and take part in role-play scenarios whereby they access all aspects of the debate.

The following questions highlight issues that can form the basis of detailed debate and discussion:

- Should scientists be allowed to alter people's genes? Would it make a difference if the genes they altered were faulty ones, so that an illness like cystic fibrosis could be cured? What if they could alter sex genes, so that the illness would not be passed on to the next generation but the human genetic pool would be irrevocably changed?

- Should we create cows and sheep with human genes so that the milk they produce can be used to treat people with diabetes or haemophilia? What about producing animals whose organs will not be rejected by human bodies, so that they can be used for transplant?

- Should it be possible to patent genes? At present genes of known function can be patented – for example, the cystic fibrosis gene is 'owned' by the universities of Michigan and Toronto, but it is not yet clear whether parts of genes or those of unknown function can be registered.

- Should food crops be modified to enable greater yields to be obtained for Third World farmers? Who should own the patents for such developments?

Pupils could have notes to support what they say, but insist that they speak *ex tempore*, i.e. they do not read from a prepared text, but speak from their understanding.

Showing a video

Many teachers use a worksheet to accompany a video. If we use the principle that pupils need to talk things through before they write, then why not give out the worksheet beforehand, but *forbid the use of pens*? Stop the video at two or three natural breaks and ask the pupils to answer the relevant questions orally using the 'tell each other' technique. This enables pupils to sort out their ideas in an easier language mode first, and takes less time, so that when the video restarts (promptly) they are all able to listen and watch.

You can then get them to return to their places, pick up their pens and complete the worksheet in silence at the end of the video.

Doing practical work

Practical work does not necessarily result in active learning. If the experiment is to be more than recipe following, pupils must know what to look out for, be involved in the planning and have a sense of purpose. The active learning comes before and after the doing, because the actual mechanics of carrying out the practical activities absorb most of the pupil's attention (see Chapter 1). Here are some ideas:

■ Get pupils to *tell each other* the purpose, the safety points, the things they must do before they actually start the practical work.

■ Get pupils to *predict* the outcome of an investigation and justifying the prediction, using 'tell each other' (especially when there is disagreement between pupils). This helps to make the practical work meaningful.

■ Get groups of pupils to report verbally to the rest of the class from a range of (practical) activities. As they are performing the investigation they can plan what they are to say and each group can then 'teach' their experiment or findings to the other groups in the class. They should report back *ex tempore* using notes, not a script.

Techniques such as these, which make practical work into active thinking activities, may appear to take more time, but if pupils know why they are doing something they are likely to be more enthusiastic and carry it out more efficiently.

Role-play

Getting pupils to act out being atoms, blood cells etc. can be a powerful way of helping them to internalise the scientific stories we tell them. Having acted these out, they are more able to write creatively about what they have done (see Chapter 10). Pupils who are actually engaged in the role-play don't always see the full picture, so divide the class into two and have half watch (and criticise), then swap to give them a turn. Here are some ideas to try:

Being atoms

Atoms do not physically change. The neat vibrating rows of atoms of the solid will give way to a seething mass (but in the same confined space) as it melts. A chalk line on the playground drawn around a 'squad' of lined up pupils defines the size of the solid. Instruct the pupils to make a tiny amount of room for themselves, and jostle about as particles of the liquid. Remember that they mustn't take up any more room, and particles of a liquid touch. Finally, the pupils break free of the mass and can walk in straight lines all over the playground as the substance evaporates. This gives a perfect opportunity to distinguish between particle words (bond, vibrate, move) and bulk substance words (evaporate, get hot, diffuse). We meet this idea again in Chapter 12, p. 88.

Displacement reactions can also be acted out; for example, where copper displaces silver or zinc displaces copper.

Circulation of the blood

The lab is laid out with desks and tables to represent the heart, the lungs, the gut and liver and three 'body' parts that need to be kept working (head, arms and legs). Pupils are placed at these organs to give or receive tokens and ensure that passwords are given correctly, and the 'blood cells' move round carrying food, oxygen and carbon dioxide. For full details see the blood circulation game in *School Science Review* (Callaghan 1997).

Sound waves

Pupils (they have to be sensible ones) make a line with linked arms. A gentle push or pull at one end passes down the line as a longitudinal wave. If the other end of the line is near a wall the pupils can reflect the wave off the wall and it comes back as an echo.

Summary

We have argued that talk should be the first medium in which we ask our pupils to express their newly acquired knowledge. Pupils love to talk, and we need to channel this into useful learning activities. From the ten-second 'tell each other' to more involved discussion and role-play activities, the secret is to provide a clear structure to allow for this reformulation that allows ideas to be embedded. We should aim to make all pupil talk purposeful, never allowing them time to chat idly and always getting them to speak from their own understanding, rather than from a script.

CHAPTER

9

Children learning through reading

In this chapter we look at ways to make reading a more active process for pupils. Scientific texts are not the same as the narrative of novels, which can be read cover to cover as the story unfolds. With our texts we need to get the pupils to pause and reflect on what they are reading – to try to make some sense of it. We deal here with the transformation of reading as a purely information receiving process (intervention) into one in which learners can make their own sense or meaning as they read (reformulation).

Directed activities related to texts (DARTs)

The aim of active learning techniques is to allow pupils to translate ideas received (by watching, listening or reading) into ideas that they *own*, ideas that are *theirs* and that they can use. Often pupils can read texts and answer questions without understanding – recall the discussion we had in Chapter 4 on *markobine gandos* (p. 28 and Box 4.3).

Techniques that give pupils the opportunity to interact with the text they are reading are called DARTs (Davies and Greene 1984; Sutton 1992: Chapters 5 and 6). In essence they all give pupils the chance to think and reflect about what they are reading. The commonest examples are *cloze* procedures where gaps are left in the text, but more demanding are scrambled texts that have to have their paragraphs reordered, diagram labelling (from text), annotations and many more.

Just as we pause in our teaching to ask questions and check understanding, so, with reading, we need to give pupils the chance to make sense of what they read. We can expect mature readers to make their own notes from published texts, but even at sixth-form level many teachers do not trust their students to do this, and so provide them with teacher-produced notes. If this happens, when do students make their own sense of it all? Are we asking them to learn these notes by heart to reproduce them in their A-level essay questions, trading it all in for a certificate enabling them to do the same thing at university? We return to the fence in Figure 7.2 (p. 57) all over again – science fails to impact on their everyday life understanding.

Our aim is to enable pupils to become students, to show them how to make their own notes, their own concept maps, their own summaries. This process should start as early as possible, and DARTs are a useful starting point. They provide the opportunity for pupils who still find reading hard and writing harder to make a clean written record of their work, but a record that they have in some way created themselves and therefore internalised. The essence is that writing is minimised. Instead of asking pupils to copy a completed text into their books we use the time to get them to read it and reflect on it. How this reflection is done is the subject of this chapter.

Which texts do we use with pupils?

Scientific writing can be broadly classified into four types:

- narrative (telling the story of a discovery);
- instructions (telling pupils what to do and how to do it, including word work and practical work);
- descriptive (describing a phenomenon, such as a volcano);
- explanatory (giving a theory, such as using particle theory to show how rocks, once solid, can become molten).

Only the first of these can be read as a story – the rest need to be worked at and internalised. Textbooks can be difficult to read if these types of writing are all muddled up. Nearly all modern texts for pupils use paragraph structure and boxes to separate different types of writing. Have a look at any double page spread in any school science text, and notice how this is done. It is worth trying to classify the text in each box or section on each two-page spread into these four types: you are likely to find that only one class of text is used in any one place.

There are two problems with using extracts from textbooks with your pupils. First, the writing may be too difficult. There are various formulae which attempt to measure the readability of texts, the simplest of which is the SMOG test (see Box 9.1). This works by asking you to choose an average sentence, and count the number of words with three or more syllables in it. If the book has short sentences and few long words it is easier to read, and gets a low reading age score. A second problem is that the subject content may not match your requirements exactly.

Writing your own texts for pupils can be equally problematic and is not easy. When we write worksheets for our pupils, it is likely that we will not have put them through the several drafts that are needed to make them readable and unambiguous. Now we all have word processors we can look at last year's worksheets and refine them for this year's class. All new worksheets should go through several drafts before they are published for pupils.

- Select ten sentences from the beginning of the text you wish to use, ten from the middle and ten from the end.
- Count the number of polysyllabic words (i.e. words with three or more syllables) in all 30 sentences. Call this number n.
- To obtain the 'readability score', i.e. the reading age for the text, take the square root of n and add 8 (the minimum age it detects).

Suppose you find one long word per sentence (for the 30 sentences), making $n = 30$.
The reading age will be $8 + \sqrt{30}$, or about 13.

The longer the sentences, and the more frequent the long words are, the higher the reading age will become.

BOX 9.1 Testing written passages for reading age – the SMOG formula (from Postlethwaite 1993: 113)

Reading for meaning

The ultimate aim is to produce students who are able to build their own understanding from the texts they read, the investigations they undertake, the things they hear and so on. All we need then, if we focus on reading, are texts to lend out to students, which can be reused each year. Table 9.1 classifies DARTs according to whether the published text is modified (by us) or straight, and whether the pupils write on the texts or not, our aim being to move towards the top left of the table as pupils become self-studying students. In the following sections we illustrate examples from all four types.

TABLE 9.1 Classifying DARTs

Types of DART	Straight text	Modified text
Reusable texts	Making notes from textbook Labelling a diagram from text	Card sort/sequencing
Texts written on or cut up and **kept by** pupil	Underlining key ideas Labelling bits of text	Cut and paste sequencing Cloze

Straight texts, reusable

- *Diagram labelling/table filling.* Pupils are given an unlabelled diagram (e.g. the digestive tract). They are supplied with a text that explains the parts and functions. They have to label the diagram using the text. A similar activity would involve filling in a table: for example, of the functions of different digestive enzymes.

- *Note making.* Our ultimate aim is that students are able to make their own sense of what they read and so are able to make their own notes with no further help from us.

Straight texts, kept by pupils

- *Underlining key ideas.* This is what many of us do when reading textbooks. In class we can photocopy a passage for our pupils – for example, about blood circulation – and ask them to underline the sentences that describe where blood is flowing away from the heart.

- *Labelling bits of text.* Pupils could ring all the scientific words to do with the circulation and link them to a short definition that they write in the margin. They could add headings to summarise what each paragraph is about.

Modified texts but reusable

- *Sequencing.* This is one of the most powerful activities linked to reading. Instructions for practical activities can be written in several steps on separate cards. Pupils have to put them in a sensible order before they can undertake the activity. Figure 9.1 is the nail-tube investigation from Chapter 1, but this time pupils have to match a reason for each stage in the practical work.

In this activity on rusting the instructions are all muddled up. We have provided a reason for each step, but these are muddled too. Before you start work you need to read and cut out the steps of the instructions, and the reasons, and arrange them in their proper order.

Instructions

Leave for one week.
Which nails do you think will go rusty, and why?

Fill the second tube half full of freshly boiled (but cooled) water, drop in a nail, pour oil on to the water surface to form a thin layer.

Take three nails and clean them with detergent, then rinse and dry them.

Put anhydrous calcium chloride at the bottom of the third tube, push in some cotton wool to cover it then drop the nail in. Place a rubber bung firmly into the tube.

Put the first nail in a test tube with 1 cm³ of water in it so the nail is half out of the water.

Reasons

This will allow the nail to be in contact with air and water.

This removes any grease from the nail to enable it to rust.

Boiling expels all the dissolved air from the water, so the nail will only be in contact with water.

This is a drying agent, and it will absorb all the water vapour from the air, so the nail is only in contact with air, and not with water.

FIGURE 9.1 Scrambled worksheet with reasons.

- *Card sort.* Pink cards could show scientific words and blue cards could have an explanation of what they mean. Pupils have to match them. A set of cards containing plants and animals has to be sorted (see Chapter 5, question 8, p. 38 for an example).

- *Loop game.* Pupils are given cards (one each) that have a question on one side and an answer to a different question on the reverse, so that as each answer is given the pupil reads out the next question. However, once a pupil has had a turn they play no more part in the loop; so as an alternative try giving a whole set of 28 cards to groups of, say, seven pupils, who have to cooperate to make the loop on their table, domino fashion.

- *Computer mix and match.* Many of these sorting and matching activities can be adapted to be 'played' on a computer.

Modified texts, but kept by pupils

- *Cut and paste sequencing.* This cut and paste activity (Figure 9.2 shows an example) is also known as a scrambled worksheet, because the worksheet will be supplied whole to the pupils to cut up and unscramble. The pupils can then simply stick the steps into their notebooks. However, this can be messy and time-consuming, so it is better to give out sets of laminated cards. When the pupils have sorted them successfully (with support if necessary) you can give out an A5 size completed version for them to stick into their books for the record.

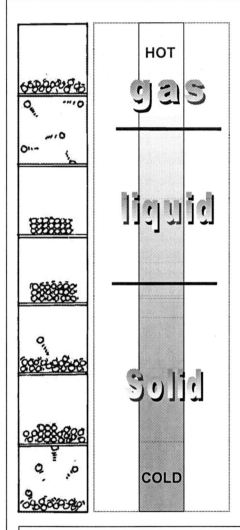

HOT

gas

liquid

solid

COLD

The increased heat energy makes the particles move about more quickly. The faster particles escape from the surface.

The particles are fast moving and are widely spaced. Their kinetic energy is more than sufficient to overcome the forces of attraction.

The particles are packed closely together in a regular lattice. The vibrational energy is not strong enough to overcome the forces of attraction.

The (heat) energy has made the particles vibrate strongly. There is enough energy to overcome some of the attractive forces and the particles, still touching, begin to slide past each other.

The particles now have so much energy that the forces of attraction are often overcome. Some particles start to leave the rest of the seething mass.

The particles are now able to move from place to place freely but are still attracted to each other and remain touching.

Heat energy causes the particles to vibrate more. The particles remain in their fixed places within a regular lattice, but they vibrate more vigorously, while remaining in contact.

Cut out along the dotted lines and mount the temperature bar (solid to liquid to gas) in the centre of the page.

Cut out the diagrams and mount in the position that best describes the state of the particles (on the left of the temperature bar).

Cut out the descriptions showing what happens to the particles at each stage and stick on the right of the bar.

FIGURE 9.2 Example of a scrambled worksheet DART.

■ *Cloze.* Leaving gaps in worksheets for pupils to fill in is probably one of the most widely used DARTs. Sometimes teachers will supply the missing words in a list, and sometimes they will supply the initial letter or the number of letters in the missing word. The aim is to ensure that the pupils read the sentence with enough understanding to supply the missing word. Leaving the *working* words (into, have, make, for) out of a cloze text can be very effective – it tests children's understanding of how the concepts are linked, rather than the meaning of words. Cloze texts suffer from the problem that pupils tend to want to find the missing word without understanding the text. Since each pupil needs to be given a copy of their own, it may be better to convert cloze passages into scrambled texts, which require a greater understanding from the pupils, and less guessing. They get to keep a neat copy of the text with no missing words, but one that they have had to read and understand in order to reassemble it in its proper order.

Summary

Reading is a powerful tool, providing rapid communication, but texts can be too demanding for pupils, and making meaning from them without help is a task we sometimes do not even trust Year 12 and 13 students to do (see Chapter 23 for further discussion). In this chapter we showed a few examples of how we could break up the reading we ask pupils to do, and allow them time, through structured activities, to make sense of what they read. Further examples of this are given in Chapters 12–15.

10

Children learning through writing

We ask pupils to do writing in most lessons. There is a tension between getting a neat and accurate set of notes 'for revision' and giving pupils more freedom, with all the major headaches for teachers: it will be full of mistakes, it will take a long time to mark, they won't have accurate notes for revision. This chapter takes a candid look at the writing we ask pupils to do, and argues that their notebook has much more value as a drafting book than as a textbook – that writing should be used to make meaning for the pupils rather than to be faultless finished notes.

Traditional approaches to writing: strengths and weaknesses

Traditionally pupils copied from the blackboard or from dictation to make a set of notes in their books, which they learnt for examinations. For bright pupils prepared to read their notes as a text-book, and make sense of them, the technique had some merit. However, lesson time spent copying is 'dead' time (wonderful for keeping the class quiet, but no good for making them think). If they have a textbook, or you have the text in a photocopiable or downloadable form, you can use this 'dead' time for a DART (Chapter 9) – the pupils not only have the text but will have begun their reinterpretation of it. You can then use their writing time more creatively.

There is some merit, however, in pupils building up an accurate written record of their work. Few textbooks will cover exactly the material at the right level that a teacher wants. In this case, unless they have kept their own record, how will the pupils review their work? An answer to this once again is for the teacher to provide 'accurate notes' in the form of DARTs, from which pupils make tables or label diagrams, and so on. The time that would have been wasted copying notes can now be used to make sense of them instead.

Much lesson time is spent writing accounts of 'experiments'. Once again, in order to ensure accuracy, we resort to asking pupils to 'write up' experiments in a standard way, often giving them help by dictating bits or writing them on the whiteboard. Is it necessary for every bit of practical experience to be written up in this way, even if we do include an *aim* and *predictions* to go alongside the *method*, *results* and *conclusion*? Our discussion in Chapter 1 of the purposes of practical work in science suggests that there are many reasons for allowing pupils to experience things practically, but only full or partial investigations need to be written up as investigations. More often the practical details are unimportant, and can cause confusion. A written record could focus on the scientific *ideas* that are being challenged or illustrated, or on the *description* of a phenomenon.

Pupils don't usually enjoy writing, especially if they have no ownership of what they write. Many may happily copy things down – a task that requires little mental effort and allows them to dream happily of what they will do that evening after school. We can, however, use pupil writing more creatively, to enable them to make sense of the science they do. How this can be done is the subject of the rest of this chapter.

Moving away from teacher as examiner: some pitfalls and problems

We have already pointed out that published written work has to go through several drafts before going to press. The first 'draft' is likely to be a verbal discussion about what you intend to say. Writing in school science needs to go through the same process: begin by asking the pupils to tell each other what they predict, what they saw, what happened etc. They are then ready to express their own thoughts in their writing.

The important factor, as always, is the *audience* (Sutton 1992: Chapter 10). Pupils writing for us as a teacher-as-examiner will wonder if they 'have got it right'. But if they are writing for a newspaper, their younger brother, the class that follows or a web page, their sense of ownership gives them confidence to write what they really understand and believe. This may, of course, contain misconceptions – and creative writing is a good *elicitation* technique too – but it is better that they expose their misconceptions early than produce writing that isn't theirs and that they don't understand. Pupils may need two notebooks, one for drafting and another for finished work. For those with a laptop the drafting can be done straight on to the computer, but it is worth asking them to save their first drafts. This provides evidence that it is their work, and it is encouraging for the pupils to see the progress they made from initial ideas to finished work.

The star numbered comment system

Creative writing (Figure 10.1) will not provide an accurate record of their work. Instead, it gives pupils an opportunity to make their own sense of the science they are studying. If pupils produced writing like this after every lesson, the marking load for their teacher would be enormous. These pieces of creative writing will contain misconceptions because not every pupil will fully understand everything you teach; nor will they be able to express their ideas accurately in writing. There are, however, ways to lighten our marking load because we are likely to know the sort of errors pupils might make.

- Pupils can read each other's writing and indicate if their partner has made that particular error.
- We can look out for these known errors as we mark. Instead of writing much the same comment in each pupil's book we simply label their errors *1, *2, *3 etc. (pronounced 'star one, star two' etc.). We introduced this system in Table 5.1 (p. 49) with some star comments given to trainee teachers. In lesson time we can explain the problems to the class, ask pupils to explain why their story was labelled with *2 and then write a modified sentence to consolidate their new understanding. Figure 10.1 is an example of creative writing from a high ability pupil, but that still displays misconceptions about blood circulation. A set of star comments is included.

If we allow pupils the freedom to write about their ideas, we must expect a few misconceptions to remain. It means we can tackle them immediately. We may not get the same set of neat notebooks, but we will get an enthusiastic set of pupils who really work hard to understand how their world works. The effort and enthusiasm some will put into their creative writing is a reward in itself, and makes the extra time we spend marking worth the effort. We consider this marking burden again in Chapter 17.

A Day in the Life of a Red Blood Cell	*(extracts)*

Yo, hi there! My name's RBC, well, it's short for red blood cell but, I don't like that name! Anyway, I'm so fit, I <u>travel round the body and all the organs about 70 times per minute</u>,[11] impressive eh?   *11
Just think how many times I go round in a day! Well, I don't really have a beginning and an end to my day, I'm always on the move, I don't stop! As I'm your tour guide today, we'll be touring the whole body, well, I sure hope you're as fit as I am good luck!!

Off we go! We are now flowing out of the lungs through the pulmonary vein. We are taking <u>a last</u>[14]   *14
<u>trip to the heart</u>, before we go round the rest of the body as I just explained. OK, we're in the heart in the left atrium, we're now going through the flap valves and into the left ventricle and wait for it LUB-DUB!!! We're being pumped up the aorta and towards the body. <u>Did you know that the lub-</u>[1]   *1
<u>dub pumping sound is the valves closing?</u> Ah, well, you learn something every-day, well, almost!

OK, we're travelling steadily towards the arms. As Tommy is almost continually moving, he needs energy in the blood[12] to keep him going. Tommy's muscles work during exercise <u>using up the</u>   *12
<u>glucose in the blood and replacing it with poisonous waste products</u>.[13] His <u>arm also uses up oxygen</u>[12]   *13
<u>in the blood and replaces it with carbon dioxide</u>. The deoxygenated blood (the blood that has had   *12
the oxygen used up from it) makes <u>it's</u>[sp] way back to the heart through the vena cava.   *sp

Righthoe! We are now <u>travelling on to the kidneys</u>.[14] Here the blood is cleaned. The <u>poisonous waste</u>[13]   *14
<u>products of respiration</u> are filtered out and the amount of salt in your blood is regulated. Again, the   *13
<u>oxygen in your blood is used up and replaced with carbon dioxide</u>[13] and the deoxygenated blood   *13
carries on back to the heart.

Teacher's star comment sheet, read out or given to all pupils with their marked work *(extract)*

*sp spelling error
*1 This is an excellent description
1–9 can be used for praise
*11 The heart beats this often, but the blood only moves a short way at each heart beat
*12 We need to explore how glucose and oxygen 'snap' together to release energy. Their atoms re-arrange to form carbon dioxide and water – see *13
*13 Carbon dioxide and water are the waste products which are removed from the lungs (see *12). Better to use 'poisons' for the materials we get from eating the wrong food or from disease. These are removed from the blood at the kidneys.
*14 If you are conducting this tour going with the flow of blood you will have to return to the heart after visiting each organ.

FIGURE 10.1 Extract from a creative writing exercise from an able KS 3 pupil, with added teacher star comments.

Learning logs

Learning logs allow pupils to become aware of and evaluate their learning: a process called metacognition, which is an integral part of a constructivist approach to learning. Pupils' learning logs need to be honest, so they are not to be marked right or wrong. They should give us an insight into what the pupils are thinking (see Figure 10.2).

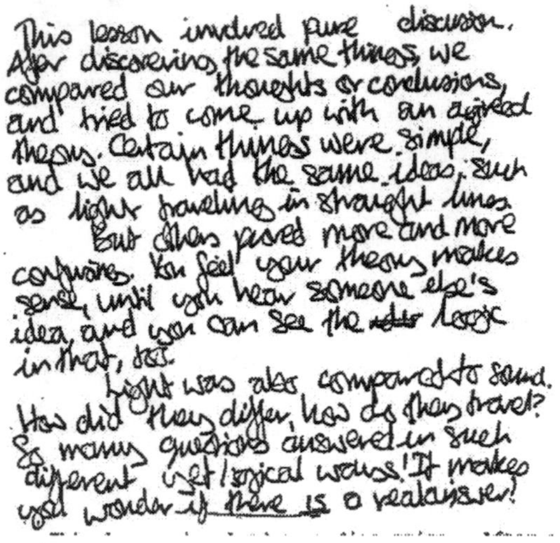

This lesson involved pure discussion. After discovering the same things, we compared our thoughts or conclusions, and tried to come up with an agreed theory. Certain things were simple, and we all had the same ideas, such as light travelling in straight lines.

But others proved more and more confusing. You feel your theory makes sense, until you hear someone else's idea, and you can see the logic in that, too.

Light was also compared to sound. How did they differ, how do they travel? So many questions answered in such different yet logical ways! It makes you wonder if there is a real answer?

FIGURE 10.2 Learning log written by a KS 4 pupil after a lesson on light.

Concept maps

Word burrs, such as Figure 5.10 (p. 47), show that there is a connection between two words, but do not explain the relationship. The real power of *concept mapping* is to label the *linking lines* (directional arrows) with verbs. It really makes you think about how the two ideas are connected. Figure 10.3 shows a map built up by someone who understands the constructive process of burning.

Pupils need to be taught concept mapping in simple stages. Begin by asking them to write a word to link two other words (concepts or ideas). Three examples are shown in Figure 10.4. Once this basic idea of linking ideas is established, additional concepts can be added to produce the completed map. When pupils construct these for themselves they can be very powerful learning tools.

Poems, films, cartoons, posters, web pages...

Writing poems is tough, but can have its rewards. These are the last three lines of a poem written by a Year 10 student who realises that microbes, despite their bad press, are an essential feature of our environment.

> So it's good in a way,
> But bad on the day,
> Let's love our microbes in every way.

Creative writing provides an opportunity for pupils to express their ideas (and make mistakes). Whether you ask them to write a film script, a cartoon strip, a scientific report for a 'conference', a poster for the science room wall or a web page for the school intranet, the message is the same. Pupils will be writing for an audience other than ourselves as teacher–examiner, and will take ownership of the task. However, they will make conceptual errors and we need to point these out while praising their creative efforts.

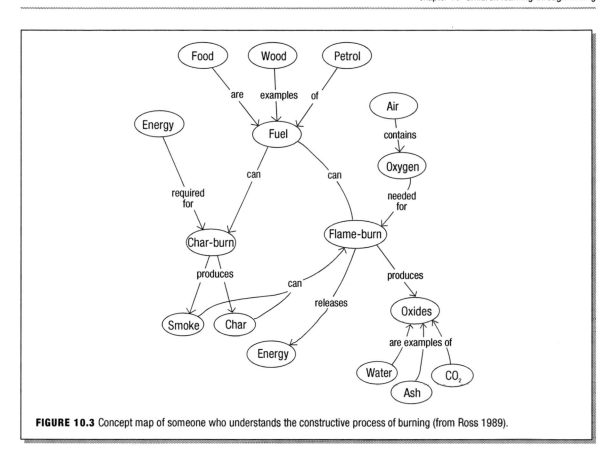

FIGURE 10.3 Concept map of someone who understands the constructive process of burning (from Ross 1989).

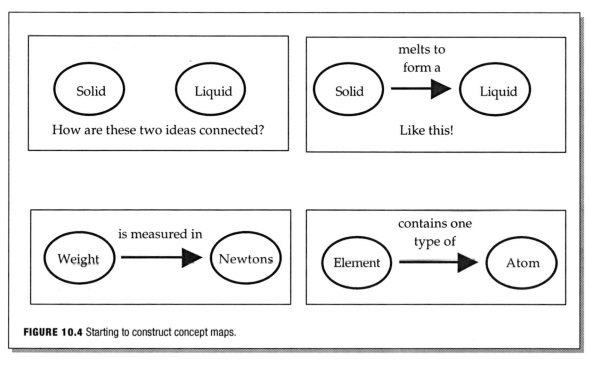

FIGURE 10.4 Starting to construct concept maps.

Summary

We cannot expect perfect writing straight off, so we sometimes resort to dictating notes or copying. These are borrowed words and ideas. We need to be far more imaginative. Do we really need pupils to make a formal record of everything they do? Can we not use writing creatively, as a means to allow them to *reformulate* the ideas they receive in class, to try to make them their own? We need to make good use of word processing at home, and increasingly in school, to make the redrafting process much easier.

When we start to use numbers

Most scientists are numerate. When ideas are tested, data are needed, graphs are plotted, statistical tests are applied and ideas begin to have substance. In contrast, pupils often find numbers daunting and unhelpful. This chapter looks at ways to help pupils make friends with numbers, and suggests ways in which we can introduce numeracy into our teaching to enhance the scientific understanding of our learners rather than baffle them.

Maths and science

The KS 3 strategy for mathematics urges maths teachers to liaise with staff from other departments in the school so that (a) there is a consistency of approach within the school and (b) pupils can see how important and useful maths can be in their everyday lives. Besides the approach to calculation, you need to agree with the maths team your approach to:

- the use of units and how to get a feel for them;
- how graphs are to be represented;
- the mathematical notation and terms to be used;
- algebraic and other mathematical techniques, such as how algebraic expressions are to be simplified or how equations are to be solved;
- how and when ICT resources such as graph plotters or graphical calculators will be used.

Maths teachers are reminded that 'almost every scientific investigation or experiment is likely to require one or more of the mathematical skills of classifying, counting, measuring, calculating, estimating, and recording in tables and graphs'. Add to that: work on decimals; calculating means and percentages; deciding whether to use a line graph or bar chart; interpretation, prediction and calculation of, for example, rates of change in cooling curves and distance–time graphs; applying formulae and solving equations. So make friends with your maths colleagues!

Figures baffle

Temperature. Consider the example, introduced in Chapter 5 (p. 37), of mixing equal amounts of water at 70° and 10°C. Many children simply add the temperatures to make water at 80°C, or, realising that this is hotter, subtract to make 60°C. Ask the same children what water would *feel like* if you mixed equal amounts of hot and cold water, and they will all say it would be warm.

Chemical equations. Science textbooks took to using 'word equations' to avoid confusing pupils with chemical equations. For many children $2H_2O$ is meaningless but they can make some sense of the same thing if we use pictures instead of the figures.

Electrical formulae. Pupils may be able to get the right answer by putting figures into $V = IR$, but how many will be able to appreciate, after that, that the higher the voltage the brighter the lamp?

Graphs. Even when we have translated the figures into graphs, they can be confusing. For example: which of these (Figure 11.1) tells the *simplest* story of a ball thrown up into the air?

Velocity

Time

Height

Time

FIGURE 11.1 Graphs of a ball thrown upwards.

In these, and many more, examples the numbers and symbols can obscure meaning, rather than enhancing it. This chapter aims to help you to make the mathematics add to the meaning.

Units and measurement

Pupils will come from the primary school into Year 7 with some knowledge of SI units, but will still need plenty of experience to realise what they mean in real life. They will be used to using arbitrary, but meaningful, measurements, such as:

- Length: finger width, paces, football pitches...
- Area: squares on paper, sheet of paper, football pitches ...
- Mass and weight: bags of sugar, house bricks, people...
- Capacity: jugs, juice cartons, watering cans, swimming-bath-fulls...
- Time: heartbeats, counting, as long as a lesson...

Imperial measures, which we still use today, are derived from these real objects: feet, stones, furlongs (the length of a ploughed furrow), barrels (oil industry) and so on. The *metric measures,* which are the basis of SI units, are arbitrary, and we need to give them meaning.

By the end of Key Stage 2 children should:

Know the approximate equivalence between commonly used imperial units and metric units:
1 litre = 2 pints (more accurately, 1³/₄ pints)
 4.5 litres = 1 gallon or 8 pints (a pint and a gallon are units of capacity)
1 kilogram = 2 lb (more accurately, 2.2 lb)
30 grams = 1 oz
8 kilometres = 5 miles (a mile is a unit of distance)

Make use of rhymes like:
A metre is just three feet three.
It's longer than a yard, you see.
Two and a quarter pounds of jam
Is round about one kilogram.
A litre of water's a pint and three quarters.

BOX 11.1 Imperial and metric units

Suggest how you could measure:

- the thickness of a piece of paper;
- the weight of one grain of rice;
- the quantity of water in a raindrop;
- the thickness of the glass in a window pane.

What units of measurement might you see, for example, in:

- a TV weather forecast;
- a supermarket;
- road signs;
- a garage;
- a railway station;
- a chemist's shop...?

BOX 11.2 Key Stage 2 activities from the National Numeracy Strategy website

The key to this is *estimation* – pupils need to get a feel for the SI units so they begin to have meaning. See Boxes 11.1 and 11.2 from the downloads available on the National Numeracy website (KS 2). Estimation plays an important part in pupils' work in numeracy in the primary school. They are taught to get a feel for what the answer to a problem will look like, so they can reject 'silly' answers (for example, where they have moved a decimal point). In the same way, any calculation they do in science needs to have this reality. Pupils need to look at their results subjectively and pick out broad trends from their figures: the warmer the water the quicker the salt dissolves; the closer the plants are planted the taller and more spindly they grow. Let's look at some examples in more detail.

Temperature

Let pupils feel water (between 0 and 50°C) before they mix or divide it. Let them estimate the final temperature and then perform the action and measure the temperatures. In this way they can relate a temperature measurement to how hot the water feels. Eventually they need to appreciate that temperature measurement starts from 0 kelvin so that a 10 degree rise in temperature from 10 to 20°C is only a small increase in energy per particle (for further discussion see Chapters 2 and 12).

Force

Let pupils feel the weight of an apple – it represents a force of about one newton. Then let them pull out newton meters to experience a range of forces. Finally, they can be given a range of forces (say 1, 10 and 50 N) to see if they can pull out newton meters to achieve that force. They can check to see how close they are.

Length, area and volume

Let pupils estimate the *length* of the classroom or a car in metres; the *area* of a room or a football pitch in square metres; the *volume* of their lungs or a bath in litres or cubic metres.

Mass (and weight)

Let pupils push a full and an empty can of beans, which are both suspended on string from the ceiling, so that they can appreciate their relative *mass* by how difficult (or easy) they are to get moving. If they are lifted the comparison will be between their weights and we are back to forces.

Power and energy

Try to relate all common appliances to a one-bar electric fire, which gives out a kilojoule of heat energy every second (1 kilowatt). Watts are actually one of the easiest units to experience: most pupils can see that a 100 watt light bulb is brighter than a 60 watt bulb, or hear that 40 watt speakers are louder than 20 watt speakers.

To get a feel for the unit of energy, a kilojoule, remember the electric fire, which sends out this amount of energy every second; a filament light bulb (100 watts) takes 10 seconds, but a 'low energy' light bulb (10 watts) will last 100 seconds on its 1kJ. A person (100 watts) gives off this amount of energy as heat every 10 seconds, but how high must someone climb to store this as gravitational potential energy (GPE) or how much sugar and oxygen must they respire to transfer this amount of energy?

A person has a mass of, say, 50 kg, and therefore a weight of about 500 N. A joule is needed to move a force of 1 N through one metre, so our kilojoule (1000 J) will lift 500 N (force of gravity on a person) through two metres.

Packets of sugar are labelled as transferring 1644 kJ per 100 g when respired. If we call that 2000 kJ, then just one twentieth of a gram is needed for our 1 kJ. Our resting bodies transfer 100 joules (0.1 kJ) a second, so to keep our bodies ticking over all day we need $0.1 \times 60 \times 60 \times 24$ kJ, which is nearly 10,000 kJ. So 500 g of sugar will be OK for a day to cover our resting energy needs – about 150 sugar lumps.

To estimate the amount of oxygen we need to respire this sugar is a little more complicated – see Box 11.3.

Respiration happens when the weak bonds in oxygen are replaced by strong bonds in the oxide products, carbon dioxide and water. 300 kJ per mole of oxygen is available from respiration. (Interestingly, this value is independent of the fuel used, because the bonds holding fuel molecules together are of about the same strength as those in the oxides.)

When resting we breathe in and out about 600 cm^3 of air every breath (tidal capacity) – a cycle of about 3 seconds. Of this about 4 per cent is the oxygen we use (which is replaced as we exhale by carbon dioxide, having reacted with the food (fuel) in our bodies during respiration). So in 3 seconds we use 24 cm^3 of pure oxygen, which is 1/1000th of a mole (a mole of gas occupies 24 litres at room conditions). 1/1000th of 300 kJ, which is 300 joules, is therefore released in 3 seconds, or 100 joules a second – which is the figure above for our resting heat output.

Clearly if we are exercising or working, we need to respire more, and we start breathing faster and deeper to provide more oxygen.

BOX 11.3 Approximating the amount of energy transferred from the oxygen we breath

Speed of light and sound

To get an idea of the speed of light talk about how long it takes light to travel certain distances: eight times round the world in a second; 3 seconds to the moon and back; 8 minutes to the sun; 3 hours to Jupiter; 4.5 years to our (second) nearest star. This also helps to give an idea of the scale of the cosmos. Compare this with sound, which travels just faster than commercial jet planes, taking 3 seconds to travel a kilometre and an hour from tip to toe of the UK.

The stories graphs tell

In the primary school pupils will have had experience of bar charts, often for discontinuous data (Figure 11.2), and may have developed the concept of a line graph by plotting continuous data in bar format (Figure 11.3). We need to find out how much meaning they can take from graphs before assuming that they can make sense of the graphs we use in science.

They need to experience the stories that graphs can tell. Much fun can be had by asking children to find meaning in graphs of 'everyday' events – see Figure 11.4.

Once pupils understand what graphs are saying it is time for them to construct their own. However, using their own data, even class data, can lead to messy graphs with several anomalous points. It is important to account for these anomalies (see the section below on 'Statistics and accuracy') but if you want to draw a clear conclusion – for example, that the more water you use the more salt it can dissolve – it may be better to give them 'clean' data, or even ask them to sketch a graph from the class results to show the trend. In this way pupils obtain a clear story in graphical form instead of getting tied up counting squares in a vain attempt to plot their points on a graph. They may complete the task just before the bell goes, but there is no time left to look at the scientific ideas behind

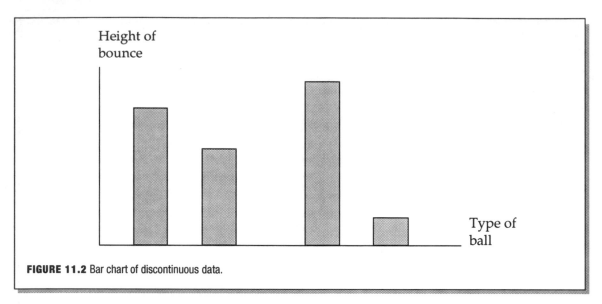

FIGURE 11.2 Bar chart of discontinuous data.

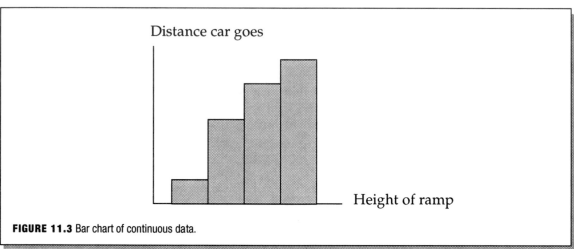

FIGURE 11.3 Bar chart of continuous data.

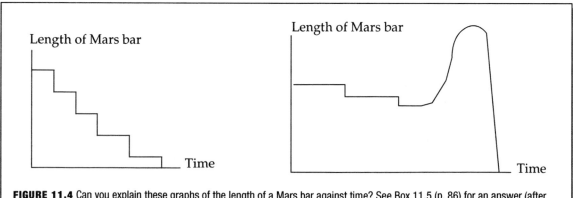

FIGURE 11.4 Can you explain these graphs of the length of a Mars bar against time? See Box 11.5 (p. 86) for an answer (after Goldsworthy *et al.* 1999).

the experiment. The pupils go away with unpleasant memories of counting squares and grappling with numbers, when they should be leaving with new scientific ideas embedded, and ready to be used. Even spreadsheets can cause problems if the data are too untidy, but clearly they can be of enormous help (see Chapter 24).

Logarithmic scales

Consider the simple question in Box 11.4. Nearly half of a sample of 100 primary student teachers who had achieved a grade C at GCSE only two years previously said the acid rain was twice as acidic, and only 5 per cent realised it was 1000 times as acidic (unpublished data, K.A. Ross, University of Gloucestershire 2003).

Acid Rain

Remember that the pH scale goes from 0 (very acid) through 7 (neutral) to 14 (very alkaline).

If some acid rain has a pH of 3 and normal rain has a pH of 6, how many times more acidic is the acid rain than the ordinary rain?

BOX 11.4 Acid rain question

Other 'confusing' scales are those for wind (Beaufort), earthquakes (Richter) and sound (decibels). In all these a unitary change in the reading denotes a tenfold change in the factor. Thus the change from pH 6 to pH 5 is a tenfold change. This issue is discussed in Chapter 12 (p. 95). The famous film, book and now CD-ROM *Powers of Ten* illustrates in pictures the scale of the universe by progressively scaling up or down in powers of ten from a person having a picnic (see http://www.powersof10.com).

Statistics and accuracy

We often tell pupils to do repeat runs so that they get three readings, but do they understand the need for these repeats? Consider the *electricity from metals in a lemon* on p. 5. Pupils who change the distance apart who *only take one reading at each distance* may get results like these:

Distance between metals (cm)	0.5	1.0	1.5	2.0
Voltage	0.82	0.77	0.79	0.73

It looks as if there is a trend here, but if repeat results were made we would find that the variation in voltage within each distance is similar to the variation between different readings. In fact the variation may be 'real' and result from the build up of reaction products on the metals; hence the drop off as the metals become contaminated (not because they are placed further apart).

Some investigations require calculations from data. These often involve the use of calculators. We must get pupils to estimate the result, preferably in their heads, rather than rushing to punch figures into a calculator following some poorly understood equation. The result may have little meaning to the pupils. 'Have I got the right answer?' they might say, and when you examine their 'answer' it is quoted to six decimal places. Rounding off so that the result lies within experimental accuracy is much easier after they have estimated what it might be – don't let them quote meaningless insignificant figures.

Summary

It was mathematics that enabled science to develop. Dalton noticed that elements combined in simple ratios of their weights, and came up with his atomic theory; Mendeleev used atomic masses not only to build the periodic table but also to leave gaps for undiscovered elements; Mendel noticed the 3:1 ratio of types of peas, which eventually led to our understanding of genetics; and physics is often called applied mathematics. As children progress through their secondary school the science will become increasingly mathematical. We must ensure that this supports their understanding, by constantly asking them 'Does this make sense?' and asking ourselves 'How can I translate this into their everyday experiences?'

The first graph is the bar being eaten in a sensible way in five bites. In the second, the person eats the chocolate off two sides, then one end, then the other two sides and the other end. They then put the bar in their mouth and pull it out before plunging the whole thing in their mouth at once.

BOX 11.5 Explanation for the graphs in Figure 11.4

PART

Knowledge and Understanding

Introduction

The KS 3 strategy has identified five key concepts that children should be using by the end of the stage. They are particles, energy, force, cells and interdependence. In these four short chapters we cannot cover all the concepts in the science curriculum, but we can focus on these key concepts and explore approaches to teaching them, explaining why children have difficulty in coming to a scientific view about them, and why misconceptions so easily build up (even appearing in textbooks). The teaching sequence we proposed in Part II of the book relies on us, as teachers, understanding the ideas our pupils already have in their minds. We must either challenge or build on these naive ideas, and then give learners the chance to reinterpret them – a process where pupils take ownership of the ideas and are given plenty of opportunity to use them. We resort to last-minute cramming when we fail in this deeper approach to learning. The chapters that follow show how important it is, in order for teaching to be successful, that teachers have good subject knowledge and a clear understanding of their pupils' ideas. They are exemplified by key concepts from chemistry, physics, biology and mathematics.

12

Difficult ideas in chemistry

This chapter shows how the big ideas in chemistry should be used as the basis for structuring learning. Sometimes the details blur the bigger picture: for example, pupils may learn how to balance equations but not understand that the process is an expression of the conservation of atoms. We begin with these indestructible particles, which lead us to consider burning as a constructive process. The oxides that form during burning produce acids and alkalis. We conclude by considering the particles again in a consideration of the rates of chemical change.

Particles that do not burn away

This is from a learning log of a primary teacher in training:

> I gradually came to realise how much of a part 'atoms' do play in matter. I have always assumed that as materials go though the process of change, the atoms from which they are made up, change too. However, this unit helped me to understand that atoms are indestructible and I can look at any substance now and judge that, regardless of what change it goes through, the atoms will remain the same.

There are only about 100 different atoms, represented by the elements of the periodic table, of which about 25 make up the bulk of what we see around us. Many people leave school 'knowing' that matter is made of particles, but believing that these particles are just little bits of sugar, iron, plastic etc. They think that the 'atoms' melt, burn, expand and dissolve, just like the materials do. One of the biggest barriers preventing people from understanding the world from a chemical point of view is the problem of seeing atoms as unchanging amid change. Melting is when particles, previously in fixed positions, are able to slide past each other; burning is where oxygen atoms from the air join with the atoms in the fuel; and so on (Ross *et al.* 2002: matter).

Although we may spend plenty of time in school getting pupils to act out being atoms of a solid, liquid or gas (Chapter 8) and doing some of the activities in Chapter 2, somehow their 'bulk matter' model persists. A popular creative writing exercise (Chapter 10) is to ask pupils to imagine being a particle in a melting solid or heated liquid. We need to make clear their confusion in using bulk descriptions (we are melting, we are getting hotter) when they should have used particle descriptions (we break free from one another, we vibrate faster). We need to spend much more time emphasising that our particles (called atoms, molecules and ions) are very different from little bits of 'real' matter. Table 12.1 emphasises this point. Remember, too, that the KS 3 strategy for science has identified 'particles' as one of its five *key ideas*.

TABLE 12.1 Bulk matter and atoms are not the same

Bulk materials	Particle model
Ice melts The solid shape turns into a pool of water	Molecules once vibrating but fixed in a regular lattice are still touching but now slip past each other as they move from place to place
Wood burns The bulk of the wood seems to disappear, as gases enter the air. A solid whitish powder remains (ashes)	Atoms making up the wood combine with atoms of oxygen in the air to form oxides; some escape as separate molecules into the air, others remain, forming a solid lattice structure (ashes)
Bulk words Solid, element, crystal, temperature	*Particle words* Unchanging, atom, bond, vibrate

Bulk materials (National Curriculum Sc3: Classifying Materials)

The matter around us comes in five forms (Ross 1997), dependent on the elements that are involved.

- Metallic elements bond with each other or themselves to form *metals and alloys*, which are typically metallic structures. They deform plastically (i.e. their shape stays changed when bent or hammered), conduct heat and electricity, are shiny and have a metallic 'ring'. Although they can be melted fairly easily they are hard to vaporise.

- Non-metallic elements bond with themselves or each other to form small self-contained molecules, giving us *volatile materials*: soft solids that easily melt and vaporise, liquids like water and petrol, and all gases.

- Metallic elements bond with non-metallic elements to form *ionic compounds*. If they dissolve in water or are melted they conduct electricity, but decompose. They have very high melting and boiling points and are brittle, cracking easily when hit.

- Carbon, the first member of the fourth group, forms linear *polymers* in which the carbon atoms form long chain molecules, sealed along the edges with hydrogen atoms, including all life structures, and polymers derived from petrochemicals. These are flexible and tough, and decompose if heated strongly (often forming a char and inflammable smoke), but some will soften and then can deform plastically (hence they are often called, somewhat confusingly, 'plastic').

- Silicon, the second member of the fourth group, also forms giant structures, usually with oxygen, but this time they tend to be three-dimensional and we get *rocks*, which are brittle and hard to melt and boil.

Our aim is to get pupils to appreciate the bulk properties of these materials, which make up the whole of our environment, and to begin to appreciate the particle models we use to explain their properties and account for their behaviour.

Chemical equations (National Curriculum Sc3: Changing Materials and Patterns of Behaviour)

It amazes people to see molten iron emerge from a furnace where black charcoal and brown rock are heated strongly – and they don't link this at all with the layers of rust that appear on garden tools left out in the damp. Chemical changes only become understandable as we see that beneath the outward appearance of change are the unchanging indestructible atoms – the Lego blocks of our real world – which we confidently express to our perplexed pupils in the form of equations. Balancing equations is often perceived as such a difficult task that it is only undertaken with the top GCSE sets and it is taught as a sort of algorithm, as if the important thing is to get the right answer. One problem is that as soon as you mention numbers pupils get frightened (see Chapter 11).

Lower down the school we make do with word equations, but these are almost meaningless to pupils and so have to be learnt by heart to get marks. They simply name the reactants and products (using obscure names), and fail to provide the underlying particle model that makes everything so clear.

The solution is that equations should be taught at KS 3, not using numbers, but actual atomic models or coloured circles, with symbols in each circle. Until pupils can count the atoms in atom drawings, you cannot expect them to understand balancing equations. Picture equations are easier for pupils to understand than word equations (which have little meaning). Chemical symbols can be introduced by labelling the circle, and the numbers we use in formulae can be introduced when children get tired of drawing out all the atoms, and need shorthand. By then they understand the conservation of atoms and have little problem in writing balanced equations.

Figure 12.1 shows a typical equation that we give to KS 3 pupils in words. If coloured atoms are used it is simple to see that no matter has been lost during the marble–acid reaction and pupils enjoy counting to ensure that every atom is accounted for. It gives the word equation a whole new meaning.

Balancing equations is not a tricky mathematical exercise, but a fundamental statement that atoms remain the same during and after chemical change – all they do is rearrange themselves.

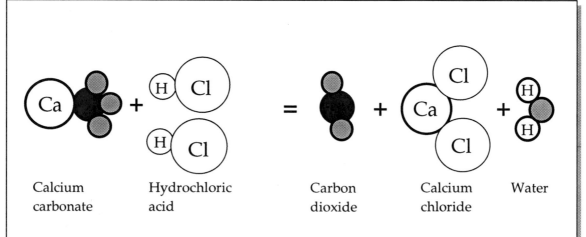

Calcium carbonate	Hydrochloric acid	Carbon dioxide	Calcium chloride	Water

FIGURE 12.1 The marble–acid reaction drawn using atomic models (even here the crystal lattice of the marble and the ionic solutions of the acid and salt are not properly shown).

Fuels don't 'contain' energy

If atoms are the same before and after a chemical reaction, what is the origin of the energy that is often transferred during reactions, either 'producing energy' as in burning, or 'requiring energy' such as photosynthesis? Chapters 4 and 5 are full of questions that help to show the distinction between matter (measured in atoms) and energy (measured in Joules). On this planet, it is the matter that gets cycled, while energy degrades. The energy arrives as high-grade photons of sunlight and leaves as low grade infra-red radiation to space. Without this energy balance the planet would not keep its constant average temperature.*

Our use of fossil fuels has allowed us to develop a technological society. Before that we had to rely on a daily supply of energy from sunlight (which drives wind and water power and the life processes that power our muscles). Careless talk suggests that these fossil fuels 'contain' energy. While it is true that the fuels are at room temperature, so the atoms within them will be vibrating, it is certainly not true that the energy that is transferred when they are *used as fuels* is contained within the fuel. The same argument applies to food, whose packets proudly proclaim they have an *energy content*.

Let us begin with a simpler system, gravitational potential energy (GPE). Again, many will say that the water behind a dam has, or 'contains', GPE. In order to store this energy water has to be pulled away from the Earth (using solar energy). The energy is stored in the Earth–water system. Like stretched elastic, the more the two are separated, the more energy is stored. Because the Earth is 'fixed' we find it easier to measure GPE simply by how far 'up' the object has been lifted, and we say that the energy is stored *in* this object. We should say, instead, that energy is stored in *the system*.

The fuel–oxygen system

We can now apply this argument to the chemical system involved with burning and respiration. It takes energy to break bonds between atoms. The electrons attract the atoms on each side of the bond. To pull the atoms apart against this electrostatic force there must be an *input* of energy. If burning or respiration is to take place we need to separate the bonds of the carbohydrate molecules and the oxygen molecules to allow them to rearrange themselves as H_2O and CO_2. The energy transferred during respiration and burning has come from replacing the weak double bond between the oxygen atoms in an oxygen molecule with the much stronger bonds in the oxides. Energy is not stored in the food or fuel, but it is available from the fuel–oxygen system (Ross 2000c; Ross *et al.* 2002: energy).

Photosynthesis

To complete the picture, we can now see energy from sunlight pulling the oxygen away from the oxides during photosynthesis. The whole process is summarised in Figure 12.2. Matter is conserved, represented by the constant thickness of the circle all the way round. Energy comes in as high-grade sunlight that 'sets' the system by pulling oxygen away from water. The biomass produced will form the substance of living things and could be passed along food chains. When life needs energy all it has to do is to take the biomass and join it with oxygen, in a process called respiration. Biomass that

---

* Greenhouse gases make it harder for infra-red radiation to leave, so the surface temperature of the Earth has to rise to restore the balance between incoming sunlight and outgoing infra-red. Another factor we need to consider is the loss of heat from the interior of the Earth, partially replaced by energy from natural radioactive decay that occurs deep in the Earth's interior. Taking this into account, the Earth actually loses more heat each day than it gains from the sun alone.

has fossilised and that we dig up as fuels can also rejoin with oxygen, in a process called combustion. In both cases energy is stored in the fuel–oxygen system. It is important to realise that it will continue to be stored as long as the fuel and oxygen do not rejoin, so you can crack, anaerobically digest, fossilise, eat, reconstruct into new cells (growth using food you eat) and still retain the fuel value of the biomass. Once you allow the oxygen back, useful energy is transferred. Eventually the energy is degraded and is radiated out into space as waste heat, to keep the Earth in balance. Energy is degraded as matter is cycled. This matter–energy distinction is nicely made in the saucepan model for photosynthesis (Box 12.1).

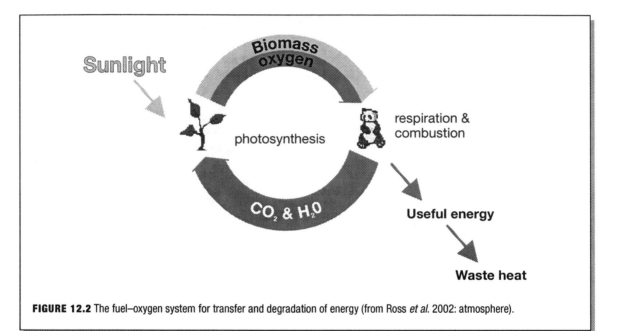

FIGURE 12.2 The fuel–oxygen system for transfer and degradation of energy (from Ross *et al.* 2002: atmosphere).

This model helps pupils distinguish between the energy source needed to drive chemical change, and the ingredients themselves (matter). In a normal saucepan the ingredients are added, and the source of energy comes from the stove from below. In the leaf (up-side-down saucepan) the source of energy comes from above (sunlight) and the ingredients enter, through the stomata, from below.

BOX 12.1 The up-side-down saucepan model for photosynthesis

The reason why we think of energy being stored in the fuel is because oxygen is 'free'. The problem for humans is getting the biomass, but whales also have a problem getting the oxygen. When we send rockets out of the atmosphere, climb high mountains or go under water, we have to take oxygen with us, just as whales do.

The model fuel cell system in Figure 12.3 is a simple illustration of this. Water is split by energy from the sun – the photosynthesis stage. The hydrogen (equivalent to biomass) is piped to the fuel cell (biomass carried along the food chain), but the oxygen is vented to the atmosphere, as in the leaf. The fuel cell obtains the oxygen it needs from the air, just as we do during respiration. The energy transferred in the cell is 'used' to power the fan, just as energy from respiration powers our muscles. We need a pipe for the hydrogen – the food chain – but not for the oxygen. This is why we take the air for granted, and why we think the energy is stored *in* the biomass. The prospect of 'clean energy' from burning hydrogen as a fuel (see, for example, http://www.hydrogenus.com and http://fuelcellworld.org/wfchome.fcm) is based on the system illustrated in Figure 12.3. What many commentators fail to say is that our current source of hydrogen is from methane, a fossil fuel whose use contributes to greenhouse gas emission. The hydrogen needs to come from a replenishable source of energy that can be used to split water.

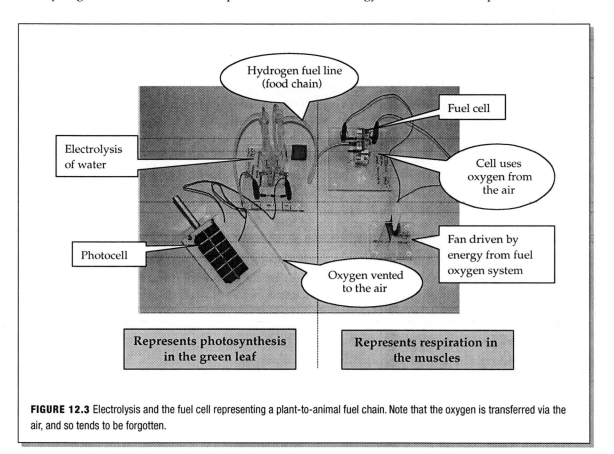

FIGURE 12.3 Electrolysis and the fuel cell representing a plant-to-animal fuel chain. Note that the oxygen is transferred via the air, and so tends to be forgotten.

Implications for teaching

It is not easy to change the habits of a lifetime, especially if the ideas we are using work so well – it is so convenient to say *fuels contain energy*. The reason why we urge a change is simple: if we fail to acknowledge the role played by oxygen, and the exhaust gases that result, we are in danger of perpetuating the myth that matter, at an atomic level, can be destroyed. Few people gain any real idea of the material nature of greenhouse gases, or of the other products of combustion such as the gases that cause acid rain. Once children appreciate the simple picture of the cycling of matter using energy from the sun (see Figure 12.2), the carbon cycle becomes as simple as the water cycle.

Emphasise the distinction between matter and energy

The main problem here is the way we call biomass (e.g. cornflakes, coal, fat, wood etc.) *energy*. Call it *fuel*, and emphasise that fuels only transfer energy when they combine with oxygen (except during anaerobic respiration of carbohydrates, where a small amount of energy is transferred by rearrangement of the bonds in the molecules).

Emphasise that gases are the material products of combustion

Flames, hot air and exhaust gases are often considered to be forms of energy; certainly the life-world view is that they are weightless. We need to take account of where matter goes during burning, by collecting exhaust gases from above a flame and seeing the water condense, or placing them over a burning candle and seeing that it does not burn in this 'used air'. Our everyday experiences tell us that burning is a destructive process – only ashes remain. We must encourage pupils to see the exhaust gases that escape to the air as being massive, and to use this as evidence of an increase in mass as oxides are *built up*. Some five-year-olds described what happens to petrol in a car like this: 'it goes into steam and it's all warm... 'cos every time we cross the road I can feel it across my legs' (Ross *et al.* 2002: energy). This is a rich and useful experience that needs to be built upon. Water is not often perceived to be a *product of combustion*, nor is the carbon dioxide that we breathe out often perceived as an oxidation product of the food we eat. Again, how many see the ashes left after a wood fire as oxides of the metals that were taken in as minerals during the lifetime of the tree? Only when these oxide products of respiration and combustion are given more prominence will pupils begin to appreciate these processes as constructive processes.

Use the atom concept primarily to explain the conservation of matter

If matter is created or destroyed then atoms must come and go. We need to use the *particle concept* to explain that during physical and chemical changes such as evaporation and burning the atoms are still there, in the same amounts. When chemical equations are written the use of atomic models or drawings allows the actual atoms to be counted on each side (Figure 12.1).

Emphasise the role of oxygen in combustion and respiration

There is plenty of evidence that we rely on oxygen every second of our lives. It is oxygen that we take with us on high mountains, in aircraft and under the sea. We pant after vigorous exercise. The three dramatic demonstrations in Boxes 12.2, 12.3 and 12.4 show the need for oxygen (air) when fuels burn.

Make holes in the base and lid of an empty metal 2lb syrup tin just smaller than a pencil. Grease the lid with petroleum jelly and replace it. Have two bits of tape ready to cover the holes after filling with natural gas (methane). Do this by holding the rubber gas tube (from a Bunsen burner) over the top hole, and waiting for 10 seconds as the methane displaces the air out through the bottom hole. Place the tin on a tripod, remove both tapes and light the gas that comes out of the hole in the lid. The flame is initially yellow, like a Bunsen with the air hole closed. Pure methane is coming from the tin. As the methane is burnt, air enters from the base. Only when there is enough air in the air/methane mixture in the tin will the flame spread into the tin. The flame acts like the spark in a car engine cylinder full of a petrol/air mixture. The bang blows the lid into the air, there is a flash of flame and the can gets hot. Ask your pupils why the gas in the tin didn't burn when you first lit the flame.

BOX 12.2 The exploding can

Fill a large gas jar with methane, and have another 'empty' one (i.e. it has air in it) ready. Light a candle perched on the top of a pole and lower the air-filled jar over it. It burns normally. Ask the pupils to predict what will happen to the flame if you lower the methane-filled jar over it. When you do lower it over the lighted candle (see safety note below) the methane will ignite, but the candle will go out. You can lift and lower the jar several times, and each time the candle re-lights then goes out, and the methane continues to burn up into the jar. Point out the condensation inside the jar (water is a product of combustion).

Safety: Hold the jar at a slight angle, down and away from you, so the flame doesn't come up over your hand.

BOX 12.3 Using methane to extinguish a candle

Hold any powdered food (custard, milk, flour …) on a spoon in a Bunsen flame, and nothing much happens (see safety note below). Sprinkle the powder from high over the flame, and the result is spectacular. The difference is that the sprinkled powder is mixed with air, so there is oxygen available for the combustion reaction. Gear wheels in flour mills were never metal on metal to avoid making sparks that could ignite flour dust. Ask your pupils why the powder on the spoon did not burn well.

Safety: All must wear eye protection, keep pupils well away, have the Bunsen burner in the middle of the bench and sprinkle from a spoon that is tied onto a pole to avoid your hand being above the flame.

BOX 12.4 Dangerous powder/air mixtures

Avoid the use of the term 'high energy bond' in ATP (at A-level)

The third phosphate group in adenosine triphosphate (ATP) is weakly bonded to the rest of the molecule. ATP is therefore a reactive molecule. By breaking this weak bond and replacing it with a stronger bond, energy is made available to do useful things in the cell. To reset the system, energy from the glucose–oxygen system is used. Energy is not released when the 'high energy' bond breaks, but comes, instead, when stronger bonds are made, replacing the easily broken weak bond.

Teaching acidity and the pH concept

The word acid comes from the Greek 'oxys' meaning sour, the acid taste. Pupils will be familiar with some natural (organic) acids, such as citric, lactic and acetic, found in lemons, sour milk and vinegar (literally *vin*, wine, and *egar*, sour, from the same root as *acrid*), but they are likely to associate acids with danger and burning. All acids will sting if you have an open wound, but it is the mineral acids, associated with acid rain and derived from non-metal oxides, that cause most damage.

If you can gain access to the food technology area of the school you can set up a tasting exercise where pupils can use solutions of sugar (sweet), citric acid (sour), salt (salt) and coffee (bitter) to detect areas of the tongue that are sensitive to the four tastes. If sodium bicarbonate is provided as a powder, they can try adding a little to their tongue while the citric acid is there, and notice that the acidity is neutralised or 'cured'. Sugar *appears* to do the same thing, but it is only the sensation that is masked; the acidity is still there.

Indicators from red cabbage

Many plant pigments act as indicators, but red cabbage must be one of the best and is certainly very easy to make. Keep sachets of red cabbage in the freezer and when required smash them with a hammer when still frozen. Boiling water or cold methylated spirit (hazard) can be used to extract the colour using a pestle and mortar.

Pupils can put samples of common household products into labelled pairs of test tubes, add water if necessary and arrange them in two test-tube racks opposite each other. The red cabbage extract is added to one rack, and universal indicator (for which a pH colour card is available) to the other. Pupils can then put the tubes in order of pH, according to the universal indicator, and can then make their own pH colour chart for their home-made indicator using universal as calibration. All subsequent experiments can use their own indicator, now that they know the pH corresponding to each red cabbage colour (Ross *et al*. 2002: atmosphere).

The pH concept: telling the story

At first pH is going to seem a rather funny numbering system: from 0 to 14, with neutral being 7. To make sense of this requires knowledge of the ionisation of water and hydrogen ion concentrations. This is beyond the comprehension of most pupils at KS 3, but it is possible to show them that the scale is logarithmic. For every change of one unit on the scale, the acidity changes by a factor of ten. There are many such logarithmic scales used in science, and all need careful introduction (see Chapter 11 on numeracy for further discussion, p. 85).

Pupils can be given a boiling tube with a tenth molar solution of either hydrochloric acid or sodium hydroxide. They should have a pH of 1 and 13 respectively. Pupils can then take 1cm^3 of the original solution and add 9 cm^3 of water, making it ten times less concentrated. The dilution can be done once or twice more. Using their red cabbage indicator, they will see that each tenfold dilution changes the pH by one unit.

Acid rain

Oxides of sulphur and nitrogen entering the atmosphere and then dissolving in the rain cause acid rain. Most books start the story from the burning of fossil fuels and consider the damage done to ecosystems. But we need to go further back than that. Again, setting the science in an environmentally important context can motivate pupils to want to understand.

Sulphur and nitrogen are an essential element to life, brought into plants through sulphate and nitrate minerals in the soil. During the conditions of high temperature and pressure of fossilisation much of the oxygen and nitrogen in the organic molecules becomes detached, but the sulphur atoms remain bonded. Millions of years later they are released when the fuel burns (animated in Ross *et al*. 2002: atmosphere).

Nitrogen oxides are produced from car exhausts. The cylinders of internal combustion engines are filled with a little bit of vaporised fuel but mostly with air – and this is mostly nitrogen, with some oxygen. Under the conditions of high temperature and pressure, similar to a lightning flash, small amounts of nitrogen join with oxygen, forming small amounts of nitrogen oxides. So the nitrogen and sulphur in acid rain are beneficial – it is the hydrogen ions that cause the damage.

Rates of reaction

This topic is another example of how we conspire to make things difficult for pupils. We give them reactions to perform that are obscure and unrelated to everyday life (e.g. marble and acid, thiosulphate and acid) in order to teach them something about how chemical change progresses.

All around us are the slow reactions of life, waiting to be examined and explored. Our aim is to share with pupils our ideas about what makes a chemical reaction sometimes go fast, and at other times go slow. We hope to develop a collision theory model to explain why reactions go faster when we increase the surface area (of a solid reactant), the concentration (of a reactant in solution) or the temperature.

We do not need to resort to test tubes and strange chemicals to experience these effects.

Particle size

- Cooking provides us with the easiest set of examples. Small potatoes, or cut up potatoes, cook more quickly than large ones (whether boiling, baking or making chips). Eggs cook faster when scrambled rather than poached, when made into an omelette rather than fried.

- Warm blooded mammals need to digest their food quickly, so they have crushing and grinding mechanisms called jaws and teeth to ensure the food is in small bits. Warm-blooded birds use stones in their gizzard. Contrast this with a snake, which swallows prey whole and needs to wait for days for the digestion process to reach the inside of the animal it swallowed.

- Small twigs burn more quickly than large logs, because the oxygen from the air can reach them more easily.

Concentration

- Bleach is more effective and works faster (and is more dangerous) when used undiluted. This is true for all cleansing solutions.

Temperature

- For every 10°C rise in temperature the rate of slow biochemical change approximately doubles. Trees in the tundra (5°C) take 40 years to mature, trees in our temperate woods (15°C) mature in 20 years and in the tropics (25°C) they take 10 years.

- Milk left in the 'fridge (5°C) lasts six days, in a cool room (15°C) three days, in a warm room (25°C) a day and a half, and at body temperature (35°C) less than a day. A similar situation occurs with other food 'going bad'. Microbial action doubles for each 10°C rise in temperature. Because these reactions are controlled by enzymes there is a maximum temperature above which the enzymes are denatured, and no reaction occurs. This allows us to sterilise food by heating it above this maximum (boiling is usually sufficient).

Collision theory

It is easy to see why a doubling of the surface area or concentration is likely to double the rate of a reaction: we are doubling the number of collisions, and reactions can only occur between two chemicals when their molecules collide.

There is a problem in explaining the effect of temperature. Many books use the idea of an increased number of collisions to explain why chemical reactions go faster when the *temperature* is raised. This does not go anywhere near explaining what we actually observe. We have seen that for reactions that are slow at room temperature, a 10°C rise in temperature causes a doubling of rate. According to collision theory we must have twice as many collisions at 20°C than we have at 10°C, but also twice as many again at 30°C as we had at 20°C. Clearly this is not the case.

What is the link between particle movement and temperature? At absolute zero (–273°C) particles essentially do not move. Their movement energy is proportional to absolute temperature. So if we want to double the energy of our particles, in a substance that is at 10°C, we need to work out its absolute temperature and double that. Room temperature is roughly 300 K. So doubling that we get 600 K or about 300°C. But our 10 degree rise in temperature, from 300 to 310 K, is only a 3 per cent rise in temperature, so we should expect only a 3 per cent increase in the rate for this tiny temperature rise, not the doubling we actually observe.

A better explanation is not easy. We need to realise that not all molecules will be moving with exactly the same energy. Some will move slowly, others faster than average. The reason why reactions between molecules are so slow at room temperature is that very few collisions are successful. Existing bonds must be broken before the next ones are made. If every collision resulted in broken bonds, the substances would be highly reactive and unstable. Bonds can only be broken (allowing a reaction to occur) if a collision is particularly energetic. Such energetic collisions are very rare, making the reaction slow. A 10 degree rise in temperature only increases the average energy of the molecules by a few per cent, but it can double the number of these particularly energetic molecules, which every so often, and by chance, have an energy perhaps ten times the average. This is sufficient to break bonds and cause the reaction. It is the doubling of the population of these very energetic molecules caused by the slight temperature rise that gives a better model for what is happening.

Should we use an erroneous model with our pupils if the better explanation is too complex? As long as we always warn pupils that our models and explanation are never true, but are there to attempt to make some sense of our experiences, pupils may be willing to accept ideas, but will be ready to develop and modify them as time passes.

Summary

The KS 3 strategy identifies particles as one of the key ideas. Without this idea of indestructible atoms all other explanations in chemistry become a closed book. We need to test our pupils continually to see whether they have grasped this idea and are beginning to use it. In a similar way it is no use explaining the constructive (building up of oxides) approach to combustion and respiration and the need for a distinction to be drawn between matter and energy, presented in this chapter, in one lesson only, if you later talk about 'food contains energy' or 'energy in a crisp' or 'oil is an energy source'. Nor should ideas of acids and rates of reaction be confined to bottles of chemicals in laboratories. Instead they should be used as a concept to help us to explain how everyday chemical changes happen in the kitchen, within living things and in our whole environment. We must give our pupils much more time to reinterpret, use and apply the ideas they meet in their science lessons. Otherwise they will be learnt for the exams, harvested as a good GCSE grade and promptly forgotten.

CHAPTER

Difficult ideas in physics

Physics has taken a large number of words in daily use and given them specific meanings. This is one reason why misconceptions with physical concepts are very prevalent and hard to remove. In this chapter we look at how the every-day meanings of words used in physics have helped to spread confusion as children try to understand scientific models in these concept areas. Our focus is on two key ideas from the KS 3 strategy for science: energy and force. Our solution is to urge teachers to get pupils not to use the words only in the scientific sense, but to realise that the words stand for different ideas depending on context. In this way they will be able to see their world in new ways.

Energy

Popular use (and misuse) of the word *energy* has led to confusions in the language associated with it:

- confusion in how the word is used by politicians and physicists, which forms our main focus here;
- confusion of matter and energy, the issue of the origin of energy associated with fuels, which we resolved in the previous chapter by our focus on the fuel–oxygen system;
- confusion between the extent and the intensity of energy – heat energy and temperature – which we examine below.
- confusion about the words we use to measure and describe electrical energy and circuits;
- (in light) confusion about the words used to describe colour.

Confusion in how the word 'energy' is used by politicians and by physicists

The word *energy* is used spontaneously even by five-year-olds – it is a part of our everyday language. Not so long ago, in school we did experiments where 'work' was turned to 'heat' by friction; we could calculate the number of joules that were equivalent to one calorie. Later we learnt that heat and mechanical movement were both forms of 'energy' and could be measured in the same units.

Nowadays, the word 'energy', in its everyday meaning, has come to represent an ability to do something *useful* and is best represented in science by saying something has 'fuel value'. As this 'energy' is 'used' it degrades into waste heat, so we have to come back for more. In this way energy can be seen as a flow: from high-grade, useful sources to scattered waste heat. This is unlike the matter cycles we met in Chapters 2 and 12, where matter (at an atomic level) cannot be destroyed, meaning that we have to develop cycles for all those materials we use that cannot be recycled by natural means. These material cycles (extraction, transport, manufacture, recycle etc.) need to be fuelled by an energy source.

Everyday conversation might say, 'Energy is being used up, so we must conserve it, and use it wisely.' A physicist, on the other hand, might say, 'When something happens the total amount of energy does not change, so the amount of energy in the universe is constant – it is conserved.' Can both be true? The problem is that the words *energy* and *conservation* mean different things in both cases. We need to consider the laws of thermodynamics to understand this.

What the physicist says agrees with the *first law of thermodynamics*, which is the law we teach in school: the amount of energy remains the same, energy cannot be created or destroyed. If you measure the joules at the start of a change there will be the same number at the end. Thus chemical energy from burning the petrol in your car is transferred into movement and heat.

What our everyday use of the word energy says agrees with the *second law of thermodynamics*: energy degrades to waste heat as it is 'used'. Thus, once the petrol has been burnt in the car engine, the energy has become scattered as waste heat and movements of air, and it cannot be used any more.

We see this progression from a concentrated useful resource to scattered waste all around us. Rooms become untidy, bath water becomes dirty, electricity lights our homes and the energy becomes scattered waste heat. It is the second law at work: the universe becomes less ordered; everything spreads out over time. High-grade energy is required to prevent this descent into chaos or to maintain order. For example, for a room to remain tidy, there has to be an input of energy (muscle power or a vacuum cleaner) so that instead of the matter in the room becoming scattered the energy you use is degraded.

Science courses on energy at KS 3 often start with an energy 'circus' in which pupils realise the 'interconvertablilty' of energy. We need to accept, at this time, that pupils will say that energy gets used up. In all the energy changes the energy we get out is never as much as we put in, because of 'losses'. Sometimes these losses are a nuisance, as in the waste heat in a car or our bodies, which we have to get rid of (through the cooling system or through sweat). This energy is not used up, but its usefulness has gone.

When dealing with energy changes we suggest you use Sankey diagrams (see Figure 13.1). The boxes represent energy, and the arrows are labelled by the process or object that causes the change. This makes a clear distinction between the contraptions, like the light bulb, that cause energy to be changed, and the energy itself. In addition, the boxes are drawn so that their size represents the amount of energy. With all boxes being equally tall you can show that there is no loss in joules. You can then show, at each stage, what proportion of the energy is transferred usefully, and what fraction is 'wasted' as heat. In Figure 13.1 it is the white boxes that represent useful energy that is transferred to the next stage. The shaded boxes are waste heat, but they all add up in the end to equal the useful energy we started with.

To make things happen, high-grade energy has to become spread out and dissipated as waste heat. Thus, in a 100 watt ordinary light bulb (giving out 100 joules per second) high-grade electrical energy is transferred into light (5 joules per second) and waste heat (95 joules per second). You can replace this with a 10 watt *energy efficient* light bulb, which transfers 5 joules a second as light, as before, but only wastes 5 joules as heat and so is ten times cheaper to run. Energy cannot be *renewed* once it has dissipated, but we can *replenish* it by burning more fuel, or waiting for more sunlight to arrive (Ross *et al*. 2002: energy).

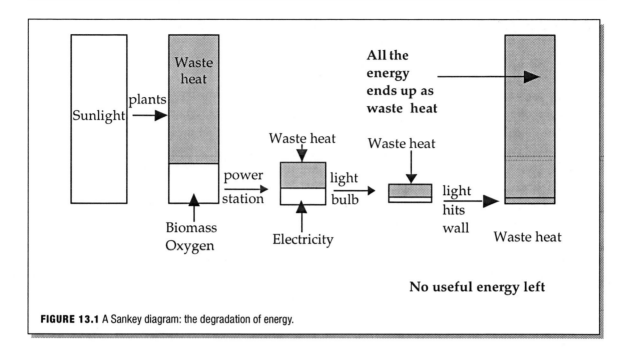

FIGURE 13.1 A Sankey diagram: the degradation of energy.

Heat (thermal energy) and temperature

Pupils in school, and the public at large, often confuse temperature and heat (thermal energy). Such terms are used interchangeably in everyday life, but it is important to realise that one (heat energy) represents an amount of energy, which may have to be paid for, and the other (temperature or hotness) applies to the intensity of the energy. You can have a red-hot nail at the same temperature as lava flowing from a volcano, but the amount of energy in the nail is negligible in comparison.

Energy that is at a high intensity can be linked with danger: a high temperature, a high voltage, a fast moving mass (e.g. a bullet), a short wavelength electromagnetic wave (e.g. X-rays), a raised mass (a loose tile) and appropriate mixtures of weakly bonded chemicals (e.g. a firework) are all dangerous. But how much useful work they can do depends on quantity, not intensity. A red-hot nail plunged into a cold mug of coffee will not do much to make it drinkable, but a red-hot poker (same temperature, more heat energy) will do the trick. However, the red-hot nail can do more damage than the hot coffee. Temperature measures the amount of energy *per particle*. High temperatures are dangerous, but may not 'contain' very much energy. A spark has a high temperature, but very little heat energy.

Heat (thermal energy), on the other hand, is associated with payment. To make your bath water hot requires buying fuel (the oxygen is free). The amount of fuel you need to burn depends on the amount of heat energy needed, which, in turn, depends on three things: the amount of stuff you are heating; the material it is made of (in this case it is water); and the required rise in 'hotness' (i.e. temperature rise). Heat (strictly 'thermal energy') is the total amount of energy transferable into your system, so we add up the energy of all the particles.

At KS 3 we should be asking pupils to measure the temperature of different amounts of water at different temperatures before and after mixing (see question 2 in Chapter 5, and the discussion in Chapter 11). They should also feel how hot or cold the water is (safety: keep the water below 55°C) so that temperature readings can be linked to their real senses.

Electricity

When we use the word *electricity* in everyday life we usually mean *electrical energy*: 'It works by electricity', 'It uses electricity'.

To most people, all words associated with electricity mean much the same. For example, people might say that electric current (measured in amps) is 'used up', so less current flows back than went out to a bulb, because they think of current as electrical energy. A physicist will say the current remains the same all the way round a series circuit. To understand the concept of current we need to think about why there has to be a *return* wire, and what it is that is conserved when the ammeter reads the same wherever it is placed in the circuit.

The *milk delivery analogy* is helpful (see Figure 13.2). The milk (representing energy) is delivered in bottles (coulombs, which measure the number of electrons) to the house (bulb). The actual current is the *flow rate* of energy carriers – coulombs per second (bottles per day) – and it must be the same all the way round, since electrons return to the cell (and used bottles to the dairy). How much energy is carried by each carrier depends on the voltage (*joules per coulomb*), or how full the bottles are (*milk per bottle*). In the case of electricity the energy is transferred by the repulsion of neighbouring electrons: the more packed together they are the higher the voltage, the more they are able to push and the more dangerous (or useful) each packet of electrons is. See http://www.glos.ac.uk/science-issues/more-details.htm for an animated version of this analogy (from Ross *et al.* 2002: energy).

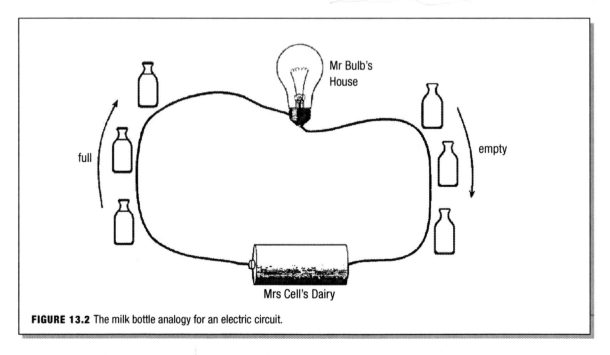

FIGURE 13.2 The milk bottle analogy for an electric circuit.

We probably teach ideas about electricity in the wrong order, and introduce current too soon. Although it appears to be a complex unit, *power* is easily recognisable in everyday terms. Power tells us the *energy transferred per second*, and is measured in *watts*, which are *joules per second*. We can all see that a 3 kilowatt kettle boils water more quickly than a 2 kilowatt kettle, and that a 100 watt bulb is brighter than a 60 watt bulb.

In the milk bottle analogy, the *power* of our supply will measure how much milk is delivered per day. That depends on (a) the number of bottles per day and (b) the amount of milk put in each bottle. Thus electrical power is measured by amps (coulombs per second) multiplied by volts (joules per coulomb). If volts and amps are introduced too early they just get muddled into a vague idea that 'they measure the amount of electricity'.

So *electricity*, in common parlance, means electrical energy, which is transferred (and dissipated) during changes involving electrical appliances; *power* is a measure of how quickly that energy is delivered; *current* is the flow of a 'carrier', which needs a complete circuit; and *voltage* shows the danger (how highly charged with energy each carrier is).

Colour vision and pigments

If all light is absorbed the object will appear black, and the light energy will be transferred to heat energy, but if only some light is absorbed the surface can look coloured or grey. Pigments are therefore *selective absorbers* of light.

Children find it hard to believe that white light is composed of a spectrum of colours – seen as a rainbow when raindrops cause light to become separated. Pigments work by selectively absorbing some colours from the white light. That is why you must look at colours in daylight to appreciate them properly, and why a blue door (which only reflects blue) looks black in sodium vapour lamps at night. The sodium vapour light has no blue in it, so all the light is absorbed by the pigment on the door.

Colour mixing by subtraction and addition

To understand colour vision, and mixing of pigments and lights, you must appreciate that the artists' primary colours – *red*, *yellow* and *blue* – are different colours from the scientists' primary colours of *red*, *green* and *blue*. There are six colours here, not four, and the names given to them by artists and some teachers are not the same as those given by photographers, printers and scientists (see Figure 13.3).

Force and motion

From the start we are struggling against common usage of language. Everything in shops is weighed in kilograms, yet kilogram is a unit of mass. How do we separate out the ideas that mass is a constant and that weight is a changing force? This force is measured in newtons and produced by the effect of gravity (or acceleration).

A more serious misconception is that objects that are moving 'have a force' in them. No matter how many times we refer to Newton's First Law, pupils will insist that as well as gravity affecting moving objects they also have a *force of momentum* driving them and they stop when this 'runs out'. They cannot see that the object slows due to the force of friction and that without this friction the object would continue forever. The problem is that there are no common examples relevant to them where there is no friction. When we push a trolley we need a driving force to keep going, only because of friction.

We began to address this in Chapter 7 (pp. 59ff) with a teaching sequence that developed the idea of 'force, gravity and motion'. Here we suggest a scheme that starts the *intervention* phase with an air track and then uses ideas developed to understand the motion of cars and footballers.

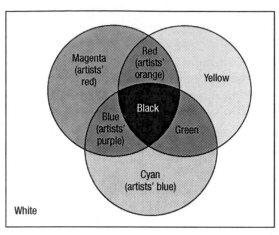 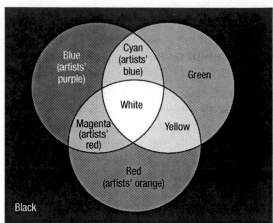

Artists: colour mixing by subtraction   Scientists: colour mixing by addition

FIGURE 13.3 Artists' and scientists' primary colours.

Air track demonstrations

The air supply to the track should be regulated by having a hole in the air line that can be gradually closed, allowing air gradually to push the trolley off the track and reducing friction essentially to zero. A very weak, stretchy length of elastic is used to pull the trolley, so pupils can estimate the pulling force. You begin by showing a trolley that needs to be constantly pulled to make it go. As soon as you stop pulling the trolley stops. We explain this by saying that there are two horizontal forces, which are in balance: your pull and friction. The more the friction the more you have to pull, but if the pull is greater than friction the trolley will pick up speed.

We now reduce friction in stages by closing the hole in the air feeder tube and show that the force we need to pull the trolley gradually drops to zero. When friction has been eliminated no pulling force is needed to maintain the speed of the trolley. We still need a force to get it going, of course, and we also need another force to stop it. This theoretical discussion can now allow us to reconsider everyday events.

Cars, football and skidding

Ask a pupil to run and stop. Talk about the need to get a grip. Talk about icy roads, wet floors and football boot studs. The idea is: to change the motion (slowing down, getting faster, changing direction) you need a force. If a footballer, or anyone else, needs to change their motion they need to get a good grip. It is only when you attempt to change your motion and can't get that grip that skidding happens.

People often associate skidding, or slipping, with turning corners, and it is true that it is during cornering (or trying to start or stop) that cars and footballers skid. But a skid happens when there is reduced frictional force from the ground, so your attempt to slow down or turn a corner fails, and you carry on in the same direction that you were going. With no frictional force (or grip) there can be no change in motion.

What force causes hot air to rise?

Air is made of atoms, which have mass, so air is attracted to the Earth by the gravitational force. If you pump air into a football the ball gets heavier (a three-litre pop bottle with a bung and valve is easier to deal with in class, and its mass will increase by about a gram, which can be detected on a top pan balance). This leads to the important idea that our atmosphere is 'heavy' and is attracted to the Earth by gravity. Why is it, then, that hot air and helium move away from the centre of the Earth, i.e. why do they rise?

To illustrate this, we can compare air and water in a demonstration. Fill a tank with water at about 35°C. A red balloon filled with very hot water is released half-way down. It will be buoyed up by the cooler water around it taking its place – this is 'hot air rising'. A blue balloon filled with ice-cold water sinks, displacing the warmer water surrounding it upwards. It is no different from a block of wood (less dense so buoyed up) and a stone (more dense so sinks).

Accounts of the weather frequently describe convection currents as being caused by 'hot air rising allowing cold air to rush in'. What they should say is that the cold, dense air moves in, buoying (pushing) the less dense hot air away from the Earth against gravity. Gases are real, massive forms of matter and we need to appreciate that if they rise, something more massive must be pushing them upwards.

Summary

We have focused on two major concepts in physics – energy and force – to show how our everyday use of words and our experiences often go against the scientific understanding we are trying to share with our pupils at school. Once again we have shown the importance of knowing pupils' firmly held everyday ideas if we are to enable them to go through a real revolution and adopt our more widely applicable scientific understanding.

Difficult ideas in biology

We begin this chapter by looking at the big ideas in biology, in particular the notion of being alive and the characteristics of life itself, then explore these ideas using plants as examples. These are sometimes neglected in our teaching and many misconceptions about how life works build up. We take a brief look at some other problems facing learners, many of which we have mentioned earlier in this book. Unlike physicists, biologists tend to invent new words when they need them, usually based on classical origins. This means that biology can be filled with strange long words, cluttered with everyday meaning. We conclude with some examples of the opposite: confusion that occurs when biology takes over existing words for its own use.

Big ideas in biology

Living things are made of cells and it is appropriate that the KS 3 strategy has recognised cells as one of the key concepts underlying an understanding of the world around us. The strategy progresses from the nature and structure of cells at Years 7 and 8, through the life processes (including the role of microorganisms and immunity) to more complex ideas of genetics at Year 9. All life starts as a single cell, and the overarching characteristic of an organism is that the single cell can divide making copies of itself. So we look first at the characteristics of life and then at cell division.

Mrs Gren: characteristics of life

At the basis of all biological studies are the characteristics of life itself: what makes something living as opposed to something that is inanimate and, indeed, something that has never lived? The 'Mrs Gren' mnemonic, representing the characteristics of livings things, is very popular, but is only a memory aid, and gives no deeper understanding. We need to start further back and 'invent' the characteristics of life afresh with our pupils. The overriding feature of life is that it can make copies of itself – it is self-replicating. We need to add, too, that it evolves. What would something need to enable it to reproduce by itself? Houses are not alive, but it is useful to think of how they come into being. They need an open space, plans (in time and space), materials, tools and energy.

- *Space*. Without space into which they can grow, living cells could not reproduce.
- *Plans*. These are held in the DNA in most life forms, providing instructions not only on how to make the parts but also on how the parts function and fit together.

- *Tools*. Life's tools are enzymes. The DNA code appears to be instructions to make enzymes, which cause chemical reactions to take place in cells and allow structures to be built and function.

- *Materials*. Some forms of life (e.g. plants, the producers, the autotrophs) are able to use non-living materials: carbon dioxide as their source of carbon, water and minerals. Others (e.g. animals, the consumers) need to take in their materials ready made: for example, as carbohydrate, amino acids (protein) and nucleic acids (DNA) from other living things.

- *Energy*. Autotrophs need sunlight as their primary energy source (except, for example, in the case of vent communities at mid-oceanic ridges, which use reactive chemicals). This energy 'sets' the fuel–oxygen system by building up biomass in the living organism and releasing oxygen to the atmosphere. Once this energy is stored, all living things can use it in a process called respiration. In turn this sets smaller 'springs' such as the ATP–ADP system to provide energy in manageable chunks where it is needed.

If life needs these things and it has to do everything for itself a number of characteristics must be present, which children can devise for themselves. If a living thing has to make a copy of itself, what must it be able to do?

M   Movement. Needed to get to empty space, to find materials and to reproduce.

R   Respiration. Recombining oxygen and biomass to provide energy.

S   Senses. Living things must have ways of telling which way is up or down, where light is, how to find other living things.

G   Growth. Growth occurs by adding cells, which is the same process as asexual reproduction. This is the 'purpose' of life.

R   Reproduction. Sexual reproduction allows a range of characteristics, which might become useful one day, to lie dormant in a population, so allowing them to respond to changes in their environment. Without this, evolution, as we know it, could not take place.

E   Excretion. Materials need to be taken into cells, but after being processed wastes are inevitable. They have to be excreted.

N   Nutrition. Getting materials for growth and to use as a fuel.

Elicitation tasks such as question 8 in Chapter 5 (p. 38), where pupils have to sort cards into life or not-life and animals or plants, become more straightforward after these seven characteristics are explored. See Box 14.1 for more teaching ideas about living and not-living.

Human biology

Following the outline above we can get pupils to think about our own body design.

- How do we get the materials to build new cells where they are needed?
- How do we get fuel and oxygen to all our cells?

Rather than telling pupils about our circulation system, why not let them design it?

- How many would think of a two-chamber heart, or come up with the design for the lungs or gut, or think of putting a liver-like organ immediately after the gut to deal with undesirable material that might get in?

■ Would they come up with the artery and capillary system to allow bulk transport followed by distribution to all the cells?

---

1   Ask groups of pupils to identify what processes the items go through when they are alive, when they are decaying and when they are changed by people into other things. Make a list or mind map of ideas about living. Questions such as the following can act as prompts:

- What is different between something that is living and something that has never lived?
- What makes a (once) living thing alive or dead?
- When does death occur?
- Is fire a living thing?
- Are seeds living?
- What is the link between the living and the non-living worlds?
- What are microorganisms and are they alive?

2   Make use of key vocabulary in your plenary session: habitat, adaptation, food chain, consumer, producer, predator, ecosystem, decay, herbivore, carnivore, life cycle, pollution, energy transfer.

3   As a homework exercise get pupils to design a 'sun' machine that only needs air, sunlight and rain to enable it to work, and then to design 'robber' machines that rely on using parts of other machines to work. They will put sensors and wheels on the 'robbers' but not on the 'suns' until they realise that the suns need to escape from the robbers. They may also decide to protect the 'suns' (plants) using spikes (thorns)!

BOX 14.1 Probing pupils' ideas about living things

Too often pupils see the alimentary canal as one long tube, which takes food from mouth to anus. It is the big idea, not the details, that needs to be emphasised. The purpose of digestion is to get food into the blood. See Box 14.2

Collect all the ingredients you would need for a simple meal, e.g. breakfast: milk, cornflakes, banana, sugar, bread, butter, marmalade, orange juice, coffee and any other soft food you can think of. Mix all these foods into a mixing bowl, explaining that this represents our mouth and stomach. Discuss briefly what is happening to the food in the mouth. A knife can be used to cut the food (the incisors) and a meat pounder to grind it (the molars). Vinegar can be added to represent the stomach acid. Using a prepared pair of tights (one leg placed into the other and toes removed to give a single tube) explain to the pupils that you are now going to allow the food to enter the intestines. Spoon the contents of the mixing bowl into the top of the tights. The food now moves into the small intestine – by squeezing the mixture you will get it to move along the tube (peristalsis). Twist the tights so that the mixture becomes compact and the juices released can be collected in a drip tray. These juices represent the 'goodness' passing into the blood for use by the body. Squeeze the remaining (undigested) mixture towards the toe of the tights and show egestion of faeces.

BOX 14.2 A simulated 'gut'

When pupils write creatively about the journey of our food, they say that the food (having said goodbye to the good bits) leaves out of the anus. Why not say goodbye to the indigestible bits and begin the real adventure as the blood carries you round? You then leave minutes or hours later as carbon dioxide at the lungs, or falling to the floor as dead skin some weeks later, having contributed to the growth of new skin cells. This approach helps to avoid confusion between *egestion* of faeces, which have never entered the blood, and *excretion* of wastes that accumulate in the blood and have to be removed by the lungs, kidneys or as sweat.

We must try to see the body as an integrated whole, not a lot of independent parts. It is this independence that leads to another serious misconception that many textbooks perpetuate. It is the idea that food 'contains' energy, rather than saying that energy is transferred when food is respired: this is a topic that we discussed at some length in Chapter 12 (p. 91).

How can two make one?

As mentioned earlier, one of the key characteristics of life is that it can reproduce itself, and this means that cells must be able to divide. But cells divide for a variety of reasons, namely:

- growth;
- repair;
- reproduction.

Division requires one cell yielding two cells, which must be identical. This is the process of asexual cell division known as *mitosis*. This process has many advantages:

- it is quick;
- it is reliable;
- it has a low energy cost;
- the offspring are always the same.

It is of course the process involved during growth, when a fertilised egg develops into an adult organism. By selectively switching genes on and off, each new cell can become increasingly specialised.

A major misconception associated with cell division relates to the structure of chromosomes. A single chromosome (obtained from either one of your parents) in a typical diploid cell, observed during the normal lifetime of the cell (interphase), would appear as a single strand of DNA capable of active protein synthesis. During the lead up to cell division, this molecule makes an exact copy of itself and the chromosome takes on the more characteristic two-pronged structure, with its two chromatids being held together at the centromere. To prevent excessive loss of material, the chromosome appears to contract, becoming shorter and fatter as it winds around the nucleosomes. During division, it is the chromatids that separate, breaking apart at the centromere. The resultant daughter cells contain a chromatid from each replicated chromosome, thus maintaining the total genetic quota.

This is all very well for growth and repair, when you want more of the same thing, but consider survival in a changing environment. All the offspring are identical and therefore susceptible to the same environmental influences.

This is where sexual reproduction takes the upper hand. It does not display any of the advantages of the above, but it does ensure that variation can arise, enabling the organism to respond to environmental effects in different ways – a factor crucial to the evolutionary process. In genetic terms, sexual reproduction causes a potential doubling of genetic material, as two cells fuse to form one. A reduction division is therefore required for the production of the sex cells, each containing half the total genetic quota and each with the potential to be different. *Meiosis* is the process by which this is achieved. Reduction is achieved by the initial separation of homologous chromosomes, which then undergo a further division to separate the chromatids. As these chromatids separate they become intertwined with one another and at the 'cross-over' points breakages and recombinations occur. This results in additional variation within the genetic make-up of the individual.

By emphasising the role of the chromatid during cell division, we can give pupils a greater appreciation of the process and how the two types of cell division can achieve the desired end results.

A teaching sequence about plants

This section outlines a number of conceptual problems associated with plants, and suggests some active learning activities for pupils.

What is a plant?

The National Curriculum refers to 'Green plants as organisms', with particular reference to nutrition, growth and the role of respiration. The most pressing issue, however, is what constitutes a 'plant'. In the *elicitation* phase of the lesson, ask a group of pupils what they think a plant is: they are likely to come up with a very restricted view that begins with 'pot plants' and may extend to vegetables, flowers and trees. The more adventurous answers include (wrongly according to modern classification systems) lichens, fungi and seaweed.

It is at this stage that you need to *intervene*. Taking the definition that plants photosynthesise, it is possible to eliminate one of the above. Fungi appear in a wide array of vivid colours, but 'chlorophyll green' is not one of them. They excrete enzymes into the surrounding medium, digesting cellulose, glycoprotein and starch before ingesting the substrate. They are saprophytes, living off dead organic material.

'Plants breathe in carbon dioxide in the day and breathe it out at night'

Pupils and adults alike hold this common misconception. It is understandable because this is what we are taught, but we need to appreciate the broader picture. Why do plants photosynthesise? What is it they are producing and what is it used for? There is a grain of truth here (see Chapter 4): plants are net users of carbon dioxide during the day, and net exporters of it at night, even though respiration goes on all the time. But, as the question in Figure 14.1 shows, many children do not appreciate that plants get their main structural material, carbon, from the air, and respond by saying its mass comes from the water and the soil.

When a plant photosynthesises it uses sunlight energy to split water and reduce carbon dioxide. The end products are glucose and oxygen. Plant biomass (its overall structure), however, is made of more than mere glucose. As well as carbohydrate, they need proteins, DNA and many other chemicals. By combining the glucose with minerals available from the soil, the plant produces these components of biomass. This process, however, requires energy. Some of the glucose will have to be

A small tree is planted in a tub.

After 20 years it has grown into a big tree, with an increase in mass of over 70 kg.

The level of soil in the tub has hardly changed over the 20 years.

The only substance added to the tub over the years has been rain water. Where do the extra 70 kg come from?

Explain your answer as fully as you can.

FIGURE 14.1 Tub tree elicitation question (based on van Helmont's famous experiment).

combined with oxygen to release the energy associated with this fuel–oxygen system. This is respiration and it takes place all the time in every part of the plant.

'But plants only breathe at night!' say the pupils. During the day the plant uses carbon dioxide in the photosynthetic process. So much is required, however, that there is a net intake of this gas. Now consider oxygen. Only some of the oxygen produced during photosynthesis is used in respiration, and the remainder is released. At one stage, referred to as the 'compensation point', the amount of gases produced equals the amount of gases required and there is no net production or release (see Box 14.3).

Roots, stems and leaves

Another clearly defined characteristic of plants is that they possess true roots, stems and leaves. Seaweed contains a simple arrangement of cells forming a 'holdfast', stipe (primitive stem) and various fronds. They photosynthesise effectively but, owing to their simple specialisation and undifferentiated cell structure, are not classified as plants. They are in fact algae and classified alongside other single-celled structures such as *Amoeba*, *Euglena* and *Paramoecium*. Pupils often describe single-celled plant-like and animal-like organisms as being true plants or animals. Lichens are a result of a symbiotic association between two groups of organism – fungi and algae – and are not classified as plants either. However, it is useful to see all photosynthetic organisms, whether single-celled or true plants, as 'producers' on which 'consumers' depend.

Introduce photosynthesis by talking about the word itself, and getting the pupils to investigate other 'photo' words to see if they can understand what the prefix 'photo' actually means. Once the connection with light is made, pupils begin to understand its importance in the plant world.

Give each pupil a card with either a 'water' or a 'carbon dioxide' molecule on it. As the teacher narrates the pupils role-play the photosynthetic process. Use a row of stools to depict the plant stem. Water molecules enter the plant through the roots and move up the stem to the leaves. Light photons enter the plant through the top of the leaves, and the molecules of carbon dioxide enter through the leaf bottom. A reaction takes place between the molecules, and the carbon dioxide cards are turned over to reveal 'sugar' and the water cards reveal 'oxygen' – the end products of photosynthesis. At this stage you need to point out to the pupils that no growth has occurred in the plant. So some of the sugar will need to be converted into other molecules to help build the plant and the spare oxygen will be given off to the atmosphere. This building process requires energy through respiration – provided by the few remaining sugar molecules and the oxygen molecules, which now re-combine (turn cards over again). This is what happens in daylight: plants become net exporters of oxygen. When no further photosynthesis takes place (i.e. at night) only respiration takes place so the plant becomes an exporter of carbon dioxide and water.

Teaching point: Note that plants respire all the time (plants die when their roots have no access to oxygen in the soil, e.g. when waterlogged).

See also the 'saucepan model' and related discussion in Chapter 12, Box 12.1 (p. 92).

BOX 14.3 Photosynthesis

Transport of materials in plants

The rooting system of the more advanced plants is complex, with a central taproot and a series of radial, lateral roots. Root hairs serve to increase the overall surface area of the system. Water and mineral salts are absorbed from the soil into the roots by osmosis. The water and minerals pass through a network of cells into a series of hollow tubes, the xylem vessels. These connect the roots to the rest of the plant.

Teaching point: take time to question pupils about what they think the small quantity of ash is that remains after plants are burnt. All the carbon and hydrogen are returned to the air in carbon dioxide and water vapour, so the ash represents the minerals taken up by the plant from the soil. That is why wood ash is such a good fertiliser.

Teaching point: there are many excellent traditional ways to demonstrate the transpiration process, such as:

- celery or carnations in coloured water showing water uptake through xylem;
- leaving several leaves to 'dry', some coated with Vaseline on the top side, the underside or both sides to show that water loss is greater from the underside of the leaf;
- observing condensation inside a polythene bag tied around some leaves of a plant.

Owing to their underground existence, roots are excluded from the light and are therefore unable to photosynthesise. Food needs to be taken to them via a second series of vessels, the phloem. This provides material for growth as well as fuel for respiration, but to release energy, oxygen is also required. This comes from air pockets in the soil, which the roots draw around them. If oxygen access to the roots is prevented, e.g. when the plants get waterlogged, the plant will die.

Teaching point: compare roots with germinating seeds. They cannot photosynthesise and so need fuel and oxygen. Both have a store of carbohydrate (and roots are continually supplied from the leaves) but both need access to oxygen from the air.

The stem links the whole plant together, surrounding the xylem and phloem and supporting the leaves and any flowers. This support is achieved by maintaining high water pressure (turgidity, like air in a football) within its cells or by forming the woody lignin, present in larger plants such as trees. The stem offers a continuous transport system from root to leaves, while the transpiration stream ensures that water is continually drawn into and up the xylem by capillary action, and out through the leaves by evaporation.

Teaching point: discuss leaf wilt and the function of lignin in supporting a plant. An analogy with blowing air into an inflatable toy is useful.

Everyday words with special meaning

We began by saying that biology is full of its own invented words, like testa, xylem and ovary. We end by addressing two problems that arise from the opposite: where everyday words are also used for a special purpose in biology.

Growth

We often ask pupils to investigate the conditions necessary for the growth of seeds, but we need to distinguish between germination and growth. Most pupils would agree that water and warmth are required. Many would suggest that light is also necessary. But this is not so for germination (although, in some cases, e.g. poppies, it acts as a regulator, like frost, in triggering germination). Seedlings require light to photosynthesise once the seed has produced its first leaves. Until this stage, light is of little use because there is no chlorophyll available for photosynthesis. The seed needs oxygen to respire its food reserves in order to germinate and then to grow. When pupils set up conditions for plant growth investigations, we need to be clear whether they are investigating the growth of seedlings (light needed) or germination of seeds (light not needed).

Teaching point: seeds can be collected from trees in the autumn. Some can be put in the freezer for a week, and others left in the classroom. All seeds are then planted in warm, moist conditions, and pupils can see which germinate most successfully. They can also consider the advantage of germinating only after a big freeze.

Fruit, seed or vegetable?

These words, especially fruit and vegetable, have different meanings in the kitchen from those they have in biology. Show the pupils a range of fruits and vegetables and ask them to identify the part of the plant from which they came and whether they are 'fruit', 'seed' or 'vegetable'. You will need to recognise, biologically, that a fruit is a fertilised ovary, seeds reside inside the fruiting body and a vegetable is any other part of a plant used for food. How many in Table 14.1 are classified differently in the kitchen and in science?

TABLE 14.1 Fruit, vegetable or seed?

Food	Part of plant	Scientific classification			Kitchen classification		
		Vegetable	Fruit	seed	Vegetable	Fruit	Seed
Tomato	Ovary (fleshy)						
Rhubarb	Stem						
Cucumber	Ovary (fleshy)						
Potato	Stem – tuber						
Onion	Leaf – bulb						
Plum	ovary (fleshy)						
Beetroot	Root						
Apple	Receptacle (fleshy)						
Carrot	Root						
Melon	Ovary (fleshy)						
Coconut	Seed						
Hazelnut	Seed						
Runner bean	Ovary (fleshy)						
Sweet corn	Seed						
Cauliflower	Flower						

Summary

We have highlighted problems with technical and everyday biological vocabulary. We have once again stressed the importance of thinking about the fuel–oxygen system, keeping ideas about material (atoms) and energy separate. The main focus was on plants. We have concentrated on the common misconceptions held by pupils and many adults. These tend to be associated with plant classification and plant metabolism. Some suggestions for practical and word work activities have been made to overcome the misconceptions.

15

Learning at Key Stage 3

The KS 3 national strategy is about classrooms and what goes on in them. It aims to raise expectations by increasing pupils' confidence and levels of engagement, and to strengthen the quality of teaching. Now established within schools, the strategy has been given a mixed reception, although the essence of the strategy is emphasising good practice, and this captures the heart of what we advocate all along. This chapter unpicks the strategy and explores its framework and philosophy, while focusing on the teaching and learning points and the implications the strategy has for the teacher.

Introduction

Every year there appears to be an ever-increasing number of strategies that need to be addressed and incorporated into teaching and learning. This can be very daunting, especially if they are viewed as 'add-on' extras. If we start with the belief that all these strategies are about good teaching and therefore good learning, then we will automatically cover the points highlighted in our 'good lesson' (see Chapters 6 and 20).

The KS 3 national strategy was introduced into English state schools in September 2001. The aim was to raise standards by strengthening the quality of teaching and learning by making it more effective, to address issues of transition and transfer within and between key stages and at the same time to raise pupils' expectations initially in English and mathematics but a year later in science, ICT and modern foreign languages. The strategy is essentially a framework built around best practice in teaching and learning with a goal that 70 per cent of the school population should attain National Curriculum level 5 and above by 2004 and 80 per cent by 2005. Essentially, it is expecting that pupils should acquire sufficient skills in thinking, analysing and absorbing sufficient information across a wide range of topics to move up two levels during KS 3. The strategy also identifies three clear parts to a lesson:

- clear aims and objectives for each lesson, to be shared with the pupils;
- activities appropriate to the class that are relevant and have pace;
- a plenary session in which all the threads of the activities are drawn together and shared, so that the class can see whether they have achieved the aims of the lesson.

The framework for teaching science

The materials that support the science framework provide practical suggestions and advice on teaching at KS 3. The framework was informed by research, Ofsted findings, the pilot study that took place between 2001 and 2002 and other sources of good practice in schools. There were key, overarching ideas that informed and directed the science framework. These included:

- *Scientific enquiry.* This should be fully integrated throughout the science programme of study, emphasising the unique nature of science, its relevance in everyday life and the contribution it gives to society. (See Chapters 1, 19 and 27.)

- *Big ideas in science.* The conceptual aspect of the framework identifies five key ideas that underpin science: particles (see Chapters 2 and 12), energy (see Chapter 13), cells (see Chapter 14), interdependence (see Chapter 14) and forces (see Chapter 13). By connecting with these big ideas, pupils are encouraged to see the interrelatedness of science: how the individual conceptual ideas they learn throughout their school career form part of a bigger, more complex picture.

- *Transition, transfer and progression.* Emphasis is given to the progressive nature of the science curriculum, both within the key stage and building on the achievements and successes of their primary work. The majority of Year 6 children will achieve level 4 in science. Secondary school teachers need to be familiar with the Key Stage 2 Programme of Study so that they can build on areas for development and avoid duplication in both content and example. (See Chapter 16.)

Generic ideas and approaches to the strategy also inform the science framework. These include:

- The use of clearly defined teaching objectives and learning outcomes (intended learning outcomes or ILOs) to plan challenging and engaging multiphase lessons.

- ILOs forming the basis for pupil target setting.

- Identification of individual teacher needs, in terms of continual professional development. Targets would be set and action plans established.

  All are examples of good practice.

Effective lesson design

From a teaching and learning perspective, effective lesson design is at the heart of the KS 3 strategy and, once again, reflects good practice. It is summarised in Figure 15.1, which links with our five or six stage lesson (see Chapters 6 and 20). This approach recognises two fundamental ideas, one being the strategy's commitment to interactive teaching and learning, the other being the developing independence of the learning. The significance of these will become apparent as we explore the various factors that impact on lesson design.

Learning objectives

The role of clearly defined and well thought through learning objectives cannot be overestimated. These will inform the pedagogic aspects of lessons and directly influence how effective lesson design

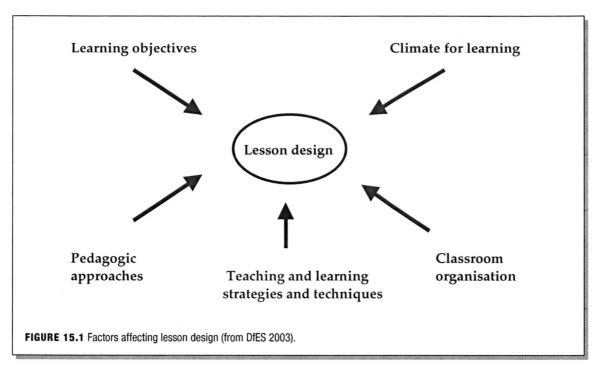

FIGURE 15.1 Factors affecting lesson design (from DfES 2003).

will be: if your learning objectives are vague then your lesson design cannot hope to be any better. The whole process of developing concise and clearly thought through learning objectives is explored at length in the assessment section of the strategy. One exercise involves the grid shown in Figure 15.2 as a prompt.

Useful words to use for defining lesson objectives and expected pupil-outcomes

Draw	State	Record	Recognise	Identify
Sort	Describe	Select	Present	Locate information from text
Decide	Discuss	Define	Classify	Explain how
Devise	Calculate	Interpret	Construct	Clarify
Plan	Predict	Conclude	Solve	Determine the key points from
Formulate	Explain why	Use the pattern to …	Reorganise	Explain the differences between …
Link/make connections between …	Use the idea of … to …	Uses a model of … to …	Provide evidence for …	Evaluate the evidence for …

FIGURE 15.2 Vocabulary for framing lesson objectives and outcomes (from KS 3 strategy *Assessment in Science*).

Teaching and learning strategies

Each teacher will have unique strategies that work best in different situations. You need to try them out under differing circumstances and learn more about them and when they are best used. The benefits of a rich repertoire of teaching and learning strategies will become evident as your teaching experience develops. The type of strategy used in a given situation is determined by a variety of factors, typically your learning objectives and the pedagogic approach used, but also by the class themselves and other less obvious influences such as room and time of day. The KS 3 strategy emphasises the importance of these strategies when presenting key concepts and ideas, demonstrating skills and processes, engaging and supporting pupils in active learning and high order thinking, establishing interactive and well paced dialogue with the class and creating the right level of challenge. It highlights three examples of teaching skills that support these strategies, namely:

- the effective and appropriate use of questioning;
- transparent and accessible explanations;
- the use of modelling as a means of presenting abstract conceptual ideas and processes.

These teaching and learning strategies may vary as you progress through the multiphased lesson: for example, the use of 'starter activities' has long been promoted. These may vary in design but all serve to focus the pupils' thinking and invariably assess some aspect of their understanding.

Effective questioning warrants coverage of its own and is explored in Chapter 5. Transparent and accessible explanations can only be achieved if you fully understand the subject matter you are teaching (your own personal auditing of subject knowledge comes into perspective when you reflect upon the transparency and accessibility of your own explanations). The use of modelling has been much debated and explored and examples of this are peppered throughout the strategy and can be extremely effective means of presenting often difficult and abstract ideas. Modelling, like any analogy, does have its limitations and these need to be identified and appreciated when using models (see Chapter 13 and the milk bottle analogy, p. 102).

All teaching and learning strategies need to take into account the preferred learning styles adopted by the pupils. Broadly speaking we express preferences towards auditory, visible and/or kinaesthetic modes of learning. As a teacher you will need to ensure that all styles of learning are catered for (see Chapter 6).

Classroom organisation

The strategy recognises the unique dynamics of a classroom environment. The implications of this are dealt with elsewhere (see Chapter 20), together with the need as a teacher to take these factors into consideration when planning your lesson.

Climate for learning

Closely related to classroom organisation, but equally influenced by all the pedagogic aspects identified above, creating the right climate for learning is your ultimate aim. The strategy reiterates the importance of pupils' preferred learning styles, and an appreciation and recognition of prior knowledge and attainment. It supports a constructivist approach (see Chapter 6) to teaching and learning, as well as the neurological understanding of learning theory.

Key Stage 3 strategy and you

The strategy offers you, as a science teacher, an insight into the wealth of training material developed against the backdrop of research and other information sources. Essentially, the material supports good practice in terms of teaching for learning, learning theory, effective lesson design, the significance of ILOs, active learning and the big ideas in science. It develops further the diagnostic use of assessment, encouraging evidence-based records linked directly to the ILOs, and promotes the use of target setting. These collectively inform future planning, inclusion and differentiation: all the key features of effective teaching. By familiarising yourself with the strategy material, attending cascade sessions when possible, discussing key approaches and ideas with teachers and trying them out for yourself, you will gain from the experience and good practice disseminated, thereby enhancing your own teaching and professional development.

Let us take a look at two different examples of lesson structure. The first is a practical investigation into current and heat.

- Set out the task on the board showing the relationship between current and the brightness of bulbs in a circuit. Have an example circuit set up and a simple table on the board with the headings 'current' and 'brightness'.

- The practical begins using two and three bulbs in a series circuit and testing the effect of increased current on the brightness of each bulb. For higher level learning, start in series and then challenge the pupils to investigate parallel circuits. There will be a number of groups who will have trouble setting up the circuit from the schematic. A quick trip around the room should identify these difficulties and sort them out. After 12 minutes or so, stop the lesson and choose one or two groups to share their results.

- Plenary session. This must be done with the equipment still out. You can turn off the electricity at the mains to get their attention. Conclusions are shared and written down and then the tidy up begins. Do it the other way around and the tidying up will take the remainder of the lesson.

The second is an elicitation session on electricity.

- Provide a worksheet set out as a mini-quiz. The aim is to find out what the pupils know. Get them to write their names on the paper.

- Ask them to answer the questions, giving them eight minutes to do this, by themselves. Get them into groups and provide a sheet with two possible sets of answers for each question. Give another seven minutes, as a group, to revisit the questions.

- Have a 'let's get the best answer' session and then collect in the papers.

The first session is a variation on the three-part lesson 'sandwich' with a major plenary before the end. The second is a standard 'sandwich' with a very 'thick part' as the plenary.

Summary

Perhaps the three most important things to emerge from the KS 3 strategy are to focus on the five key ideas, the need for effective lesson design and the need to ensure that you as a teacher are well prepared for the lessons you are going to teach. This includes not only knowledge and understanding of the subject area but a myriad of other things as well. In this chapter we have touched on many of them: the need for clearly defined learning outcomes; careful and productive transition from one stage to the next; establishing an environment conducive to learning...so many things to consider when planning, but all of them expressions of good practice.

PART

IV

Planning, Assessment, Teaching and Classroom Management

Introduction

This part addresses the requirements set out in *Qualifying to Teach* sections 3.1, 3.2 and 3.3. In Chapter 16 we discuss the different approaches to planning in both the medium and short term and the effective use of tracking. Being well prepared for the class does not guarantee success but failure to plan usually ends in disaster.

In Chapters 17 and 18 we show that however important assessment is, it does not need to take over your life. The discussion includes the use of elicitation exercises and a discussion of the differences between formative and summative assessments. The chapters cover: how to respond to the pupils' work and why we mark; different tasks and the marking load; in-class marking; and self-assessment and learning. Chapter 19 looks at the assessment of investigations.

In Chapters 20 and 21 we look at classroom management. There is no magic formula that guarantees success when applied, but there are approaches that nearly always fail (like confrontation). It is important to note that certain strategies only work when the relationship between the pupils and the teacher has matured to a level where the group will accept something new. So if something does not work in the early days, do not abandon it for ever: bring it out and dust it off later in the school year. You will find some useful tips on 'what to do in the event of' situations. In Chapter 22 we discuss the practicalities of resourcing and teaching in a science lab with a close eye on our health and safety responsibilities. Chapter 23 has a focus on the older student, but we advise you to retain your strategies that worked well with the younger pupils.

16

Planning, progression and tracking

This short chapter addresses different ways of looking at medium-term and short-term planning to enable you to track a pupil's progress and set targets with a view to progression. This covers the QTS requirements of section 3.1 of *Qualifying to Teach* (DfES 2002).

Tracking

There are a number of possible ways to plan a set of lessons and ensure progression. More problematic is to incorporate the *tracking*. This is where you record the results of elicitation tests and summative tests and compare them to each other and to the students' predicted levels of attainment. If tracking is seen as an extra chore on top of the day-to-day marking then the tasks can become meaningless and irrelevant. If it is taken on board as a key element in the elicitation, formative assessment and summative assessment cycle then not only is it relevant, but it becomes a useful tool to help you to set learning objectives within the topic or set of lessons.

Tracking is really no more than marking and assessing with a purpose. We need to be able to identify what the students have covered and at what key stage level they have covered it. In a school that 'sets' students, this can be easier than in mixed ability sets. The key thing is to keep it simple and involve the students in the process. Some schemes of work have student self-assessment forms, like the Heinemann scheme for Key Stage 3.

Let us look at two different approaches.

Approach 1

- Read the scheme of work.
- Complete each task in the order presented.
- Plan each lesson with an appropriate activity to achieve the outcomes required.
- Set a mini-quiz or test.
- Record the class test results.
- Compare results from test to test.

Approach 2

- Photocopy the pages from the syllabus followed by the school and National Curriculum requirements for the topics being covered.

■ Cut out specific tasks from the syllabus and learning objectives from both.

■ Arrange these pieces of paper into a sequence of tasks that you feel comfortable to follow.

■ Create a task grid in *Excel* (see Figure 16.1).

■ Plan the sequence of lessons and identify appropriate activities to achieve the outcomes required starting with an elicitation session.

■ Share the grid with the group.

■ At the end of the sequence mark the tasks against the grid.

Name	Elicitation (a) The nature of friction Start level	Practical (b) for problem solving and consolidation	Practical (c) to investigate practical aspects of friction	Lesson (d) Project to extend understanding	Overall level at the end of topic	Progression Column 6 – column 2
	Level 3, 4, 5, 6 or 7	Level 3, 4, 5, 6 or 7	Level 3, 4, 5, 6 or 7	Level 3, 4, 5, 6 or 7	Level 3, 4, 5, 6 or 7	
Alice	6	6	7	Excellent	7	+1
Brian	5	5	6	Excellent	6	+1
Charlotte	4	5	3	Not done	4	=
David	3	3	3	Not done	3	=

FIGURE 16.1 Setting up a grid for tracking progress.

Approach 1 is an entirely satisfactory approach as long as the lessons are 'good'. It does mean that your medium-term plan has been done for you as you are following a pre-planned route through the topic. The three disadvantages are:

■ you are trying to follow someone else's progression of ideas and links through a topic from their start point;

■ there is a danger that you will have to adjust the level and content of the lessons part way through the topic;

■ you may get too involved in the process of getting through the topic and only discover at the end that little progress has been made by the pupils.

Approach 2 has more work at the start of the topic but has three major advantages.

■ because you already have your tracking grid set up it is easy to see whether progress is being made;

■ because you have planned your elicitation, you are more likely to identify a better starting point for the group in front of you;

- because you are constantly in dialogue with the group regarding progress, there is a more natural flow as you respond to the needs of the group and adjust your future lessons accordingly.

Figure 16.1 shows how such a task grid for tracking might look.

Progression

As long as you have started from a sensible point that the pupils can relate to, and the *shared* aims are met, then the pupils will make progress. If they have been *engaged* in the learning then new knowledge is more likely to stick and they will also be able to apply this knowledge more effectively. When the pupils have learnt new ideas or have a better understanding of the topic and can move up the rough guide to attainment, as in Table 16.1, we can say they have *progressed*. Checking previous attainment and elicitation at the start of the topic are key to finding the sensible point to start from and to identify, later, if progression has really taken place.

Record keeping

Every school has data available electronically for you to download. This is more suitable for electronic mark books than for transferring into traditional hard copy mark books. Many teachers today have only electronic mark books, or they keep the attendance register in hard copy and the 'marking and assessment' information electronically. This is advisable as it makes statistical analysis and transfer of information so much easier.

In your mark book you need to keep a list of tasks and the individual outcomes. When you are marking, you should use the 'rough guide to attainment levels' (see Table 16.1) to build up a picture of each pupil's attainment and their progress. 'Good work' comments or '8/10' are less useful.

TABLE 16.1 Rough guide to attainment at Key Stage 3: a simple set of indicators providing a guide to attainment, without the need for formal testing

Level 3	Has difficulty in completing simple tasks. Needs support to follow instructions. Has limited understanding of the topic.
Level 4	Can follow simple instructions. Has a basic understanding of some of the principles being discussed.
Level 5	Can work independently and has a sound understanding of the topic. Can accept new ideas and explain how they relate to the topic in question.
Level 6	Pupils at this level have a good knowledge of a lot of the topic and are able to investigate independently. They can apply new ideas to different situations and are able to work on open-ended tasks.
Level 7/8	These pupils have an in-depth knowledge of the topic. They need to be given tasks that allow them to gather detailed information to analyse, problems to solve and information on where this new found knowledge can be applied. They can transfer skills across subject areas, are open to 'new' ideas and can suggest ideas of their own.

From medium-term to lesson planning

Now that you have your lessons in your own preferred sequence, the next task is to decide on what style would suit the main focus of the lesson. To do this you need to identify clearly what the aims of each lesson are and the desired learning outcomes for the class and for each of the sessions. Differential targets are good, and 'all *must*', 'some *should*' and 'a few *could*' statements can help. Box 16.1 gives an illustration from a lesson sequence on friction.

Start with an elicitation exercise. Find out what they know and are interested in and you may be able to 'create' a task together for future lessons. Involve any adult in-class support you may have: they have usually had experiences of successful lessons they have seen before and they may also be able to give you a good indication of the level of ability of each pupil.

While activities are in progress you have the opportunity to talk to each group, confirm their level of ability and help them to move on in their understanding, i.e. *reformulation*.

Finally, the plenary session can be driven by you from the front: for example, by getting each group to share their findings in turn. Remember that a plenary session does not have to be at the very end of the lesson. As you monitor the pupils' work from lesson to lesson you can complete your mark book/tracking grid very easily. You have pre-planned the learning outcomes and will be able to assess the progress made by the pupils. Retain high expectations for each group, but don't make them unreasonable lest you fail to get any progression, because the tasks and concepts are too demanding.

A lesson sequence on friction

The main aim is to get the pupils to recognise friction in different situations (from brakes to air resistance), and how to either increase or decrease the effect it has: they should be challenged to discuss 'good' friction (Would we like to be walking on ice all the time? How would our clothes stay together?) and 'bad' friction (How do we reduce air resistance?).

Elicitation: Give examples of good and bad friction, imagine a world without friction.
Intervention: Interactive plenary to set the scene for development.

Here are two examples of practical tasks that will help pupils get to grips with friction (sorry!)

1 Use a bench pulley and mass carriers to investigate the friction between the bench and different materials.
2 Use string, plasticine and card, to measure the effect of surface area and wind resistance on a pendulum.

Reformulation: Working from the book to gather information using a DART. Revisiting the exercise 'a world without friction'.

Using ideas: Project – describe a bicycle, parachute, a pair of shoes etc. in terms of friction.

Set up your tracking grid to monitor progress and ensure:

All *must* understand the nature of friction and that it is a part of everyday life.
All *should* be able to identify a number of examples of friction. They *should* also be able to identify methods of reducing friction.
A few *could* identify a range of circumstances where frictional forces are either too high or too low and the consequences.

BOX 16.1 Linking planning with tracking

Summary

By unpicking the schemes of work and creating a tracking grid at the start, you create a better personal understanding of the flow of concepts and skills. The number of tasks can then be identified and adjusted to fit into the time allowed. Once the elicitation identifies the starting point for the group, a sensible progression target can be set. By the end of the topic you will easily be able to tell how much progress each pupil has made.

17

Formative assessment: responding to the pupils' work

There are many reasons why we need to mark and keep up with marking. Some are management issues, some are good practice issues and others are motivation issues. In this chapter we identify differences between formative and summative assessment and then examine ways to find out what sense the pupils are making of our teaching and their learning as they progress through topics. While agreeing that we need to give feedback to pupils, for a number of reasons, we also consider ways to reduce the marking load.

Professional requirements for marking

As a professional you are expected to have a marking routine, as you need to give encouragement to your pupils, compare your groups with others at a glance and be able to provide snapshots of progress. This is particularly relevant when you are discussing progress with parents at a parents' evening or with colleagues.

The statutory marking requirements that teachers are expected to carry out are:

1   SATs at KS 2.

2   KS 3 teacher assessment of National Curriculum levels.

3   Coursework marking at GCSE.

4   Coursework marking at A-level.

These are all *summative* assessments, and they are discussed further in Chapter 18. We may argue that the results can be used to inform our opinion of pupils' levels of achievement. It may not be a true indicator of their level of understanding, or their real potential.

A new pressure introduced in 2000 is the Threshold Award Scheme, part of a wider appraisal system now in place in all schools. In order to go through the *threshold* you have to provide evidence of the marking and assessing of your pupils and their work, and show that you can compare their attainment to a national figure at the appropriate Key Stage. The rules require a positive set of statements pointing to how each pupil can improve, in the form of SMART targets (Specific, Measurable, Attainable and Realistic within a Time frame).

Why do we mark?

When we mark we need to keep in the forefront of our minds the reasons why we are marking the work. What is it that we want our marking to achieve? We suggest that in *formative* assessment, discussed in this chapter, the aim of the marking is to elicit a response from the pupil that results in a change of thinking and working.

Formative assessment and summative assessment: the differences

Formative assessment allows us to challenge the pupils' understanding as they learn, and to check the breadth and depth of their subject knowledge. This is done at the beginning of a topic or as a progress check. It is imperative that we clear up misconceptions as we launch into the topic. If we do not then pupils will fail to accept new ideas or block them because they are not relevant, or they do not fit with their existing model. Box 17.1 gives a simple case in point.

In summative assessment we are normally drawing a line under a topic and publishing the results. It is the end-of-topic assessment, and is the subject of the next chapter.

The girl asked:	Why do we spend so much time on photosynthesis?
Answer:	Because it is the way plants grow and they are important to us.
The girl:	How are they important?
Answer:	We eat them.
The girl:	Don't be silly, we don't eat plants!
Answer:	Yes we do, we eat carrots, potatoes, peas and tomatoes and things.
The girl:	They are not plants. They are vegetables!

BOX 17.1 The importance of formative asessment to inform your teaching

How to mark: styles of formative assessment

This section refers to different marking strategies and their appropriate use. There is little point in spending a long time responding to pupils' work if they do not read what you say and take no action on the comments. Not all the work produced needs to have a detailed response. You may only need to record the fact that the work has been completed on time. You should save your marking effort for the types of homework in which there is a high possibility of misunderstanding surfacing. This is most likely to be in creative writing activities.

It has been noted that where only a mark is given pupils do not search the text for comments about where they went wrong. Positive comments and suggestions for improvement at the end of the piece are far more valuable to both the pupil and the teacher. Over a period of time the comments will string together and give a good indication of the progress, or otherwise, of the pupil. We can reduce the load on ourselves by adopting the annotated script method. Figure 10.1 (p. 75) contains an account of the adventures of a blood cell. It does show a lack of understanding by this able KS 3 pupil, but it may be poetic licence. We need a quick and unobtrusive way to point out the errors and a way to make the pupils realise their own misconceptions and correct them themselves. This is where the star or annotated system works well. Pupils know that if they get 'sp' they must look up the word and write it correctly. Stars, merits or house points can be awarded to those pupils who complete their corrections no matter what level the work was at, to start with.

In-class marking

This can be effective and useful when used sparingly. There is a significant amount to cover in any syllabus and there is not sufficient time to carry out substantial amounts of marking during lesson time. It is useful to check that specific notes or drawings required have been completed before progressing further. It is a good idea to get pupils to open their books for you so that you can make a cursory check that the work set has been completed before embarking on the next task. This is a quick and easy method of picking up those who have not completed the tasks on time.

In all instances, however, there is far more satisfaction for the student and peace of mind for the teacher if a marking routine is set and adhered to. There is nothing worse than allowing a huge wave of marking to build up, because it invariably clashes with a pre-booked outing or event and the marking may be compromised. It is better to allocate time to do the job properly and complete it in a positive frame of mind rather than complete it under time pressure. In the last resort, either take in the books to enable you to note whether the work has been done, with a promise for detailed marking, or mark the last piece of work in detail, again with the promise of detailed marking in the future.

Differentiated tasks and the marking load

In the past, teachers might have dictated notes or asked pupils to copy from the blackboard. Such activities needed only cursory marking for completeness and neatness. They cannot be used to judge a pupil's ability. To replace this activity we suggest that you provide the notes in a scrambled form so that the pupils need to decipher the messages. This is referred to in Chapter 9. To do this they will have to read and digest the phrases and think through the problem to rearrange the statements. You cannot uncover misconceptions or discover learning from notes copied from the board.

Creative writing

Of all the tasks, this is probably one of the best ways to assess whether the concepts have been accepted and embedded correctly. It does, however, demand more time than any other marking task. See the annotated script method in Figure 10.1 (p. 75).

Project work

Again this is a good activity to set as homework on a completed topic, particularly over a weekend or half term or over a number of lessons in class. There are problems with this, however, as different pupils spend different amounts of time on project work and some get more 'help' at home than others do.

It is always more valuable to monitor the research carried out by pupils and oversee the creation of the first draft document rather than waiting until the final 'writing up' has been completed. When marking in this way the teacher has a good overall picture of all the abilities, strengths and weaknesses of the pupil and thus the overall mark will more accurately reflect both the commitment and the ability of the pupil.

Some pupils put in great chunks of material that they have not digested or considered. These types of projects need to be given less credit than those where pupils have used the information gathered to construct their own report.

An example of 'good practice' in marking a project on vertebrates is: 'A well presented piece of work that covers nearly all the key areas. Next time, could you include the key to show how you differentiate between the five major groups and use a ruler when drawing topic boxes? Two merits.' Some teachers suggest that red ink is not the best colour to use and that in some groups personal touches such as 'smiley' faces are preferable to official merit marks.

Classwork

As indicated earlier, children learn at different rates and in different ways. The most valuable assessment technique is to be involved with the groups as they are working. A huge amount of learning goes on while the group is actively involved in good classwork tasks. It may be difficult to assess individual pupils against levels of attainment during these tasks but it is here that the teacher can get a good feel for the general level of understanding. Shorthand notes made during the lesson in the mark book can help to keep a log of pupils' attitudes and attainment: for example, 'A', provided a good answer; 'Ch', chatters; 'N', neat work. It goes without saying that classwork is also where most of the teaching and learning take place and is an important part of developing relationships between pupil and teacher. This is where the good teacher takes pleasure from a task well done or responds to a 'crisis' in order to rescue the learning.

Self-assessment and learning

Pupils can learn a lot from marking their own or each other's work. We find that where they are involved in the marking, they will argue and discuss every point so that they can get the best mark for themselves, or not make a mistake when marking someone else's script. It is time consuming and often frustratingly slow to do this, but a well managed session will produce dividends in the long term and save you time in the short term.

Marking informs you, the learners and other staff

Marking pupils' work is your way of getting to know what they can do and how much they have understood. But you have a choice of marking strategies to use through the year. There are times when you need a breather, and picking the right strategy can be a life-saver. In a week with lots of evening activities use class marking and self-marking, or set mini-tests. Do not set 'projects' for all your groups over half term: they will take weeks to mark, and the pupils will all want them back quickly with lots of merits.

Motivating pupils and setting individual tasks

We wish to motivate our pupils positively. With continuous, good quality formative assessments, we can improve pupils' attitudes to learning, self-assessment and the learning outcome. Marking work is vital to both teacher and pupil. There is no doubt that despite the time required to mark, it can be rewarding for the teacher to see that the pupils have absorbed and accepted new ideas successfully. There are a number of ways to enhance the reward for the pupils over and above the SMART target. Smiley faces work well. You need to find others. Gold stars work for some groups even if they are not keen on the official merits. The reward system is a valuable tool to use to build a good relationship between pupil and teacher.

You will put in a lot of time marking pupils' work, and giving them feedback. You want to ensure that they read and act upon what is essentially your personal tuition to them. So always give *action points* for the pupils to follow up, and only give merits when they have *responded* to your comments: add an equation, label the diagram, add a sentence about x, correct spellings etc.

Informing teachers

Formative assessment helps us in several ways.

■ It identifies where the misconceptions in individuals or groups of individuals are. This is the 'critical moment' when you can decide how to proceed with your next set of lessons.

■ It helps us in planning. This may be regarding the style and pace of the lessons to come, or even the order in which we need to place the lessons to ensure the desirable learning outcome.

■ It establishes on a regular basis where the pupils are in their learning. It is easy to misjudge a group and dive in too deep. The pupils will not stop you unless you are sensitive to their glazed looks or indifference if the topic was not at the right level. Chin (2003) provides a useful comparison between deep thinking and surface learning. Formative assessment needs to recognise and reward deep thinking.

Summary

Marking pupils' work is mainly a formative and evaluative process. It helps them to develop their understanding of science and it helps you to evaluate the effectiveness of your teaching. It also lets them know that you are on to them and you will not accept poor quality work. Letting them off could send the message that you do not care, or that the work is not important.

■ Choose an appropriate marking style for the task you have set.

■ Keep up to date on a two-week cycle with all pupils. They like to see that their work is marked and appreciated.

■ Give praise as you are scanning their work.

■ Remember that the aim of formative assessment is to improve pupils' learning.

■ Set time slots for marking and stick to them. Do not let it take over your life.

■ Give tasks to complete to ensure that your comments are read, and reward those who respond and do their corrections.

The next chapter deals with summative assessment and its association with national assessment procedures.

18

Summative assessment

In this chapter we address issues related to summative assessment and, as in Chapter 17, address some basic questions concerning the reasons for marking. We suggest how you can manage the marking load more efficiently and help to reduce it. The Threshold Pay Award scheme currently affects those teachers who are about to go on to point 6 on the pay spine, and there are specific targets to be met in order to go through the threshold.

Introduction

Bearing in mind the strategies for marking in Chapter 17, we can use these again when we are marking terminal tests. As we enter into the summative marking mode for these tests we need to address the same question posed in Chapter 17: 'Whom are we marking for?' Is it for the school, the parents or the public at large? Are we marking to track the pupils' performance to assess our own ability as teachers? In this chapter we concentrate on tracking the pupils' academic progress.

We have to remember that even in these days, when the number of examination boards is diminishing, the number of courses available is mushrooming and their entry requirements vary widely. Once again we ask the question: 'Why do we assess?' We have already suggested that these are some of the reasons:

■ to check progress, to enable us to report to parents and outside bodies;

■ to establish starting points for future work;

■ to help the learning (formative);

■ to help the teaching (evaluative);

■ to inspire improvement.

Formative assessment is discussed in Chapter 17, and covers three of the five points mentioned. Summative assessment is mainly about drawing a line under a topic or a level so that we can move on to the next topic.

Assessment and pupil learning

As teachers, we have to question what we do and why we do it, even though we are aware that we may have no choice in the matter. In this way we improve our effectiveness. We are assuming that we have already carried out our formative assessments and we are now producing final or summative assessments. We assess for the following people:

- For the pupils, so that we can help motivate them to continue learning.

- For ourselves, so that we can assess the quality of our teaching and their learning, and check for misconceptions overlooked, to inform our planning.

- For parents: we collect evidence to write reports.

- For outside bodies for moderation: if we were to mark pupils' work in another school, would we give the same marks as their teachers?

- For outsiders: we provide evidence to future employers.

National summative assessment

This section covers the type and scope of national assessments currently in use in state schools.

Roughly every half term you need to use end of topic tests or internal exams to assess the success of your teaching and the pupils' learning. No matter how motivated and able a group of individuals is in the class or with group or project work, there is still a need for assessment under exam conditions. Tests and exams should be designed to show off the strengths of the pupils, not highlight their weaknesses. The skill of the teacher is in choosing the right standard of entry and 'selling it' to the individuals.

A grade D at GCSE may not please the senior management team but it may be a big success for the pupil who needs it to progress further on the NVQ or GNVQ front. There is a wide range of external assessment tasks that schools can and must use. It is up to departments to identify the correct level of assessment for each pupil or set of pupils. Examples of the following tests are given here:

- YELLIS, Year 11 Information System.

- SATs, Standardised Attainment Tests.

- GCSE, General Certificate of Secondary Education.

- GNVQ/NVQ, (General) National Vocational Qualification.

YELLIS

This is a system that provides a broad band academic 'score' for individual pupils. Schools use the results in four main ways:

- to justify the setting of individual pupils;

- to predict the potential GCSE grades of individuals and cohorts;

- to identify the under-achievers;

- as statistical evidence of the 'value added' provided by the school.

SATs

At the end of KS 2 the average level of achievement for the majority of pupils is a level 4. 'Good' pupils will achieve a level 5 and only a few across the country will achieve a level 6.

At the end of KS 3 the majority are expected to achieve a level 5 or 6, with the 'good' pupils achieving a level 7. A small minority will achieve level 8.

Care is needed when analysing the data from these tests. In the first instance a child achieving a level 5 at KS 2 will not have the breadth of knowledge of a level 5 at KS 3. Secondly, the progress in levels across KS 3 is not as rapid as at KS 2. This reflects not only the non-linearity of children's learning, but also the extra breadth in the body of knowledge associated with the higher levels. In the following section on SATs and GCSEs, we have included examples of the different types of questions that are employed to test different types of learning. When comparing SAT levels of achievement and expectation at GCSE, the common assumption is that a level 8 at KS 3 is already equivalent to a GCSE grade C. We have to practise marking at this level so that we are in step with external assessments.

In the National Curriculum (DfEE 1999) there are specific guidelines to follow when assessing levels of attainment.

- AT 1, Scientific enquiry (p. 75).
- AT 2, Life processes and living things (p. 77).
- AT 3, Materials and their properties (p. 79).
- AT 4, Physical processes (p. 81).

SATs and GCSE questions

These national tests set out to check four basic criteria:

1   Can the candidate recall information?

2   Can the candidate understand this information; data handling?

3   Can the candidate manipulate this information; reasoning and interpretation?

4   Can the candidate apply the knowledge to everyday situations?

These tests use many formats or structures to achieve these aims. Multiple choice type questions are the quickest for pupils to answer (but difficult to set) and can be used to check for all four of these criteria, not just recall. The SAT question in Figure 18.1 illustrates these four criteria, all in one question. See if you can assign criterion number 1, 2, 3 or 4 to each part (a, b, c and d) of the question (see Box 18.1).

Terminal papers such as GCSE, as well as having these short-answer style questions, have more open-ended ones that test for scientific thinking. In particular, the Section B questions of GCSE papers are designed so that candidates can show an understanding of the subject and can apply it in unfamiliar circumstances. An example of this could be 'Discuss your understanding of the laws of circular motion' in a question related to a theme park ride.

GNVQ

The GNVQ is assessed continuously. Topics are presented to the pupils and they treat these as areas to investigate. The pieces of work are marked as they are produced and are assessed internally against key skill criteria. The internal assessors in the school are then moderated by external assessors and the marks awarded are verified. Pupils can achieve pass, merit and distinction grades.

A GNVQ pass with merit at intermediate level equates to two GCSE grade C passes. A GNVQ pass with distinction at higher level is equivalent to two A-level passes. Further comment on the 14–19 curriculum pattern is contained in Chapter 23.

The drawing shows what happens to most of the energy in the food that a hen eats in one day.

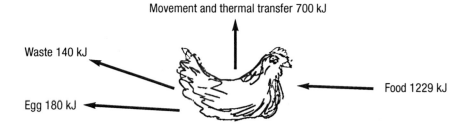

Movement and thermal transfer 700 kJ

Waste 140 kJ

Food 1229 kJ

Egg 180 kJ

(a) In the cells of the hen's body, energy is released from food by respiration. Complete the word equation for this process. (one mark)

Glucose + _____ ⟶ _____ + _____

(b) (i) Calculate the energy that remains in the body of the hen. (2 lines provided for one mark)
   (ii) What is this energy used for? (2 lines provided for one mark)
(c) Suggest how farmers might reduce the amount of energy that hens lose each day by thermal transfer. (2 lines provided for one mark)
(d) Farmers can reduce the amount of energy that is transferred by movement and thermal transfer from hens. Suggest **two** reasons why this is cost-effective. (4 lines provided for two marks)

FIGURE 18.1 Example of a SAT (from paper 1, 1998, tier 5–7, question 9). Note the common but unhelpful practice of saying that food and biomass 'contain' energy, which we deplored in Chapters 12 and 13.

In part (a) the candidate must recall information (1).
In part (b) the candidate must manipulate numbers (2).
In part (c) the candidate must show reasoning and interpretation (3).
In part (d) the candidate must apply their knowledge (4).

BOX 18.1 Suggested response to activity on p. 134 relating to Figure 18.1

Review

This has brought us full circle. We have identified that the constructivist approach helps to break the barriers between classroom science and real life. In this chapter we identify one of the main reasons for assessment as being to provide society with individuals who can interpret and apply the skills and knowledge gained in their years in school.

You should be aware of the responsibility you have both legally and morally to take marking as seriously as planning and executing the lessons. You should also be aware of the benefits of a well organised marking timetable for both you and your pupils. In conjunction with the ideas discussed in Chapter 17, you should be able to identify and use different types of assessment appropriately.

As a teacher you are responsible for mapping the terms and preparing your students for the challenge of assessment, in whatever form it is designed. The way in which you record the progress of the pupils in your charge and the level of their progress will be a major part of your interview when you apply to go through the threshold.

The testing debate will continue as long as there are pupils in the classroom. Our position is that good tests, either internal or external, help to support good learning outcomes, and we recommend that you use them.

Do not create too many of your own tests, because, as with all creative writing, it will take a number of drafts before it is 'right'. The majority of schemes of work have good tests available. Use them: they save time. A good CD that is widely available is *EXAMPRO*.

Summary

There is a wide variety of summative tests that are used at each Key Stage. These are there to provide information about levels of achievement to outside bodies. Setting test items is a very skilled job, whether you are testing for the recall of facts, understanding of scientific texts, manipulation of information or application of knowledge, so our advice is to recognise good test items and use them. Further details concerning the KS 3 strategy can be found at http://www.devon.gov.uk/dcs/ict/ks3/. In the next chapter we discuss in more detail the issues concerned with marking Science 1 assignments.

19

Assessment of scientific enquiry

This section explores all aspects of scientific enquiry (Sc1), which includes ideas and evidence as well as investigative skills. Investigations are essentially problem-solving exercises, carried out by pupils in groups or individually. They form only one aspect of science – supplying the evidence – and they need ideas to focus them. This chapter begins by looking at the 'ideas' strand of Sc1 and moves on to the investigations aspect, exploring assessment on the way.

Origins of scientific enquiry

The 1991 National Curriculum introduced an assessment procedure for Science Attainment Target 1 (Sc1). The 1991 SCAA Science Criteria for GCSE states that all syllabi should give pupils opportunities to 'Develop experimental and investigative abilities' and must require pupils to demonstrate their ability to:

> carry out experimental and investigative work in which they plan procedures, use precise and systematic ways of making measurements and observations, analyse and evaluate evidence, and relate this to scientific knowledge and understanding.

In order to standardise the assessment process, rigid criteria were applied to the marking procedure. Critics emphasised its prescriptive nature, which left little room for professional judgement but wasted time as teachers mulled over the level indicators. Changes were introduced to the GCSE syllabus in 1995, to be assessed for the first time in 1998. These were applied across the examining bodies and a common assessment pattern was adopted in schools. The result was a more flexible assessment procedure, less prescriptive than its predecessor, with an emphasis on the teacher's professional judgement. Rather than being concerned specifically with the process skills of investigations, it recognised the outcomes of an activity by giving credit to pupils who critically analyse their results. It also gave more opportunity for pupil initiative in practical work.

National Curriculum 2000

The National Curriculum was revised in 2000, with the requirements for KS 4 operational in 2001.

QCA (DfEE 1999) explained that 'At all key stages, the revised programmes of study place greater emphasis on the development of a wider range of enquiry skills, and on contemporary science and the applications of science.'

Scientific enquiry

Attainment Target 1 consists of two subsections, one encompassing the nature of science and its ideas and the other covering the investigative side of science and the testing of ideas. Both are to be taught through contexts taken from the three other programmes of study, and they account for 25 per cent of the assessment at KS 4.

Ideas and evidence in science

This focuses on how scientists work, how their ideas are presented, evaluated and disseminated, and how controversies can arise as a result of data interpretation. Great emphasis is placed on enquiry skills, contemporary science and the application of science. Finally, it emphasises the value-laden nature of science and its power and limitations in addressing everyday issues, which we brought out in Chapter 1, and return to in our final chapter. Ideas and evidence are examined during the written examination and opportunities for inclusion within the other three attainment targets are clearly identified in the different examination boards' syllabi. Different icons are used for each board: OCR, for example, uses a bell.

The KS 3 strategy emphasises the interplay between ideas and evidence, whereby ideas are formulated in the theoretical world, forming initially theories and then hypotheses. These are tested in the empirical world, so that predictions developed from the hypothesis give way to empirical evidence. This in turn informs the theory and helps to mould the hypothesis. This interplay is not always complete or as simplistic as explained here. Our description in Chapter 1 is far more realistic.

There exists a wealth of tales from the science archives that can be drawn upon to illustrate the nature of science and its unique peculiarities (Williams 2002). Contemporary science has a great deal to offer as well: think about the development of our understanding of modern-day genetics and the controversy that surrounds that. To promote and understand this interplay between the theoretical and empirical worlds the KS 3 strategy suggests some interesting activities (see Box 19.1).

Stimulating pupils' ideas – thinking about more evidence

- *Lemonade fizz.* Sometimes people can be seen adding a spoonful of sugar to lemonade or cola to make it fizz more. Why do you think this happens? Is it only sugar that has this effect? What would you do to find out?
- *Pineapple jelly.* Jelly made with tinned pineapple sets, whereas that made with fresh pineapple doesn't. The tinned pineapple is superheated in the production process; do you think this might affect its performance in the setting process? What do you think might be going on here?

(For those people who need an answer, see Box 19.2, p. 142.)

BOX 19.1 Ideas and evidence

Investigative skills

This subsection covers the process skills of scientific enquiry: planning, obtaining and presenting evidence (with an emphasis here on the use of ICT), considering evidence and analysing data in terms of earlier predictions, evaluating the process and data obtained and suggesting improvements.

At the end of each Key Stage, a section entitled 'Breadth of Study' emphasises the need to relate science to everyday life, to explore everyday occurrences through whole or partial investigations, to communicate findings and interpretations effectively and to consider all aspects of health and safety when conducting such investigations. The work of Goldsworthy and Feasey (1999), which helps to make the planning and conduct of investigations clearer, was mentioned in Chapter 1 (p. 5). What we need to discuss here is how these investigations, which form such a central part of science, can be assessed in school.

At present 25 per cent of a student's marks at GCSE are from the teacher-assessed investigations by course work. This reflects the equal weighting that each of the four Attainment Targets carries. The other 75 per cent of marks at GCSE are derived from the examination, which focuses on the concept Attainment Targets 2–4.

How does the Science 1 assessment procedure work?

Science 1 assessment is teacher-marked and carried out in school, and is intended to encourage open-ended investigation, putting emphasis on planning and providing the students with a clear understanding of the procedure for carrying out an investigation. The assessment focuses on 'general performance descriptors', with marks being awarded in hierarchical fashion against performance indicators. The performance descriptors are in four skill areas:

- skill area P, planning experimental procedures;
- skill area O, obtaining evidence;
- skill area A, analysing evidence and drawing conclusions;
- skill area E, evaluating evidence.

For teachers to exercise their professional judgement effectively, it is important to identify connections between the objectives of investigative work (taken from the Programmes of Study in the National Curriculum) and the assessment criteria (the performance descriptors in GCSE syllabi). As we saw in Chapter 1, scientific investigations are needed to test ideas and models. Ideally they will be ideas the students have developed or established in response to an observation or question, or ideas the teacher has suggested to the students as a possible explanation of what they have seen. Students should therefore have expectations and they will be able to make predictions, which need to be identified. These predictions are used to evaluate the investigation.

How do schools use and assess investigations?

There is clearly a range of practice followed by different schools due to circumstances and the freedom given by examination boards. The data that follow relate to a selection of Gloucestershire secondary schools.

Help and guidance varied considerably from school to school. Most schools spent time at KS 3 developing investigation techniques before these were perfected at KS 4. Many schools introduced investigation booklets containing detailed sections on the various skill areas, prompting the pupils and guiding them in the required direction. Different skill areas can be assessed at different times. In all schools, basic data sheets and the examination board's guidelines were available to the pupils.

A total of between eight and ten investigations over the two years at KS 4 was typical. Some schools operate a preparatory period during Year 10, where the marks from investigations do not contribute to GCSE (perhaps because the students get too much support, or work in groups) and the full-blown investigations take place in Year 11. Others have a range of partial investigations throughout the two-year period, focusing on specific skill areas. To obtain an overall score for the individual student, scores are aggregated and the best ones for each skill area are used. Each pupil presents a minimum of two or three samples of work as evidence.

The skills of 'planning' and 'observation' tended to be assessed with pupils working in groups. The skills of 'analysis' and 'evaluation' were assessed for individual pupils. Many schools encourage group work during investigations, a factor important to any scientific activity as a means of encouraging teamwork and discussion. It is the pupils' best performance in skill areas and not the best group investigation that counts. The teacher has to ensure that individual work is identified within the group effort, a task that is not always easy. Concentrating on one skill area rather than all four during the same investigation often eases the burden.

A partial investigation

Students are given the following information (with a set of results): 'This particular piece of work forms part of the GCSE coursework and assesses skill areas A (analysis) and E (evaluation).' Students are given an outline method (involving equal sized pieces of potato and a range of molar concentrations of brine solution) and a table of results. Students are expected to include the following in their comments:

- Key concepts. Osmosis: what is it?

- Key ideas. Do different concentrations of brine solution affect water loss? Do potato cells work in the same way as onion cells (they are both food storage organs)?

- Prediction. What might the student who undertook the investigation expect to happen?

- Analysis. What did the results indicate? Was the prediction right? Could a graph be drawn and if so what could be concluded from it?

- Evaluation. Identify what was 'good practice' and what needed improving or altering to substantiate a conclusion.

- Conclusion. Could a conclusion be drawn and if so how reliable would it be?

If students are given the results, they all get a reliable and complete set of data and the teacher can focus on their ability to analyse and evaluate.

Marking procedure

Marking Science 1 investigations is detailed and complex, although specific guidelines are given. Within each skill area a maximum of eight marks can be awarded, with the exception of skill E, which has a maximum award of six marks. All marks are given on a scale of increasing student understanding, involvement and activity, with appropriate criteria identified at each level (2, 4, 6 and 8), referred to as *assessment identifiers*. All criteria relate directly to relevant sections in the National Curriculum. The final mark for the investigation is then obtained from the sum of the individual marks for each skill area.

Using teacher-produced grades for a National Assessment Examination weakens the reliability of the results. To overcome this all examining groups require stringent moderation of the assessment process, subject to external inspection. To this end, schools moderate internally and externally on an annual basis.

As with all summative assessment procedures there is a danger that the assessment tail will wag the dog. Students do the investigation in order to get the marks rather than for improving their scientific understanding. We must assess, for all the reasons we have discussed in the preceding chapters, but we need to ensure that the assessment tasks form a real and useful part of pupils' understanding and experience in science. The process of being scientific, which we introduced in Chapter 1, needs to be at the heart of students' investigations: the ideas that we have about the world need to be tested. Students need to be fully involved with expectation and prediction. Why are they doing this? What are they expecting? Did what actually happen agree or disagree with what they thought?

21st Century Science

This pilot GCSE was introduced in 2003 because of concerns about the inflexibility of the present system (see Chapter 27 (p. 208) for further details). In 'real science' the data you generate through experiment allow you to test your ideas and develop your theory. In 'school science' the data are less important: they have to confirm the theory. If the experiment 'goes wrong' then there must be something wrong with the data, not the theory! This 'tail wagging the dog' syndrome, together with the process being heavily assessment driven, has been one of the biggest criticisms of the system. Twenty-first-Century Science sets out to change that.

The GCSE adopts a three-tier system aimed at catering for all pupils:

- Core: basic scientific principles important for everyday life.
- General: these additional units are for students wishing to follow the formal academic route to A-levels.
- Applied: these vocational units offer a work-based approach to science (see also Chapter 23 for details about applied science at GCSE).

The assessment procedure has also attempted to adopt a more flexible approach, with an emphasis on the quality of the procedure. All pupils submit a literature-based case study accompanied by a portfolio of research evidence using standard scientific procedures for investigations. The investigation itself can be on any topic but must demonstrate the ability to design an experimental strategy, underpinned by background theory, capable of giving reliable and good quality evidence. The emphasis, however, is not to plough through the theory to support the investigation, which tends to limit the range and flexibility of investigations. It is to demonstrate how theory supports the investigative design, but not to inform the outcome. The assessment criteria consist of five strands, which include planning, observation and analysis and a separate strand for presentation. The days of partial investigations are numbered under this system, but some pupils may enter a 'part-score' only, depending upon the aspects of the investigation that they contributed to.

The pupil as scientist

Research scientists spend months or years developing ideas and methods and going up blind alleys. The results which actually achieve what they want often come over the course of a few frenzied days. There is little time in school for this blind alley, rather messy, pilot work. The more we leave pupils to devise and carry out their own investigations, the messier they get, so we resort to helping them by providing recipes of things that we know will work and get GCSE marks. Partial investigations are important, therefore, in allowing pupils to plan (without having actually to do their experiments) and then to analyse (with 'clean' data provided by the teacher).

Recognising the importance and significance of this, not just to science education but to science as a whole, several research councils have developed and funded the Pupil Research Initiative (PRI). This initiative aims to:

- raise pupil motivation and achievement in science;
- improve the teaching and learning of science, particularly investigative and ICT skills;
- increase the interaction between schools and the science and engineering research community.

To achieve these aims the PRI has developed curriculum activities and materials for use specifically in Sc1, which have been well received by teachers and pupils alike, and can be accessed through the websites of the research councils. We return to this theme in Chapter 26 (p. 199).

Summary

In this chapter we have seen how pupils can assume the role of being a scientist within the constraints of the school laboratory. Much of the process involved, however, is not practical. As we saw in Chapter 5 (Figure 5.1), there is a need for the pupil to predict what will happen and then test these ideas and expectations. It is this testing that forms the practical aspect, and even then, unless pupils are blindly following a recipe, thought and preparation form a fundamental part of this.

For any of the above to be successful the investigation needs purpose – something that the pupil can relate to and have empathy with. Investigations need to be seen as a part of the activity of the wider scientific community, not a way of getting marks at GCSE, however important that also has to be. 21st Century Science is a step towards that.

Ideas and evidence – some answers

- *Lemonade fizz.* This happens when any solid is added to a fizzy drink – the solid particles allow small stable bubbles to begin to form. The process is referred to as *nucleation* and is used in several processes, e.g. seeding clouds.
- *Pineapple jelly.* Superheating the pineapple denatures the enzyme pectinase, which breaks down pectin, a carbohydrate responsible for setting jellies and jams. The fresh, untreated pineapple contains pectinase so the jelly doesn't set.
- *One to try for yourself.* When a can of diet coke and one of ordinary coke are immersed in a tank of water, the diet coke floats, but the ordinary coke sinks. Why do you think this is?

BOX 19.2 A response to Box 19.1

Preparing for classroom management

There are few professions that have as much contact time with other human beings at a time when they are undergoing large physical, intellectual and emotional change as teaching. This can be a real roller coaster ride. The ideas in this chapter aim to help new teachers to prepare for this 'organised chaos'.

Introduction

This chapter is in five sections covering things we need to do to prepare for the task of managing pupils in the laboratory.

1 Getting to know the school systems.
2 Knowing your pupils.
3 Getting to know your subject.
4 Being organised.
5 Relationships with adults in the school.

Getting to know the school systems

We begin with an introduction to things you need to do before you set foot in your new classroom and, indeed, before you officially set foot in your new school. You need to gain as much information as you can about the school: for example,

■ the catchment area and location;
■ school routine (each school has its own daily structure).

Before you start full teaching

Trainee teachers will have plenty of opportunity to observe before they begin teaching. As a newly qualified teacher (NQT), or when starting a new post, you need to give yourself the same advantages that this classroom observation gives. You can watch parts of lessons on your pre-employment visits, and department members will invite you into parts of their lessons if you ask. The aim is to observe as many science teachers as you can.

Knowing the school and its systems is vital for your successful teaching. The lists that follow should help you to get ready. You need to:

- Find out the times during the week when you can: try out all practicals and demonstrations (Chapter 22); meet your head of department to discuss your lesson plans (see 'Getting to know your subject' below). It is important that you set these periods aside and treat them as part of your science timetable.

- Obtain a copy of the schemes of work, set lists, IEPs (individual educational programmes) and homework timetables.

In terms of pupil organisation, find out the prevalent school management style for:

- Entry and exit of pupils to and from the laboratory: how is it sanctioned; how is it kept orderly?

- Storage of coats and bags: is there a system?

- Layout of the lab: is it always the same?

- Organisational techniques for demonstrations, use of video or other resources: how do the pupils 'gather round' safely?

- Distribution of books and equipment: how is it done to avoid 'scrummages'?

- Reward and punishment systems.

In terms of safety procedures (Chapter 22), find out:

- the *safety* procedures for the science department and school;

- what system is used to communicate with the laboratory technician.

Day one

No matter how many times you have been told what cold water feels like, you will not be prepared for the physical and psychological effects of diving into freezing water. Remember that individual children can be perfectly rational and pleasant in normal circumstances, but do not be surprised to find that collectively these individuals can behave very differently.

As a tutor and teacher you are *in loco parentis*. It is in this area that using your own experiences can help you. The children must feel that you empathise with them when they are in trouble – it is your job to guide them through difficult times and help them to improve. There are times when you must be the disciplinarian, but this should not be your main role. Children will always be testing individual and collective rules; this is how they learn. Your job is to be firm and fair in setting out and enforcing these rules. Most important of all is to be consistent. If you are not you will only confuse them and cause problems for yourself. You need to create an atmosphere of trust and self-respect within the group.

Keeping the momentum going: personal and professional management

In school you have a number of rights.

- *Support*. You will receive support from the deputy in charge of staff development and NQTs. She or he will be able to provide advice, assist with strategies and arrange for you to observe other lessons. This is normally discussed and agreed in the summer term prior to you starting in the September.

- *Non-contact time*. NQTs are entitled to half a day per week (10 per cent of your timetable) that is free for further professional development.

- *A suitable base to work from*. This may be difficult with more and more pressure on laboratory provision, but as the new teacher you must check that your timetable provides as few changes in your teaching and tutor base as possible. It is not easy to manage, especially in your first year teaching in 11 different rooms.

- *Agreed schedule for lesson observations*. As an NQT you will be observed at least three times in the first two terms. With continuous professional development (CPD) and threshold payments, you can expect to be observed throughout your career. Do not treat this as a threat: look on it as an opportunity to receive help and advice from other good teachers and to show off how good you are.

- *Staff handbook*. This contains specific information on school policies, or where to look for them.

We have listed those rights we feel are absolutely necessary. You may have to negotiate others. You also have a number of responsibilities:

- *Professionalism*. It is important to remember that if you wish to be treated as a professional then you must act like one. Listen to and cooperate with other colleagues (you do not know it all yet).

- *Preparation*. Have well prepared lessons, suitable for the pupils, with relevant resources and support material.

- *Directed time*. Be punctual and reliable. You are expected to attend on every day the school is open: INSET days, parents' evenings and open days, with the odd extra duty thrown in for good measure. As mentioned previously, there are some activities where attendance is compulsory for the teachers. This is called directed time.

- *Smile*. Enjoy your own lesson and the time spent developing relationships with the pupils. Give 100 per cent during term time.

- *Keep a diary* of curriculum progress and events.

- *Be available* to cover lessons in other subject areas for absent teachers.

- *Keep up to date with marking*. Most schools have a marking policy. This is discussed fully in Chapter 17.

- *Meetings*. You must attend staff meetings, department meetings and house/year meetings. This is directed time. Keep your powder dry. You may have opinions about items on the agenda but wait your turn; others may have seen it all before and you may not have the whole picture.

Saying 'no'

In dealings with other colleagues, saying 'no' with a smile leaves a more acceptable image than saying no after a session of hair pulling, teeth gnashing and wailing. In your first year you will feel that to succeed you have to do everything that is asked of you. This is not true. There is an ongoing debate on the 'work–life' balance.

Knowing your pupils

It is difficult for you to teach if you don't know your pupils. Much can be done before you meet a class to get to know the group. The more quickly you get to know each pupil as an individual, the better will you be able to help them to learn at an appropriate level.

Getting to know your class before you start to teach

Before you teach the class you should try to take in pupils' notebooks from the previous year, to assess their standard of work and the progress they have made. Some schools have formal links with their feeder schools and you can view the pupils' previous work. Record the quality of their work in your *mark book*. Once you start teaching you will need to record any absences from the lessons, whether they have completed work set (e.g. homework) and to what standard, their test scores and other assessment results. All this will help you to build up a set of pupil profiles. Keeping an accurate and complete mark book is an art form – ask for advice.

Class lists are usually provided in the starter pack you will receive with your timetable. You will also have lists of pupils who are on the register of special educational needs (SEN) and information about the support available for them in the form of individual educational programmes (IEPs). You will be involved in drawing up IEPs for pupils, in conjunction with your head of department and SEN coordinator (see Chapter 25).

Tutor lists will enable you to learn the names of your tutor group quickly. It is expected that all teachers on main scale will take responsibility for a tutor group. There may be photographs of the children in the house head's or year head's office. Although this will be the first class you will get to know well, you need to plan your strategy for getting to know the pupils in all your classes as soon as possible.

One thing to remember: it is all too easy to dive in on day one and start 'teaching', but they need time to accept you as their teacher and they will not always share their knowledge immediately. You can gain their confidence by establishing the working rules in the first few lessons.

Getting to know your pupils as you teach

Pupils respect a teacher who calls them by name. Knowing your pupils is essential and you must put as much effort as possible into achieving it – preferably within the first six lessons. Set yourself a target of five new names each lesson until you can remember them all.

The following suggestions may help you to get to know all the children:

- A roll-call may help you to recognise pupils in the class at the beginning of your teaching (but it is time consuming and it is difficult to look at the pupils and at your register at the same time).
- Take notebooks in regularly, and hand them back yourself. Put the notebooks of the five pupils whose names you want to learn at the top and make a note of who they are. You will also know the quality of their written work.
- Have seating plans, or ask pupils to put name labels out at the start. Tell them that if they think you know their name they can put the label away.
- Write comments about pupils at the end of each lesson in your mark book.
- Study the class list in advance and make memory links. There may be three Janes in the class: make it your job to see who they are and distinguish between them.

- Always address a child by name. If you do not know them all, during the 'tell each other' phase of class question-and-answer sessions walk round looking at the covers of the children's notebooks and note the names of three pupils you will ask. Pupils are impressed when you address them by name: they want to be known and they respect a teacher who takes the trouble to get to know them. A pupil who knows that you do not know their name can get away more easily with disruptive behaviour.

It is easy to pick up the names of a few trouble-makers and a few other 'keen' pupils in a class. There is a double danger if you leave things here. The trouble-makers will always get the blame and become labelled (because you can't tell off someone else whose name you don't know) and the amorphous bunch 'in the middle' never get asked to respond to a question, feel left out and so become unmotivated.

They know more than you think. Once you can fit a name to each face, you can begin the process of getting to know them as individuals. Do they have problems in school or at home? What is their preferred learning style? They all come with ideas of their own, and we need to draw on this knowledge. Make sure you ask them about their primary school experiences if you are teaching Year 7 or 8, or their experience lower down the school in science or other linked subjects. Many will have travelled, or had family members with jobs with a scientific interest – experiences you need to draw upon. At the same time you need to look out for alternative ideas, taking care that the appropriate scientific vocabulary is used and encouraged.

Getting to know your subject (schemes of work and lesson plans)

A difficulty with operating in a 'science' atmosphere is that links with 'reality' become less easy to make. The focus at KS 3 and 4 is not on training future scientists, but on giving the next generation a way of looking at and understanding their environment. In this respect, the laboratory setting can be alienating, and pupils see 'science' as something that happens only in this room. If nothing else, lessons need to be seen to be relevant to the pupils. Your scheme and lesson plans for each class should be available for your head of department in good time for discussion, comment and approval.

Schemes of work

Under the law each department has to satisfy the requirements of the National Curriculum in substance and content as specified. Your department should already have a programme of study laid down, with relevant schemes of work available to cover all statutory requirements, stating the topics to be covered and giving an idea of pacing. You should use as many existing resources as you can until you have established yourself in the eyes of both pupils and teachers, but you must *unpick* them (see Chapter 16 for details) and put them together in your own way so that you are absolutely clear about your objectives. You need to take ownership of the lessons, just as you encourage your pupils to take ownership of the new ideas you are teaching. The more prescribed the scheme of work, the more care must be taken to identify lesson aims.

Unless you have an idea of the demands of the term as a whole it is easy to get swamped. Therefore you need a medium-term plan. You can use either your diary or a suitable logbook for this. A medium-term plan is usually for the half term and can be in a simple bullet point style. See Figure 20.1 for an example.

Week number	Aim	Topic	Activities	Homework
1	Concept	Gravity	Theory/numbers	Text questions
2	Practical skill	Gravity	Finding g 3 classic practical	Sc1 Write up
3	ICT	Circular motion	CD-ROM Red Shift	Essay on Kepler etc.
4	Models	Electric fields	Compare concepts with Gravity	Posters on field shapes. Text questions
5	Practical skill	Electric fields	Practical circus	Past paper questions
6	Section B skill	Atomic structure and radioactivity	Student presentations on concepts and models	Preparation for presentations

FIGURE 20.1 Medium-term plan.

Timing, strategies and style

Once you have decided on a sequence of lessons you will have aims for each of the lessons (with intended learning outcomes identified) and this will then help you to choose the approach required at each stage for these outcomes to be achieved.

Entering into teaching you will have already developed a style that seems to suit you at this stage. You will be encouraged to emulate a colleague whose style/approach you respect. Remember that, like a diet, teaching needs a balanced approach. Even though egg and chips may be your favourite meal it won't be long before you become sick of it. The successful teacher will use a variety of approaches to the subject. The style or approach depends on the point that needs to be emphasised or the skill to be practised. You need to build into your personal medium-term plan and lesson plans a variety of approaches to keep your subject fresh, relevant and interesting. (Lesson structure and techniques were explored in Part II.)

Keep lesson plans to a minimum and be prepared to adjust them at a moment's notice. Be warned, as mentioned before, that even apparently tried and trusted schemes of work need to be unpicked before each lesson to ensure that *you* can follow the continuity of concepts and the links between them. The pupils need to feel that *you* are driving the learning, not the book.

The level of subject matter must be suitable for that class. The outcomes must be achievable and measurable. The lesson must have relevance. Involve the students: use their ideas, their words and their work. The lesson must be structured. It is entirely possible to have an open activity that is structured only in terms of time, where the students are investigating in their own style but are given time targets. With the introduction of both literacy and numeracy strategies in the infant and junior schools, there is pressure on secondary schools to include this structure in the introductory phase of the lesson.

What makes a good lesson?

Good lessons will produce a feeling of well-being in the teacher and pupils, of time usefully and enjoyably spent. Good lessons:

- are planned, well structured and flow with confidence and purpose;
- have clearly identifiable messages, with shared aims and objectives;
- capture imagination by being interesting and related to everyday experiences;
- build on pupils' ideas and experiences, challenge misconceptions (elicitation);
- introduce new concepts and challenging ideas (intervention);
- cater for a range of learning styles (see Chapter 6);
- involve questions, discussions and problem-solving;
- provide mental activities pitched at a suitable level for the range of pupils present (reformulation), and contain physical activities involving as many senses as possible;
- include plenary sessions.

The three part sandwich proposed by the KS 3 strategy is a simpler version of this.

Follow-up

The lesson forms part of a larger story and to this end you must ensure that you illustrate to the pupils any continuity and progression in your next session. This can be done very briefly at the beginning of the next lesson: 'Do you remember how we explored the reaction of several metals with water last lesson? Well, we are going to take this one stage further today and see if they react with something stronger. Think of a reagent that is stronger, that metals might react with. Whisper it to your neighbour.'

Follow-up also applies to your own personal evaluation of the lesson and is absolutely essential for all concerned. The following all-important questions should be answered while the session is fresh in your mind:

- What went well?
- How could you improve certain aspects and how did your timing go?
- What have you learnt from the lesson?
- What would you do again? What would you do differently?

Tools of the trade and personal organisation

You will need: a diary, schemes of work, toolbox, back-up activities, differentiation, medium-term plan, lesson plans, rewards and punishments. These are the mental and physical items that will help you in your day-to-day battle to survive. Personal time management is vital. You need to remember what you need to do and where. For this you will need the school calendar, your diary and the schemes of work.

Keeping a diary is your lifeblood. This document is where you store *all* information regarding timetable, curriculum, meetings, attendance and assessments. Retrospective comments on the outcome of different lesson styles are a goldmine for inspiring improvements in lesson sequences for next time. Getting the format of your diary right can save hours of pain and extra work when it comes to assessments, end-of-term reports or finding out who returned the book with the interesting cartoons. Electronic diaries are good, as the transfer of information is so much quicker (see Chapter 17).

Remember that there are disruptions through the year. You need to be aware of those specific times when the demands on the pupils' extracurricular activities and the extra demands on your time need to be managed. In order to do this, you need to have the full school calendar in simple form to refer to (see Figure 20.2).

Calendar	Term	Topic	Date	Notes
	Autumn	Preparation	September 4/5	Lessons/class
		Day 1	September 6	Department
	Week 1	Staff meeting	September 6	
	Week 2			
	Week 3	Y7 reports	September 20	interim
		Y9 reports	November 12	Complete Nov 5
Christmas holidays			Dec 18 to Jan 6	
	Spring	Parents' eve	January 10	Y7
		Parents' eve	January 15	Y9
		Y8 Reports	February 5	Complete Jan 23
		Parents' eve	March 8	
Easter holidays				
	Summer			

FIGURE 20.2 Part of a typical school calendar.

A real toolbox may be needed if you are teaching in different classrooms or laboratories. Not all rooms are equipped with what you will want and a small box with chalk, whiteboard pens, spare paper, pencils, merit slips, punishment slips and marker pens can save time and embarrassment.

To ensure that you remember everything, including your differentiation (see Chapter 25), you need to draw up your own lesson plans, much as you did as a trainee teacher. You may keep these with the overheads, texts and worksheets that you are using and you will only need a brief summary in the diary.

Being organised

As the leader in your classroom you have to learn to get your own way. This requires interpersonal skills. For your own professional development you must have good personal organisation and for the benefit of the teaching and learning you must be able to feel the mood of the class. We focus here on things you can do before the lesson starts. The chapter that follows looks at real-time management once the lesson has started: making those instantaneous decisions that can make or break a lesson.

Preparing the classroom

As a teacher, you are performing. You need to know and understand the subject matter and how it applies to the broader arena of life. Here the teacher-as-actor analogy stops. In the classroom the 'audience' are expected to play an active role in the lesson and in their own learning. To achieve this you need to ensure that the sequence of the lesson is well planned: you know what the pupils will be doing and when; you have clearly identified learning outcomes and how they relate to the working curriculum.

Here are a number of things to think about. You need to have answers ready, so it is all about good preparation.

- *Get there early*. It is your territory, into which they are invited. Organise the room as you want it for each lesson; it may take time but it is worth it. It strengthens your position as the teacher. Do not always let them sit where they wish, even after you have control of the group.

- *Board work*. Clean the board between each topic. Write legibly and check that it can be seen from the back of the class. Use OHTs where you can, with standard diagrams. Prepare your digital projector or interactive whiteboard.

- *Voice projection*. When you speak do so clearly, audibly and naturally, to the whole class; above all try to smile, and look and feel confident, even if you're not. Be aware of all the pupils, especially the disruptive element in the far corner. Do not expect to speak for longer than a few minutes without involving the pupils in some interaction: a quick 'tell each other what you have heard' reinforces the learning. The class should listen to other pupils' contributions too. The voice is a powerful weapon. It is not always what you say but how you say it. If you start off by shouting, then shouting becomes the norm. Where do you go from there if you really wish to make a point? Be *positive and assertive*. 'Today we are going to . . . and this is what I expect you to do' is far better than 'Sit down . . . stop that.'

- *Personal appearance*. You should be smart but comfortable. A new shirt two sizes too small, or a fashionable pair of shoes that give you blisters or squeak, will not do your confidence any good. It is worth paying attention to your 'sock drawer': you may not notice the strange and varied combination you have put on in the past, but pupils are guaranteed to notice and comment. It is examples like these that fuel distraction, so it is best to avoid them. This applies equally to mannerisms such as fiddling with your keys or earrings or swaying from side to side while talking.

- *Embarrassment*. If the pupils cannot read the books you have given them they will use any displacement activity to avoid being caught out in front of their mates. Neither do they like to be the centre of attention from the teacher. It is not 'cool' to be clever. Good preparation will ensure your materials match their abilities.

- *The pack*. You are a new teacher and they will automatically 'try you out' to see where your limits are. Come in with the confidence of having done your homework. Don't let them catch you out, even though they have been at the school far longer than you have. Do not try to confront them, divert them by engaging them in something interesting.

- *Hidden agenda*. You may not be aware of pupils' home or friendship situations. Outside influences are often far stronger than any influence you may think you have and will affect their classroom behaviour. Be prepared to find out what these are and act accordingly.

- *Food*. If a group of pupils are hungry (the lesson before lunch) it is entirely possible that your words of wisdom may be falling on deaf ears.

- *Times of lessons*. Experienced teachers will tell you that when you are planning your lessons you must take into account the time of day and the weather. A class that is normally well motivated to work may be impossible to manage if you try to introduce a brand new topic on a wet and windy Friday afternoon. The first lesson on Monday morning is likely to produce a number of extremely tired pupils who have stayed up too late for one reason or another. There may also be a few sore heads among the pupils in the upper school (usually Friday morning).

- *Their previous lesson*. It is important to remember that when the pupils arrive in your class, you have no idea what they have just experienced unless you ask. Knowing which lesson(s) they have come from is easy to find out and can be written in the notes section of your lesson plan. Note that sometimes they will all be coming from different options. The key to settling them quickly is to adapt your style to suit the mood. If they are all hot and sweaty from PE, then a few minutes of quiet reading or time to settle would be better than charging into a new topic at full speed. Whenever possible, link your topic to the lesson they have just come from to show the integrated nature of learning.

Relationships with adults in the school: interpersonal skills

Because we are successful human beings we already have skills and tricks we use to get what we want, physically and emotionally, from others. As a teacher you will have to learn to 'play the game' and identify, use and develop these conscious and subconscious skills and strategies. In our lesson preparation we must always be sensitive to the intended audience. Set 8 on Friday afternoon is a different animal from set 1 on a Monday morning. In dealings with other members of staff, either formally or informally, be aware that you are always on duty and on trial in the first year. Some of the tips here appear obvious, but it is difficult to keep the recipe for success at the forefront of the mind at all times.

Smile

You will be perceived as a pleasant positive individual if you try to be cooperative. Even bad news can be delivered and accepted when done as a part of a positive plan for improvement, as true for the NQT receiving advice as for the NQT giving positive plans for improvement to pupils. Predictions of eternal damnation delivered at full volume serve only to raise blood pressure further and when viewed in hindsight produce feelings of guilt and unease in the teacher and resentment in the pupil. It is difficult to rebuild relationships from this platform, so keep things positive.

Experiment

Remember that this is a year in which you are allowed to make mistakes, so try things out. Ask to see lessons of other members of staff you admire and those who do things differently.

Be reliable

It cannot be stressed enough that being in the right place at the right time is probably your number one priority. The stress of being late can destroy a whole day. You must get to lessons on time. Be early when you can. You are expected to be there every day, every INSET day, every parents' evening and open days. It may not be fair that you must be on duty at the other end of school when the bell goes, just after your most difficult class, but that is the way it is. Do not teach right up to the bell: try finishing five minutes early and have a relaxed exit for both you and the pupils.

Cooperate

Teaching can be a lonely profession. For 80 per cent of your day your only company will be the children you teach. As an NQT you are usually very focused on your classes and tasks and it is easy to misjudge the overview or 'big picture'. Cooperating with colleagues is vital in the game of scoring and storing Brownie points, which can be 'cashed in' when you need help. Doing 'cover' may be a pain but it is an opportunity to see other departments and develop relationships with a wider range of children, so it needs to be done with some enthusiasm, and with the knowledge that much can be learnt from it. Listen to advice from colleagues.

Avoidance of conflict with parents

When there is likely to be conflict with a parent, because of either poor behaviour or lack of achievement, you must prepare well in advance and carefully structure the meeting. Pick a suitable place and time for the meeting (not a corridor between lessons). Write down a list of the facts and stick to them.

- Start the meeting by sharing these facts and invite a response and/or clarification.
- Set the agenda as one of improvement.
- Ask for positive suggestions for actions needed from all parties for improvement.
- Set a review date.
- Put it in writing.
- Have a witness present.

Keep things in perspective

Although we are professionals, teaching is still a job. Keep things in perspective – you have a right and a responsibility to look after yourself.

- Have a life outside school. Hobbies are vital, as it is too easy to become totally obsessed with preparation, planning and marking. Set specific times for schoolwork at home.
- Keep physically fit. Go to bed at a reasonable time during the week.
- Keep one day free from schoolwork and keep it for yourself.
- Take a break at lunchtime. Go for a short walk on your own if possible.

Summary

This chapter has provided information and guidance for you to prepare to teach. Most problems teachers have in maintaining control can be solved by careful preparation: knowing the pupils, knowing the school systems, knowing the science, talking things over with colleagues. This allows you to teach in a firm but enjoyable and fair way, so that the pupils feel safe in your lessons and feel that you are confidently in charge. In your class you need to develop an atmosphere where most pupils want to learn; those that don't must realise that it is not worth causing disruptions. The next chapter looks at management of pupils 'as it happens'. You have done your preparation and the lesson has started . . .

21

Managing pupils in the laboratory

Chapter 20 covered everything you can do to prepare for your lesson. When the bell goes and you are there with your 30 pupils, planning stops and real time management starts. Although we deal with safety issues in Chapter 22, there are a number of crisis management points that arise from considerations of safety, and these are covered in this chapter.

Starting the lesson

You have done your preparation, you are there on time, you have a well prepared lesson, you have invited them in and they are seated and ready to start. You now have to introduce the lesson. All lessons need a short sharp introduction in which the task or activity is set and the learning outcomes are identified. It is at this stage that the ground rules are set and the strategies used to avoid potential dangers. Box 21.1 lists a number of possible incidents that form the basis of our discussion.

Starting work quickly

Ideally pupils should have work to complete to provide evidence of the learning outcomes. Always set too much rather than too little, to avoid the boredom factor. Get involved in all the groups or activities equally. Sometimes it is useful to stand back and watch the learning happen. Patience is a virtue and allowing pupils the time to find their own answer is always more effective than diving in and providing the answer. Pupils need time to accept new ideas and models. When they have to accept that their old ideas may be limited or incorrect they can display strange or unacceptable behaviour, e.g. silence, aggressive behaviour and language, sulkiness, elation, tiredness, anguish. You will sometimes see pupils clutch their heads and moan, 'Sir/miss, you're doing my head in.' When this happens, you have got to them.

Crisis points and critical moments

It is when the unexpected happens that you are put to the test. Pupils will be watching to see how each incident is dealt with: are you in control, are you confident? Children can sense weakness and they expect a higher standard from you than they do from themselves or their parents. There are crisis points when drastic action is needed to maintain the integrity of the lesson and critical points when the focus of the lesson and the learning outcomes need to change. The incidents in Box 21.1 will occur from time to time. For each of them think how you would react. Would it depend on the class at the time, or are there universal answers? How many of these would not happen were your preparation better (see Chapter 20)? As we work our way through this chapter, we use these incidents to illustrate some basic principles of classroom management.

---

1   It starts snowing and they all stare through the window
2   You hear breaking glass from across the lab
3   Someone burns their hand on a hot tripod
4   Someone trips over a bag
5   Someone offers you a match to light the Bunsen burner
6   A pupil asks, Did I see you working in the supermarket last summer?
7   When the class has left you find one of the hand lenses is missing
8   Someone carries on chatting as you try to address the class
9   Someone carries on with their work whilst you are talking to the class
10 A 'rugby scrum' forms round the front bench as pupils try to get their apparatus

BOX 21.1 Critical incidents to consider

Critical moments or misconceptions exposed

There are times in a lesson when you have introduced a topic well and the pupils are on task and working enthusiastically, then someone drops a bombshell, displaying a misconception that shows a complete lack of understanding of the topic covered in the lesson. It is important to identify these 'critical moments' and to respond appropriately. One appropriate response may be to abandon the planned lesson and attack the misconceptions.

It starts snowing: no. 1 in the list

This is beyond your control. Do not fight it, as it may provide a better focus for your lesson and a good vehicle for learning. If it is just a distraction then a three-minute diversion may be what is needed to satisfy curiosity. Make a virtue out of necessity.

Patrol your room: nos 2 and 3

The more quickly you can reach an incident, such as no. 2 (broken glass) or no. 3 (burnt hand), the more easily you can make a judgement as to whether you need to stop the whole class for a safety warning, or to keep calm and deal with the incident locally (send for the dustpan, or get the pupil to put their hand under the tap). By agreeing on the standard procedures at the start, you can prevent a lot of these minor accidents.

Only one rule: no. 4

'Behave appropriately' should be the laboratory rule. We deal with safety precautions more fully in the next chapter, but incident no. 4 (tripping over a bag) is a case in point. Bags are put under the benches not because it is a rule of the teacher, but because it is dangerous to leave them in the aisles. It is appropriate behaviour to put them somewhere safe.

Pretend to be angry: no. 5

There are times when we have to be 'angry'. It can be an effective weapon (if you really do get angry then you will have lost). You are on stage and you can 'act'. Remember to be angry at the behaviour, not the child. If you are offered a match (no. 5) you must be 'angry': it is against school rules for pupils to be carrying matches or lighters around. Try not to be drawn into an argument. Postpone the discussion and drive the lesson forward. One often regrets knee-jerk reactions. These can be avoided by being prepared: bring your own lighter.

Use humour: no. 6

Use humour to defuse or deflect possible problem situations and to stir up interest in the topic. You have to judge this carefully if you do not wish to lose control or trivialise the subject. If someone asks you if they saw you in the supermarket in the summer (no. 6) do not get sniffy: laugh it off but show that personal comments are inappropriate in lesson time.

Delegation of tasks: no. 7

Delegating tasks as part of a recognition/reward system can be very effective. They love handing out books, a task involving status and trust. Problems such as no. 7 (hand lens missing) are avoided by adopting clear systems for handing out and counting back apparatus. You may not have time to count everything, but your pupils will do it diligently for you. Most schools will provide small items of apparatus in trays with slots. You can easily see how many empty slots there are at the start, and you can ensure they are the same at the end. Once the pupils have left the lab, getting the item back is a tall order.

Homework

They love it really! Remember to follow the timetable. Do not be conned into being nice to them and not setting it. Homework gives them the opportunity to show you how good they really are, and the chance to reformulate their ideas. They will moan, but that is expected. Be prepared to negotiate the deadlines as more and more pupils have part-time jobs. As a teacher you may feel that your subject is the best one on the timetable, but this is not an emotion shared by all your pupils or their other teachers. See Chapter 17 on marking.

Disruptive pupils or disruptive behaviour?

How to deal with disruptive pupils is usually the problem that is foremost in a new teacher's mind, and taxes some teachers well into their careers. You need to know, first of all, whether there are any pupils in your group that most teachers in the school find hard to deal with – these you will need to find support for from the school management system. However, most pupils behave well for most teachers, and they will respond to a firm but fair approach, especially if you make the lessons interesting and useful. Remember to criticise the behaviour, not the pupil, and take an opportunity to praise the pupil as soon as possible after the incident for behaving appropriately. The next set of incidents provides examples of disruptive behaviour.

Not paying attention: nos 8 and 9

There are many reasons why pupils disrupt lessons. They may be bored, or your lesson may lack structure or pace, or be pitched at too high a level for them to achieve. You will learn to identify the major causes of disruption in the groups you are teaching and take the appropriate action. Disruption begins quietly: for example, when pupils continue talking when you have asked for silence (no. 8 in our list). You need to take action, because it can only get worse if it is not checked. The action may be a simple pause and a quiet 'please . . . '. If someone carries on working (no. 9), are they really a distraction? This time you can be gentler, but still insist that everyone is listening: if you (or a pupil) address the whole class you should expect that everyone is listening to you or them.

If there are persistent talkers or disturbers, you can use different seating plans to reduce disruption. You can dictate groups for learning rather than friendships. If all else fails hit them with a snap test (they love tests) and spread them out. In this way you are not 'picking' on any individuals.

Moving pupils round the lab: no. 10

Manage the distribution of apparatus carefully to reduce the potential for fights in the scrum that could form (no. 10). Several techniques make things easier: distribute the apparatus around the lab and ask one pupil from each group to collect various bits; have pupils take trays of apparatus around, giving each group their 'bit'; only allow collection to take place once the group has drawn a blank table for results, so they don't all come together.

For bringing them round to see a video or demonstration, or just to have them close so that you can discuss better, you need to teach them where to go so that it becomes routine: 'Front row stay where you are, second row bring your stools to the side, third row . . . '

Merits and sanctions

Rewards and punishments should be in the ratio 20:1. If you give punishments for poor behaviour always give rewards for good work. They defuse the situation and help to modify behaviour. Rewards systems, e.g. merits, must be used. Be more careful with sanctions. You need to be careful that you are consistent, and that the one pupil who is getting punished deserves it more than others who were excused. If you have had to reprimand a pupil in the lesson then you should praise them at the first sign of good behaviour. You may then be able to say 'I am pleased with what you are doing now and if you continue to work like this I will withdraw the punishment.' At all costs do not punish the whole class for the bad behaviour of the few.

Positive reinforcement

It is easy to forget or ignore those students who are getting on with it and wrestle with the attention seekers. You need to praise the quiet ones and the workers as well. A real plus is when a 'naughty' pupil gets something right. Managed carefully this could be a turning point in behaviour. Instead of saying 'George, don't do that . . . ' say 'George, will you help by giving out the books, please?' Other phrases to use are 'It is nice to see you settling quickly' and 'Thank you for listening', even though you may have to talk over a couple of chatterers.

Active learning and some danger points

You can 'lose' the pupils in many ways. Talking above their heads and not involving them in the learning are two. Becoming too involved with one small group in the class is another. There are practical hurdles to overcome as well. Be aware of faulty equipment that is set out for you, or of circuit boards with flat batteries. Slides may be in the projector carousel upside down and your video may not be wound back to the start. A mad rush for apparatus causes a 'scrum' (no. 10) around your pile of apparatus. Providing a purposeful, challenging and useful set of learning activities is the best answer for a happy and well behaved classroom. This is about you and the well structured lesson – being prepared (Chapter 20). You have made an impact. You have elicited the pupils' ideas and you have taught the new material through a video, demo or presentation. It is now the pupils' turn to be active in their learning. They need to make sense of the new information that they have seen and heard. Your role is to give them the time and the structure to do this *reformulation* effectively. Keep them busy and focused and they will have no time to be disruptive.

Ending the lesson

The last 15 minutes of the lesson are probably more important than the 30 minutes in the middle. Many a good lesson is spoiled or the main aim is lost because of bad timing. If you leave the plenary session too late, the effect will be lost. To consolidate a good lesson you need to allow time for:

- reviewing the aims of the lesson;
- clearing up;
- setting homework;
- discipline issues.

Teacher intuition

This is a very personal section in which we discuss the 'higher order' skills you will need to hone during the year to establish who you are, how you teach and what your personal and professional rules are. You need to establish rights, responsibilities and rules for yourself and others around you. We discuss those critical points that affect your inception into the school and the route to pupils accepting you as their 'teacher'.

Pacing

It is not just in the lessons that you must get the pace right. You must pace yourself physically during the term too. The first year is a marathon, not a sprint. If you are tired or stressed, the pupils will quickly pick up on the fact. This will provoke them into pushing you further. You do not need to have every lesson as 'all singing and dancing'. *They* need to be working hard, not just you.

The voice

This is a very powerful weapon in the 'body language' arsenal. The level and tone of your voice pass on huge signals to the pupils. You need to modify the tone and level of your voice to suit the situation or even to create the desired environment. Shouting is not usually a good option: it means that you have lost control and it is hard to get it back with this method.

Peer pressure

There is a culture that expresses the view that it is cool not to be 'clever'. The 'in crowd' may be a cool gang to be with, and swots or boffins need not apply. In this case the motivated pupil can be the focus of ridicule and the object of bullying. We need to address this by including all pupils in the lesson. It is not 'cool' to be seen to be too enthusiastic, and we may find that pupils do not interpret our requests as we would wish (see Table 21.1).

TABLE 21.1 Different expectations

Teacher's command	Teacher's expectation	Pupil's response	Pupil's thoughts
Hands up	Hands high	Indifferent	I'm mot making a fool of myself
You at the back	All at back to stop	None	It's someone else in trouble
Come out and draw it on the board	Pupil comes out and draws it on the board	Terror, no movement	I'm gonna look a right idiot
Can anyone tell me...?	Three or more hands should go up	No response	I'm not gonna make myself look like a boffin

Family worries

You do not know what the home situation is for any of the pupils. You must be sensitive to the realities but it is neither necessary nor desirable to know all the problems. Tone of voice, not the words, is a key issue in this situation. Never be tempted to try to sort out their problems. All pastoral care issues must be reported to their tutor or house/year head.

Frustration

Bright pupils who are not being pushed will react differently and some will resort to disruption to show their disaffection. Less able pupils will indulge in any displacement activity when set work that is too difficult, rather than fail and be seen to fail.

Attention seekers

Develop a knack of ignoring low-level unacceptable behaviour and over-praising acceptable and desirable behaviour. In this way the pupils learn that they need to be *good* to attract attention. This only works if used consistently over a long period.

Setting and reading the mood

Pupils pick up your mood as soon as you and they enter the room. If you are tense and edgy, there will be an atmosphere. If you are comfortable and relaxed with yourself and the atmosphere is warm and conducive to work, there is less likelihood of disruptive behaviour. Well structured lessons, aimed at their needs and with achievable outcomes, help to ensure this.

Your body language (e.g. smiles, thumbs up, nods, 'good') shows pleasure at success. Very small signals are powerful ones, which they pick up on. You can set the mood by the activity you choose.

Privileges

Privileges, such as helping the teacher, can be a useful means of including certain characters in the class. This is not just for the academic achievers. Drawing on the board, doing 'tough' work and using 'expensive' equipment are positive ways of encouraging active learning. All pupils at all levels want to be trusted and included. Active learning tasks are good activities to help to build this mutual trust.

Sharpening your intuitive skills or retuning your lessons in this way is a very useful strategy and it does gain the unspoken respect of the pupils if you have responded to their needs. In order that you can effortlessly steer lessons to good learning outcomes without stopping or having sharp changes of course, you must develop the ability to *listen* patiently, and *absorb* and *act* on criticism objectively. The comment 'Sir this lesson is boring' may be infuriating but true. So what are you going to do about it? You now have some strategies. What would you do?

We have provided a further table of mismatches for you to consider (Table 21.2). They may appear to be amusing but they are a reflection of what is really happening.

TABLE 21.2 Instructions mean different things to different people

Instruction to class	Meaning intended by teacher	Interpretation by pupils
Quiet please!	Stop talking	I am talking quietly. So I am quiet
Sit down	Sit at your place	In a minute
Sit down	Sit at your place	The desk will do
Can anyone tell me . . . ?	I want someone to answer	I am not going to make a fool of myself by being a boffin
Have you done your homework?	Show me your homework	I'll answer yes and hope he/she doesn't ask to see it
Make notes on . . .	Read the text and make bullet notes	Read the text and copy it
Do questions 1–10	Write out complete answers for questions 1–10	Do 1–4 and then copy the answers from my mate
Start work now	Start working with a positive attitude	Chat. Look for pen. Search for book. Look out of the window
Face the front	Turn round and face forward	Swivel eyes to the front
Class dismissed	Leave the room in an orderly manner	Charge the door in a mad scrum
See me at break	Report to me at break wherever I am at the beginning of break	Turn up if it suits at the end of break
Listen	Stop talking and pin back your ears	He or she cannot mean me
That work was OK	Improvement needed	I'm brilliant!

Summary

The key points to good management are ensuring that you plan and execute a well prepared lesson that is aimed at the specific needs of all your pupils. To help you we have identified some areas where you need to be sensitive in order to keep the group motivated, and times when you need to question whether you stick rigidly to the lesson plan. At the end of the lesson, you need to reflect on what went well and learn from mistakes. Ask for advice: no one can resist a call for help. Your head of department and other colleagues can help you to become a better teacher, if you let them. Tell them about your successes as well as the failures. Talking is great therapy.

To continue the management theme, the next chapter is concerned with the Health and Safety at Work Act and other aspects of safety.

22

Health, safety and laboratory management

Evidence shows that school science is safe and, indeed, the science laboratory is one of the safest places in the school. Only 2.3 per cent of all reported incidents in school took place in the science lab (HSE 1997) and only 0.8 per cent of those resulted in significant injury. However, accidents do happen and legislation has been introduced to minimise them to protect staff and pupils and to maintain the high standard of safety that already exists. In this chapter we begin with general aspects of safety and safety legislation and then consider particular problems arising from bio-hazards and very reactive chemicals.

The law and the science teacher

In 1974 the Health and Safety at Work Act (HASAWA) was introduced. This enabling legislation allowed Parliament to introduce new regulations imposing a duty on the employer to 'ensure as far as is reasonably practicable the health, safety, and welfare at work of all his employees'. There is also a duty 'on every employee while at work, to take reasonable care for the health and safety of himself and other persons who may be affected by his acts or omissions at work' (Hull 1995: 131).

Within the umbrella of HASAWA is a myriad of other legislation, but the greatest impact on schools comes from the 1989 COSHH (Control of Substances Hazardous to Health) regulations. These aim to protect employees and others from substances that might be hazardous to their health, ranging from microorganisms to all uses of chemicals classified as being harmful and corrosive. It also covers explosive, flammable, radioactive and oxidising agents. In order to assist in this procedure, documentation was produced by a variety of bodies, including the Association for Science Education (ASE) and the Consortium of Local Education Authorities for the Provision of School Science (CLEAPSS). The latter, in association with the Scottish Schools Equipment Research Centre (SSERC), produced a series of *Hazcards* summarising relevant information about the range of chemicals used in school. Included are suggestions of alternative activities and chemicals that could be used to minimise risk.

Issues of health and safety should therefore feature prominently in your lesson plans and you should be aware of training opportunities during the early years of teaching. The ASE publication *Topics in Safety* gives some comprehensive examples of how you could control risks in basic KS 3 science laboratory work, as well as illustrating how safety notes can be incorporated in a scheme of work (ASE 2001). At the very least you should familiarise yourself with these, but spending time with the laboratory technician, talking to other teaching staff, trying out the practicals for yourself and generally seeking advice on healthy and safety are musts.

The Management of Health and Safety at Work Regulations (1999) outline explicit requirements placed on the employer in terms of managing health and safety issues. These relate to the following areas:

- assessment and recording of risks;
- making arrangements for the effective control and monitoring of those risks;
- providing up-to-date and relevant information to all employees on matters to do with health and safety in the workplace;
- appointing appropriate health and safety officers responsible for their own department, usually the heads of department.

The science department safety policy

In many PGCE programmes trainee teachers are advised to spend a day with the laboratory technician early in their first school experience. This helps the trainees to become familiar with the workings of the department, where everything is and the importance of getting your preparation requirements in on time.

By law employers must have a safety policy and all science departments will have one. All science teachers must be familiar with it. It defines procedures and areas of responsibility in order to promote safety within the department. The 'procedures' apply to the day-to-day running of the department, as well as to specific emergencies, listing where safety resources are and what to do in the event of an emergency. It identifies regular checks that need to be made and who is responsible for carrying them out. Such checks may include:

- fume cupboard;
- portable electrical appliances;
- autoclaves, pressure cookers and steam engines;
- radioactive sources for possible leakage;
- chemicals that are likely to deteriorate;
- eye protection;
- first aid boxes;
- fire extinguishers and other safety equipment.

Although certain members of the department will be given specific responsibilities, it is important that you are familiar with the department's policy and know what to do if you notice anything untoward, or an accident occurs.

The procedure for reporting and dealing with accidents

- All incidents of injury to a person or damage to clothing have to be logged in an incident logbook according to procedures in the school's safety policy.
- Designated, qualified members of staff, the names of whom will be in the staff handbook, deal with incidents requiring first aid.

- Any incident requiring treatment by the school nurse has to be reported to the head of department and logged in the 'main book' in the school office.
- All serious accidents are to be reported to a qualified first aider or the school nurse.
- If a child is not seriously injured, but is distressed, they can be sent to the school nurse accompanied.

Managing safety and risk assessments

A major part of the 1989 COSHH regulations is dedicated to 'risk assessment'. This is a procedure that all employers are obliged to carry out before hazardous substances are used or made. Owing to the enormity of the situation, your employers (the governing body or the local education authority) delegate responsibility for this to the teachers involved with the specific subject area. The head of department has to ensure that risk assessments are carried out on every activity involving potentially hazardous substances or equipment. Consider these two questions (Borrows 1998):

- What is the difference between a hazard and a risk?
- How can risks be eliminated?

A 'hazard' is anything with the potential to cause harm. This will include many chemicals, where the hazard is inherent within the material. In other instances it is associated with the use of that material, i.e. such activities as using a scalpel. On the other hand, a 'risk' is the probability that harm will actually be caused by the hazard. There are two elements to risk:

- How likely is it that something will go wrong?
- How serious is it if something does go wrong?

Risk can be reduced by good safety management: for example, strict adherence to wearing eye protection (using acids) and good discipline when using scalpels (dissecting plants). If the outcome of an accident is likely to be serious it is better not to take the risk, however small, and to use a teacher demonstration or video instead.

General risk assessment

General risk assessments (GRAs) have been compiled by a variety of authoritative bodies, and are models against which activities can be compared. There are two main aspects of the GRA:

- the thinking process;
- the informing process.

The first aspect involves answering a series of in-depth questions concerning the activity:

- Is it educationally necessary?
- Is there an alternative, less hazardous substance or procedure?
- Is it a teacher demonstration, or pupil activity?
- What are the age and experience of the pupils?
- What personal protection or control measures are necessary?
- How will residues be disposed of at the end?

The other aspect of a GRA involves recording and informing others of the outcomes of the assessment. It is not necessary for each teacher to conduct a detailed GRA on the same activity every time it is used. Risk assessment forms giving this general information can be attached to schemes of work, available to staff to make use of. Remember, it is not just the teaching staff who need this information: the technicians play a fundamental role in this, and their related work in the preparation room needs to be considered as well. Before we consider how pupils are to be warned about hazards, we need to consider our own preparations.

Preparing to meet your class

Before even starting to teach we need to be fully prepared.

■ We need to know where the gas taps, water taps and electrical switch-off points are for all labs. If the school policy is to turn off all the mains at the end of the day it is important to check that all bench taps are closed in the labs before the mains are turned back on and the pupils enter the room.

■ We must never do an experiment for the first time in front of a class, however simple it may seem. If there is no chance to practise first, then it should be left out.

■ No hazardous substance should be placed in front of pupils (or anywhere in the school) unless it is labelled. If you decant, say, propanone into a beaker, the beaker needs to have the same hazard warning as the original bottle.

Sharing good safety practice with the pupils

The Science National Curriculum (DfEE 1999:36) at both KS 3 and 4 emphasises the importance of health and safety in science education by stating that pupils should be taught to: 'recognise that there are hazards in living things, materials and physical processes, and assess risks and take actions to reduce risks to themselves and others.' Traditionally pupils have been given a set of rules by which to abide while they are in the science laboratory. Is it the set of safety rules or the sharing in the making of them that is important? Is it better to introduce them gradually as they are needed (and thereby seen to be relevant) or all at once at the beginning?

Telling children what to do, or how to be safe, is not the same as them knowing: the 'tell each other' technique (see Chapter 8) is valuable here in allowing pupils to internalise what they are to do and how to be safe. For example, after agreeing the aim of an investigation, get the pupils to 'tell each other' about any potential hazards that they need to be aware of (15 seconds needed) and what precautions need to be taken. These can then be compiled as a list on the board. Some schools have a small 'safety board' alongside the white/blackboard especially for this.

Pupils should not have to wear eye protection all the time; it can alienate them from an experience they can easily relate to. They must, however, be worn if there is a hazard. Eye protection has to be taken seriously and when you ask for goggles to be worn you will need to keep reminding pupils of the requirements. Eye protection is for eyes, not for the upper forehead.

Too often safety is blamed for the decline in 'exciting' science. This need not be the case. Many of the practical activities that enthused and excited generations in the past can still be performed today, but in a safer, more controlled and perhaps more familiar environment. One problem of operating in a 'science' atmosphere is that links with 'reality' become less easy to make. We are not training future scientists, but giving the next generation a way of looking at and understanding their environment. In this respect, the laboratory setting can be alienating, and pupils may see 'science' as something that happens only in this room. We conclude this chapter by looking at two particularly hazardous areas of science teaching: dealing with microbes and with very reactive chemicals.

Biohazards: handling microbes and other biological hazards

What do we mean by 'microbes'? The term 'microbe', or microorganism, covers a wide range of organisms that cannot be seen with the unaided eye, yet live all around and within us. With the aid of a hand lens, binocular microscope and laboratory optical microscopes, we can enter a world of mystery and intrigue. Members include: protozoans, algae, lichens, slime moulds, viruses, bacteria, fungi and yeasts.

Why do we teach about microbes?

Microbiology enters the National Curriculum as early as KS 2, when the use of microbes in decomposition is introduced. A wide range of exciting and interesting work can be tackled with minimal specialist equipment and in perfect safety if the organisms studied are known to be non-pathogenic (not harmful to humans). These include:

- brewer's and baker's yeast;
- bacteria in yoghurt;
- edible mushrooms.

Microbes play several important roles in our lives. Perhaps their most fundamental role is in the cyclical changes involved in decomposition, enabling the cycling of nutrients needed for life. Although they are involved in diseases, they are also used in the production of important medicines, e.g. human insulin for diabetics. Industrially and economically they are important for the production of everyday substances such as vinegar (ethanoic acid) and lemon juice (citric acid). They play a significant role in food production, including mycoproteins (Quorn), bread and alcohol.

Are microbes safe to use in school?

If microorganisms other than the three listed above are used, there is a risk of infection. As long as safety precautions are adhered to the risks can be kept to a minimum. The use of hay infused with liquid for the purpose of studying protozoa and animal life is a case in point. An infusion of this kind will provide nutrients for bacteria, which in turn are eaten by other bacteria and protozoans. Particular care has to be taken when sampling the medium and disposing of the culture, because unknown bacteria may be present. When preparing such an infusion, animal faecal matter must not be used to enrich the sample. Equally reliable and just as fascinating results can be obtained using leaf mould and bread mould, but we still need to take care.

Special risk assessments (ASE 2001)

When using microbes in class, it is necessary to make sensible adaptations to the general risk assessment described earlier in this chapter. Suppose, for example, an unspecified culture of microbes, isolated from the school pond, was to be grown in jam jars of nutrient broth. These were to be opened by an unruly, unskilled Year 9 group supervised by a newly qualified physics graduate teacher. This is a hazardous situation, accompanied by some risk. In general, there are certain factors the teacher would need to consider before deciding whether or not to continue:

- The nature of the organisms. Are they 'harmless', such as yeast used in baking or fungi that are likely to release spores and cause allergies?
- The source of the organisms. Was it a pure culture purchased from a reliable supplier, or an unknown sampled from the environment?

  Never use potentially dangerous sources such as the following: human mucus; pus from spots; faecal material; drains and toilets. All air, water and soil samples should be treated as containing potential pathogens and dealt with accordingly.

- Temperature of incubation. Cultures of 37°C are likely to contain human pathogens; incubation should be between 20 and 28°C (a week at laboratory temperature is usually sufficient).
- Culture medium. Media which selectively grow pathogens, e.g. blood agar, MacConkey agar and broth for studying coliform bacteria, should normally be avoided. Use nutrient agar for bacteria and malt agar for fungi. Successful results can be achieved by using bread as the culture medium, but the same safety procedures must apply. The plates must be sealed, must remain so and must be disposed of properly when finished with.
- Type of investigation and facilities available. Unless you are specially qualified and working with sixth-form students, all investigations should be with sealed containers. Inoculated plates should be taped with small pieces of sticky tape at intervals around the plate. This will allow access of air and help to prevent the growth of anaerobic organisms. If there is a risk of opening, the microbes should be killed before the plates are viewed, then sterilised.
- Correct disposal of the used containers is of fundamental importance and should be considered before the outset of the investigation. They must be placed in sealable plastic bags and autoclaved to sterilise. They can then be disposed of in the normal way, wrapped in sealable plastic bags.
- Expertise of people involved. Never assume anything, check that the technician has had suitable training, consider your own level of training and the age, discipline and skills of the pupils.

Under the circumstances it would be unwise to proceed with this Year 9 lesson, mentioned earlier.

Levels of practical work

Topics in Safety (ASE 2001) identifies three levels of work:

- *Level 1*. Organisms used have little, if any, known risk and no specialist training or knowledge is required. Work may include investigations with baker's and brewer's yeasts, protozoans, algae and lichens.
- *Level 2*. Bacteria and fungi from recognised suppliers or organisms cultured from certain aspects of the environment can be grown on appropriate media. Incubated containers must be taped closed, labelled and not opened by pupils if they contain living cultures. They must be disposed of correctly after use.
- *Level 3*. The growth of known microorganisms from recognised sources and subsequent transfer of live samples from the incubated cultures, e.g. serial dilution techniques.

It is envisaged that only work at levels 1 and 2 will be carried out by pupils aged 11–16. For level 2 work the teacher should have experience in the basic techniques, precautions and disposal procedures. Level 3 work would normally be restricted to post-16 education, where facilities are appropriate. A more extensive knowledge of microbiology and sterile procedures is required for activities at this level. It would be inappropriate for such work to be supervised by non-specialist staff unless suitably qualified.

Working with very reactive chemicals

Most of the materials we use around us are giant structures based on two elements from group 4 of the periodic table: carbon gives us living materials and plastics (life polymers), and silicon gives us rocks. There are three other basic sorts of material: metals (elements from the left and bottom of the periodic table), volatile materials such as water, wax and oxygen (made of the non-metallic elements at the top and right of the periodic table) and ionic solids, formed when a metallic element combines with non-metallic elements. This simple classification system has been called the structure triangle (Ross 1997, 2000a). The triangle is built up from all the possible combinations of pairs of elements from the periodic table. Although group 4 with carbon and silicon is the most significant group in the periodic table, containing the elements of both life and the rocks, it is helpful for children to experience the extremes of metallic and non-metallic reactivity (giving experience of the other three substance types: metal, volatile and ionic). This is provided by an exploration of the elements of groups 1 (the alkali metals) and 7 (the halogens).

Safety

On no account should KS 3 or 4 children be allowed to handle these elements themselves. Do not attempt to react the metals in air by heating them. Only use sodium for the reaction with chlorine and bromine. All routes from the metals to the eyes must be blocked. Safety screens must be used in conjunction with eye protection in case metal explodes over the screen. A mobile fume cupboard is safer and gives a good view. A petri dish on the OHP, covered by a large sheet of glass on a supporting ring, is also good, with pupils seeing a shadow on the screen of the reaction with water. Many schools now have flexible video cameras, so pupils can see the reaction on the TV screen.

Reactions of the alkali metals

Most teachers will demonstrate the reaction of the metals with water and when left in air. The three demonstrations that follow provide additional experiences for the pupils, but must be tried out only with the support of an experienced teacher or technician. What follows is only a guide, and you need to take all the normal precautions provided by the Hazcards, your technician and colleagues.

Lithium has small atoms (hazardous: try out beforehand with your technician)

To show that the more reactive metals have larger atoms, cut pieces of lithium (Li), sodium (Na) and potassium (K) of equal size, about that of a match head. Now ask which of these will contain more atoms? If you react these pieces with water and collect the hydrogen, which will produce the most? Pupils may understand this better if you ask them how many fruits are in three equal-sized boxes: a box of satsumas (Li), a box of oranges (Na) or a box of grapefruit (K).

The lithium has the smallest atoms, so will have the most atoms in the piece we have cut and therefore we expect it to produce a greater volume of hydrogen than the others, even if it is generated at a slower rate. To collect the hydrogen, hold, with one hand, an inverted boiling tube (Figure 22.1) full of water (no air bubbles) steady against the side of a pneumatic trough and release the metal from tweezers under water so that it rises up the tube. This reaction is animated in Ross *et al.* (2002: matter).

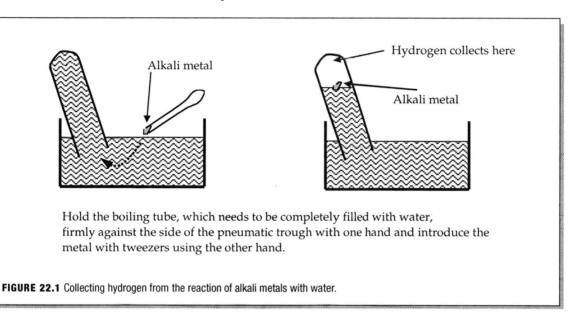

Hold the boiling tube, which needs to be completely filled with water, firmly against the side of the pneumatic trough with one hand and introduce the metal with tweezers using the other hand.

FIGURE 22.1 Collecting hydrogen from the reaction of alkali metals with water.

Making salt (hazardous: try out beforehand with your technician)

Have a Pyrex boiling tube of chlorine ready before the lesson. The sodium must be free of its protective oil (which reacts with chlorine) by immersing a freshly cut rice-grain sized piece in octane, or a similar solvent. Leave it on a filter paper for 30 seconds to allow the solvent to evaporate, then drop it to the bottom of the tube of chlorine, using tweezers, as you briefly remove the bung. Exchange the bung for a Bunsen valve (Figure 22.2) and it is now safe to heat the tube in the open laboratory, as long as you are all wearing eye protection. Use a hot Bunsen flame and heat the sodium directly through the tube. Keep the hot flame firmly directed at the tiny piece of sodium. You may see a feeble yellow flame and soot if there is oil left, then suddenly the sodium catches fire. Remove it from the Bunsen and hold it up to watch it burn with a brilliant yellow flame in the chlorine, producing a white smoke of solid salt (sodium chloride).

Making an alloy of sodium and potassium (hazardous: try out beforehand with your technician)

What will happen if we react two of these reactive metals together? Some may say they will react violently, but sodium is only reactive towards non-metals. When two similar elements 'react' together they form a material remarkably similar to the original elements – thus Na and K form an alloy that still behaves like an alkali metal, but with a melting point lower than either. Compare this with solder (an alloy of lead and tin). To make the alloy place equal rice-grain sized pieces of sodium and potassium into a dry ignition tube and gently warm until the metals melt together. Carefully (eye protection) place some of this alloy on to water, and it will burst into flame (like potassium) but burn yellow (like sodium).

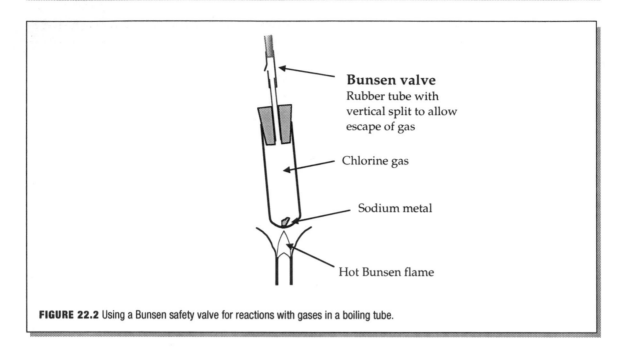

FIGURE 22.2 Using a Bunsen safety valve for reactions with gases in a boiling tube.

Making a new halogen: the reaction between chlorine and iodine

The same principle of two similar elements reacting together to form a material remarkably similar to the original elements applies if you react the two very similar elements iodine and chlorine with each other. Drop a few iodine crystals into a tube of chlorine with a Bunsen valve (similar to Figure 22.2). A brown liquid (and vapour) of iodine chloride (ICl) forms, which looks and behaves like bromine, also from group 7. The yellow crystals are iodine trichloride, and decompose as you gently heat the tube. You can tell the difference between this brown halogen (ICl) and bromine itself by dropping a strip of real tin foil (Sn) into the tube. Bromine vapour will slowly attack the tin, forming tin bromide, with the colour fading, but the iodine chloride attacks the tin more rapidly, forming tin chloride and iodine vapour, so the brown colour turns purple. Dispose of these carefully, in a fume cupboard, because the tin bromide and chloride are corrosive and fume as they react with water vapour in the air.

In contrast, when the two elements are from opposite ends of the periodic table you get a compound that is completely different, as we saw when we reacted sodium and chlorine.

Summary

On the whole laboratories are safe places, and they become safer when pupils understand why they are asked to take various precautions, and when we undertake risk assessments for all our practical work and demonstrations. We have a duty, as teachers, to understand these precautions ourselves. The following documents make essential reading, and are collected here for ease of reference.

References

ASE (2001) *Topics in Safety*, 3rd edn. Hatfield: ASE.

CLEAPSS (1997) *Laboratory Handbook*. Uxbridge: CLEAPSS School Service.

DfEE (1996) *Safety In Science Education*. London: HMSO.

HSE (1997) *Health and Safety Executive 1996/7*. London: HSE.

SSERC (1997) *Hazardous Chemicals Manual*. Edinburgh: SSERC.

23

Teaching and learning at 14–19

In this chapter we emphasise the importance of active learning and the constructivist approach to learning at all levels of education. The revised NVQ and GNVQ approach for 14+ takes on board the idea that all students need to be self researchers by the time they are 18, but with support. We look at the post-16 continuum for the new 14–19 initiative.

Introduction

The standard approach at KS 4 for a lot of schools is to put everyone in for GCSEs and achieve the 70 per cent pass rate at grades A* to C. Research has indicated that this is possibly not the best method of teaching and learning for all candidates (21st Century Science Team 2003). There are two groups who are disadvantaged by this approach: those who do not perform well in tests and a small but significant group who are disaffected with the school system in general. It has been proposed that a vocational approach may address their needs more effectively and the emphasis placed on responsibility and ownership of one's own learning not only marries well with the NVQ approach, but also prepares sixth-form students for life and learning at university. An active learning style suits the needs of all pupils.

Reform at post-16

Post-16 education has been under review for some years, with several attempts being made to reform the A-level. The narrow, specialist course of two or three subjects of study during a two-year period was retained. This was mainly due to the high academic standards claimed for A-levels and their use as the university entrance examination. September 2000, however, saw the introduction of a revised system offering a new range of qualifications to the students.

What are sixth-form students expected to do?

- A/S-levels (advanced/subsidiary), worth half a traditional A-level, are studied in the first year sixth. Most pupils will take four A/S-levels during this year.
- Pupils will normally drop one subject after the first year. During the second year of the sixth form, most will continue with three subjects to A-level (so-called A2s). Some will do a fifth A/S-level; others may start three new A/S-levels.
- Most students will study *key skills* as well, i.e. the application of number, communication and IT. This is a feature that started life in the GNVQ (see below). They will receive grades for their efforts.

- In addition, the most able will be offered 'super A-levels', advanced extension papers retaining the high academic rigour of previous A-levels.

In a few subjects, there will be a free-standing AS without an A2, but A2s are all full qualifications and must follow the AS route. Learning and assessment opportunities for some or all of the *key skills* will be signposted in the specifications of all AS and A2 qualifications.

The reform has been received with mixed feelings. The concern is that pressure is mounting on students and teachers. This is because it is becoming more difficult to choose the right course out of so many options and to ensure that the qualifications will be acceptable for the students to progress effectively. There is also the question of quality when we compare our system with those in the rest of Europe. It is important for all students to have a grasp of scientific issues, even if they are not following a science degree. The new proposals for an AS in 'science in context' (Hunt and Millar 2000) are an encouraging step in this direction. This gives non-scientists a grasp of the big scientific ideas and their effect on society.

Reforming vocational learning 14+

There are General National Vocational Qualifications (GNVQs) available in 16 different subject areas. They are equivalent to 2 A-levels and range from art and design, hospitality and catering, to performing arts, leisure and tourism. Pupils may begin some GNVQs at KS 4, but most subjects are post-16 and have a three-tiered structure: foundation, intermediate and advanced. There is a common infrastructure running through the various levels: each consists of mandatory units addressing the subject content. Several *optional units* and *additional units* are included for extended study depending on the level of study, but all levels address the *core skills* of:

- communication;
- application of number;
- information technology.

David Blunkett announced plans to expand the vocational system (Gadd 2000). The government aims to raise the status, attractiveness and effectiveness of work-based training. The GNVQs will see a name change, to Vocational Levels, and undergo a review of the standards of the advanced tier. The Modern Apprenticeship scheme was also reformed. There will be a greater emphasis on knowledge, understanding and off-job learning in a college or with training providers. This may cause conflict between the needs of the school and the needs of the pupil. This is because some senior managers may wish to promote GCSEs rather than GNVQs. There is an excellent discussion on the merits of the 14–19 review in MacKay (2003).

Teaching and learning 14+ and applied science

The natural lines drawn between the Key Stages can create boundaries through which some students find it hard to progress. The pressure to perform in SATs can lead to a higher percentage of didactic-style lessons than normal, to ensure coverage of the syllabus, but these may not include time for *reformulation*, allowing pupils to gain a deeper understanding of the topics. This can affect the enthusiasm of lower ability students or late learners and some of these who do reasonably well at SATs then do not progress further during the next two years and underperform at GCSE.

It is hoped that the new *applied science* course will address this concern and provide an opportunity for these two groups to be included in science education, and to achieve their potential. Under the direction of the QCA all four main exam boards have produced almost identical specifications for this new course. But it is in the assessment and tracking that the difference between the boards lies.

1 It is a two-year course.

2 There are three parts (units).

3 Units 1 and 3 are wholly coursework based. They are internally marked and externally moderated.

4 Unit 1 must include both a portfolio on health and safety in the workplace and a lab book with six complete practical tasks: two biology, two chemistry and two physics. This is presented and marked in the May of Year 10.

5 Unit 2 is the core knowledge that is taught alongside the practical work to inform and extend the students. This is examined in January and/or June in Year 11.

6 Unit 3 is a further coursework portfolio which is presented and marked in the May of Year 11.

The advantage of applied science is that the students have more involvement in how and what they learn. The emphasis is more on 'doing', 'finding out' and reformulation following teacher intervention, rather than 'learning through listening'. This is very well suited to active learning styles of lessons. It also ensures that there is more opportunity to improve *key skills* as required by the National Curriculum.

Another advantage is that students know very early on not only what GCSE grade their standard of work is likely to produce but also what they need to do to improve on this. A favourite question of pupils is 'What do I need to do to get a C or B grade?' Both teacher and pupil can be realistic about the target grade and it may not be A* to C. The course lends itself to industry links and this is encouraged, but it is not an absolute necessity. Each unit can be taken, or presented, twice. Most important is the emphasis of the course on how science is used or applied in the world of work and how it affects us as citizens.

Whatever the approach at KS 4, traditional syllabus or new NVQ style, the important point to remember is that we all wish to help students to become better at the thinking skills they will need not only for their further education but also for life. Students need to be able to :

■ locate, sort and classify information;

■ process information, store it and recover it;

■ think creatively;

■ evaluate and make judgements;

■ plan, predict and pose relevant questions.

They can only do this at 14+ if they have been actively encouraged to do so from early on and we avoid the 'cramming' that can begin to feature as pupils move through SATs and on to GCSEs.

Teaching and learning post-16

The optimists among the teaching profession highlight the positive aspects of students as they enter post-16 courses:

- they are older;
- they have chosen to be there;
- they have chosen their subjects;
- they are well motivated to work;
- they have been successful and will continue to be so.

But the pessimists warn us that:

- they are only a vacation away from Year 11;
- they are entering the teenage roundabout of love and angst;
- they regress in enthusiasm as the social scene offers far more attractions than academic achievement;
- they are under additional pressure from part-time employment to pay for their social 'needs'.

Whatever the view, it is our job to help them to achieve their best. We are privileged as teachers to be involved with helping the development of these young adults; the time can be rewarding for both teacher and student.

Teaching post-16 is different from teaching further down the school and your approach will need to reflect this. The pupils are mature, but we must still be the teachers and we must not ignore those active tasks that worked so well at KS 3 and 4. We can and should try to recreate the 'awe and wonder' response in post-16 students as they are at the beginning of a journey that could lead to a life centred on your subject, rather than at the end of an exam trail. Post-16 courses are for specialists now, but with the broadening of the number of post-16 exams that students take, we must also cater for those who are less confident and enthusiastic in science.

Examples of these different styles are given below and echo the active learning ideas from the previous three chapters.

- Creation of *mind maps* for display (poster work).
- *Teach the class*. Get the students to research a topic and 'teach it' using only outline notes. They could prepare a few *PowerPoint* screens to assist themselves, and help to put over the message.
- *Mastermind/Millionaire quiz*. No one can resist the challenge of winning a quiz show (they can even phone a friend or ask the audience). This needs a lot of preparation but can be used again with subsequent groups.
- *Hot-seating*. Like a talk show guest, the pupils must prepare to discuss issues with the interviewer and audience. They must also decide where they stand on issues like genetically modified food or the use of nuclear power stations, and support their position with research data.
- *Q card construction*. Each individual or pair takes one topic area and creates a miniature revision guide on A5 sheets. These are then edited by peer review to pick up misconceptions and omissions, and published on the school's intranet.

- *Pub quiz*. Once again we rely on the competitive spirit in the students. Set them homework to revise a topic and then split them into groups to answer sets of questions you have prepared; this is tough but rewarding. You can also get them to prepare a set of questions.
- *IT lessons* as discussed in Chapter 24.

Students at 16+ need the same learning cycle as everyone else. Using different styles in this way can also help you to prepare for the other considerations of differentiation and different learners. Not all your pupils will achieve the top grades. Indeed, it can be argued that getting a weak pupil to a C or D grade is as valuable and rewarding as guiding the A grade candidate through the course. However, teaching for understanding is vital, and the way to achieve good grades is to have students who are motivated by the subject. If they retain their misconceptions their only ploy is to learn by rote for examinations, an activity that is tedious, unrewarding and likely to lead to poor exam results and an inability to progress further.

Crossing the continuum

As a teacher you need to be aware that the teaching and learning styles needed at A-level are those to be practised at KS 3 and 4. It may be quicker and easier to provide didactic teaching at KS 4 to 'get through the curriculum', but in the long term the harder option of getting them to think for themselves will be a winner. You need to adopt an active teaching/learning style to help you and your pupils have a seamless transition between Key Stages.

Summary

In this chapter we have recognised a continuum in the learning and teaching styles in science education advocated for all pupils. It is important for all pupils to challenge their own ideas and understanding, building a holistic picture of science and the various facets associated with it. We also need to ensure that, whatever the route we take, the students are given the opportunity effectively to hone their thinking skills with reference to:

- communication;
- application of number;
- IT;
- working with others;
- improving their own performance;
- problem-solving.

PART V

Professional Values and Practice

Introduction

This part covers the 'professional values and practice' section of the standards for initial teacher training. It stresses the need for our science to appeal to everyone and be relevant to the world they live in. ICT (Chapter 24) provides a web of information that pupils and their teachers can use to inform them about their world. More generally, ICT provides a resource for teachers to support the learning of their pupils. 'Science for all' covers issues of race, gender and special educational needs (Chapter 25). In Chapter 26 we examine the importance of linking science to the everyday lives of our pupils. In particular, we examine the educational value of working outside the classroom.

Our final chapter discusses a philosophy for science and the growing awareness of the need for the public to understand science. We re-examine the purpose of an education in science by considering the origins of science teaching in British schools.

We need to educate the next generation to understand the need for sustainable development on this planet: this final part of the book shows the role that science education can play in this.

24

Use of ICT

This chapter is about the use of ICT (information and communications technology) within science at all levels of ability. There is an acknowledgement that not all schools have access to the same level of ICT, but here we explore what is reasonably possible.

Introduction

Four major changes have occurred over the past few years.

1   Hardware and software for ICT are more readily available.
2   Both teachers and students have better skills in certain areas of IT and ICT.
3   The pace of change is increasing.
4   There is almost universal access to the world wide web.

There is, however, a trap set for all teachers and that is that there will inevitably be two divides in any class. One is *financial*, where the pupils from more affluent families are likely to have computers available at home with internet access, while others don't. The other is about *attitudes*. Some students will have a natural desire to explore, use and become expert in all aspects of ICT, while others, when they do get to a computer, will just want to log on and surf. It is expected that all NQTs will be computer literate and be able to promote and use ICT within their subject area. 'There is considerable research evidence that learners are more highly motivated when their learning is supported by modern technologies' (Newton and Rogers 2001, cited in Denby 2003: 41). This chapter explores these opportunities for using ICT to enhance learning.

IT or ICT?

Some confusion exists about these two terms and how they are used. IT is a subject in its own right on the National Curriculum, whereas ICT is the name given to its application in learning.

Information technology (IT)

Put simply, the job of an IT teacher is to teach the pupils the skills associated with using computers, either standalone PCs or networked machines. This involves keyboard skills and use of the three main types of program, namely spreadsheets, word processing and database packages. The pupils will learn how to open and manipulate these packages by using standard IT tasks, which will be identified in the IT scheme of work.

IT skills are taught at all levels in schools. Pupils are taught keyboard skills and how to use the mouse. They are introduced to word processing packages and how to use the menu buttons to 'word process' a document. At secondary school they are expected to learn how to enter data into spreadsheets and how to use formulae to manipulate these data. They are shown how to present the resulting information in a variety of different ways, including charts and graphs. Once again the pupils using computers at home will develop their IT skills far more than is possible if pupils have access only during IT lessons at school.

Information and communications technology (ICT)

The focus here is on communications. Incorporating ICT means that we, as teachers, can use the students' ability to manipulate the package we intend to use to communicate, i.e. as a teaching and learning tool. It is important that we coordinate our work with the IT department and check that the pupils are able to operate the package we wish to use. If they take place at the right time, these lessons will be useful as both teaching and learning tools for science, and for consolidating pupils' IT skills.

ICT skills allow us to select and use appropriate IT packages to speed up the learning process or provide more accurate, better presented data than in the past. They also enable us to provide pupils with more experience of a technology they will be expected to use when they leave school.

Starting points

We can assume pupils will enter KS 3 with some IT skills. Those skills will include using documents, saving their work and editing text. They are likely to know how to access specific Internet sites for learning. The difficulty is that different feeder schools will have covered different amounts of ground in this area. We can also assume that all pupils will have specific IT lessons in KS 3 to underpin the ICT in all subject areas.

Bearing in mind that the IT department has its own scheme of work to follow, the timing of coverage of certain topics may not suit you; you need to liaise with the IT department to get a feel for their agenda. Another point to remember is that even though students may have covered 'spreadsheets' in IT, they have to be taught how to use them in science and which type of graph or chart is appropriate for each task.

Before you decide to use ICT you must decide whether it is the best way to support the lesson. Is it saving time, enhancing the learning, teaching a skill or having a positive impact?

Teachers may ask: 'Do I have to use ICT in every lesson?' The simple answer to this is no. A few ICT tasks per half term is something to aim for. It is also counterproductive to try to use ICT where it is not appropriate. Sometimes it is quicker and more appropriate to use a book or a magazine in the library.

Hardware

The majority of schools now have the first three in this list and they will have some of the rest too:

1   Standalone computers in each class. These are good for data-logging activities but not as good for the students to carry out tasks which span lessons.

2 An integrated school system, where all the computers are linked to the central server. This is great but can cause problems when the system 'crashes' or you have to wait to get particular subject-specific software installed and made available.

3 Data-logging. Great for data capture in real time.

4 Class sets of laptops. Great for data-logging and for long-term tasks as long as you have lots of floppies or flash memory pens to download the work at the end of each session.

5 Digital projectors. Wonderful for whole-class interactive teaching.

6 Interactive whiteboards. Great for whole-class reformulation and interactive teaching.

7 Palmtops. Portable and great for field trips and data-logging.

Software

Whichever operating system they are running, all schools will have packages for word processing, spreadsheets, database, publishing and webpage design. These basic packages are cross-curricular but you need to ensure that the specific science software you need is installed and made available to the specific machines or rooms you wish to use. It is important to check that they do work before you take the class on a journey of discovery.

Benefits of using ICT in science teaching

ICT can be used on several levels, from support for the teacher in record keeping and lesson preparation, through supporting the lessons themselves (e.g. creating worksheets or *PowerPoint* presentations), to actual use by the pupils (e.g. in individual data-logging). In the sections that follow we examine these in more detail.

ICT and teacher administration

Computers can help enormously in your day-to-day administration: electronic spreadsheets of pupil records help you to track progress, assess value added and analyse test results; e-mail can enable faster and more efficient communication between staff; lesson plans can be amended from year to year if they are word processed, and evaluations can be stored electronically where you can find them again when you need them; ideas for lessons can be downloaded from the web.

ICT supporting teaching directly

Most lessons will need material for the pupils to read: it may be a worksheet, a homework exercise or a *PowerPoint* presentation. All these can be prepared on your computer and amended from year to year. Many published schemes now provide worksheets in electronic format, which you can amend to suit your class.

Data projectors are making their way into classrooms either as part of an interactive whiteboard or simply as a way of projecting a large image of the computer screen for all to see. These are a tremendous leap forward in the presentation of lessons. They can be used in a number of ways. The teacher can produce really professional *PowerPoint* presentations to introduce topics, or use them to clarify worksheets. This eliminates the problem of having your back to the class as you write on the board. It also allows you to skip from one sheet to another and once a good worksheet has evolved it can be used again with other groups. The video played through the projector is also far more effective. CD-ROMs and data-logging software can be demonstrated to the whole class before they have a go individually or in small groups.

For those lucky enough to have these available they are fantastic for prepared presentations, templates with drag and drop activities and CD-ROMs. However, a lot of preparation work needs to be done and specific lessons must be picked for their use. They are not something that can be used in every lesson, as they will lose their impact. See box 24.1 for a couple of ideas. The websites of the companies that produce interactive whiteboards are full of resources for teachers to download – make use of them.

With a lower set the teacher can produce a Cloze procedure template and have the missing words in individual text boxes on the side. The groups can then discuss which words fit where and a pupil can drag and drop the appropriate words into the correct space.

With higher sets the teacher can produce a set of templates for use on progression of ideas: for example, the construction of the periodic table, the building of electron-layers in atoms or the build-up of food webs.

BOX 24.1 Using the interactive whiteboard

ICT and the pupil

In this section we summarise a range of applications of ICT to support pupils' learning when the pupil is the one actually using the equipment.

Word processing

With descriptive tasks, encouraging the pupils to use a word processing package has a benefit for both teacher and pupil. The presentation allows poorer students to produce work that you can read. The better students will usually extend the work for themselves. You can also include a specific vocabulary to cover literacy requirements within the subject areas. The huge advantage over asking the pupils to write it by hand is that it allows them to redraft their work without having to rewrite it. It also becomes feasible to ask pupils to redraft it yet again after responding to teacher comments. Pupils will always display misconceptions (some may be poetic licence) and the approach in Chapter 10 (Figure 10.1, pp. 74–5), using numbered star comments, allows pupils to produce, after redrafting, a 'perfect' story, which can be posted on the school's intranet. Another good tool to use is *Word Art*. In the materials topic with Year 7 you can get pupils to use the art to describe the word (Figure 24.1).

Spreadsheets and data capture

There are many different skills required to use spreadsheets effectively:

- data input;
- manipulating the keyboard;

FIGURE 24.1 Word Art used to illustrate a property of a material.

- using formulae;

- producing charts, pie charts and graphs;

- using graph drawing packages within spreadsheets to support the analysis of results from experiments.

There are a number of activities that can be chosen: calculation of speed and production of speed–time graphs; production of rates of reaction graphs for chemistry. The example given in Figure 24.2 was created by asking pupils to enter planetary data into a spreadsheet and then generate graphs showing the relationship between the order of distance of the planets from the sun (x axis) and their temperature, or time to orbit.

Getting to grips with graphs was the first publication from the AKSIS Project (**AS**E and **K**ing's College **S**cience **I**nvestigations in **S**chools). This book and compact disc pack aims to teach KS 2 and 3 pupils about graphs. Their research suggests that pupils do not pick up how to construct and use graphs properly, and we need to provide support before they meet them through investigations. The discs contain exercises for pupils, to enable them to overcome the major graph-drawing problems uncovered by the project; only then are pupils asked to apply what they have learnt in an investigation. Full details are on the ASE website (http://www.ase.org.uk). Mention has already been made in Chapter 11, pp. 83–5.

Of course if the data can be captured on a data-logger pupils can see a graph of their results directly. There are several commercial systems available and one of the best sources of ideas for practical work involving data capture is Roger Frost's website at http://www.rogerfrost.com.

Internet searches

This is an area fraught with problems. The lesson must have a clear structure and outcome or it can descend into 40 minutes of surfing time. Ensure that the pupils have a worksheet to complete and a maximum of three sites to visit. Patrolling the room to ensure that the toolbar contains only the pages identified is the main task for the teacher. Have a fall-back lesson ready in case the system crashes.

CD-ROMs

There are at least three ways in which CDs can be accessed in the class:

- The facility can be installed with a site licence and then placed in a CD tower so that the whole class can access it from the computer suite.

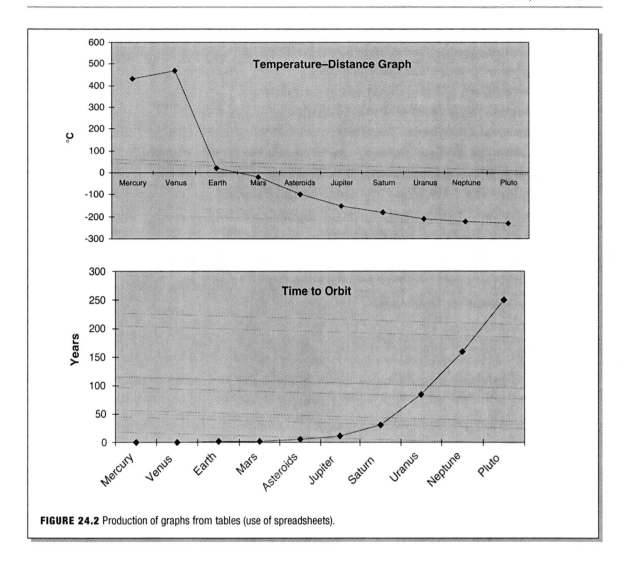

FIGURE 24.2 Production of graphs from tables (use of spreadsheets).

- It can be installed on one machine (for example, in the science lab) as one 'station' in a circus of activities.
- You can use a data projector, or big TV screen, to give a demonstration when only one CD is available, and all the class see it together.

A few CDs that are of specific value are listed here but the market is now huge and you need to keep your eyes open, especially for those where the learning theory is embedded into the CD design.

- Crocodile Clips. For the virtual electricity and mechanics lab and many more, visit http://www.crocodile-clips.com/index.htm
- RedShift 3. For work on the planets.
- Multimedia Science School is expensive but well reviewed. Visit the web site, http://www.scienceschool.com/

- The CD that is linked with this book (Ross *et al.* 2002) has a number of animations and models that are useful as a teacher demonstration or as an interactive activity. The following list gives an example of one from each section of the CD.

  Matter. Atoms animated during boiling and burning.

  Genetics. Protein synthesis transcription from messenger RNA.

  Atmosphere. Animation of cycling of sulphur atoms used by life and acid rain.

  Biodiversity. Predator–prey model and effect of camouflage on evolution.

  Energy. Using milk delivery in milk bottles to explain electric circuits.

  Radioactivity. Animation of how carbon 14 dating works.

  Agriculture. Step-by-step explanation of the cloning of Dolly.

  Health. Animation of the path of food from mouth to cells.

  Home. Interactive model of materials that enter and leave our homes.

  Transport. Balanced forces on a car travelling at speed.

  Visit www.glos.ac.uk/science-issues

The pitfalls

Even though there are many advantages in using ICT in our teaching we need to be aware of some of the pitfalls. Think about each in turn before reading our suggestions for overcoming some of them.

1 It can be counterproductive for teacher–pupil relationships if the task is too hard or too easy for the pupils.

2 There is a danger that because we use the IT packages infrequently, we are not as expert as we would like and are reluctant to expose a potential weakness to the pupils. This possibility increases as pupils move through the school and have more opportunity and time than the teacher to keep abreast of improvements and changes in IT.

3 Time can be wasted by pupils who are interested in decorating the title rather than completing the content.

4 Pupils may be tempted to play games in the 'background' while pretending to work.

5 The system may crash during lesson time.

6 It is difficult to monitor 30 demanding pupils with different problems all at once.

7 What do I do if there are only a few computers?

Overcoming the pitfalls above

Here are some strategies that may help to overcome some of the problem areas listed above.

- 1 and 2. Familiarise yourself with the task you wish to use and ensure it matches the pupils' abilities and the intended learning outcomes. Check with the IT staff that this group (and you!) are capable of using this package. Talk to other staff members about their approach.

- 3 and 4. Have a tight structure: either hand out a worksheet to follow with the tasks broken down into a 'recipe', or deliver a 'whole-class' lesson and give tight time limits for each part of the task.

- 5. Have a back-up plan in case the system crashes.

- 6. Identify the expected lesson outcome and ensure that all the pupils are aware of this at the outset. Keep it *simple*. Make sure that the task is straightforward.

- 7. If there are only a few computers you need to split your class into groups and 'book' all the machines you can, while putting pressure on the head of department to drive the school forward in the quest for improved ICT availability. Another way is to use them as single workstations in a circus of experiments. Bear in mind that more and more pupils will have computers at home, so make use of them.

Summary

Teachers are divided into two camps when ICT is in focus: those who are confident to include its use in lessons and those who are not. If you are prepared to accept that there will always be someone in the class who is more competent at IT than you are and use their expertise, then you can have good ICT lessons. The secret, as with all lessons, is good planning. You need to try out the resources well ahead of time, and provide structured activities for the pupils.

CHAPTER 25

Inclusion and science for all

The focus of this chapter is on the need for our science curriculum to cater for everyone. We begin with special educational needs (SEN) and the history of provision. We recognise the unique benefit science has to offer SEN and emphasise the importance of differentiation and equality of opportunity for all. The major role of assessment and recording, as a means of informing planning, is discussed. We then consider issues of race and gender. We conclude by considering the role an education in science has to play in promoting sustainable development in the world and recognise our role as teachers within this.

Science for all: SEN

> Pupils differ with respect to characteristics such as gender, ethnicity, class, the extent to which they have special needs, their preferred learning styles and other aspects of their personality and home culture. Not only do pupils differ in all sorts of ways, but you, their teacher, will have differing expectations of them from your previous knowledge of pupils. What is a science teacher to do with this diversity?
>
> (Reiss 1998: 34)

The 1988 Education Reform Act lays down that pupils, regardless of their differences, are entitled to receive a broad, balanced education and that teaching is differentiated according to their needs. Pupils have individual needs at different times during their schooling. The term special educational needs (SEN) refers to pupils who have been identified as requiring special support, which is initiated through a process called 'statementing'. SEN covers the entire spectrum, from children with severe learning difficulties and those with physical and behavioural difficulties to the gifted and exceptionally able child.

Unique benefits proffered by science education

Science education, by its nature, includes a range of characteristics:

- a practical approach, nurturing first-hand experiences;
- potential for group or collaborative work and peer support;
- conceptual development in sequential steps affording opportunities for success;
- development of understanding of the big ideas in science, i.e. those broad conceptual areas that allow for internal differentiation and individual progression.

Nicholls and Turner (1998: 107) support this view and list perceived benefits of science that assist pupils with learning difficulties, which are:

- the importance of first-hand experience;
- the links between science and everyday experience;
- knowledge and skills that can be acquired through practical activity;
- many skills that are acquired in small steps, e.g. investigations include many subskills that can be taught separately and successfully;
- activities and phenomena that capture the imagination of pupils, enhancing motivation.

As teachers, we need to recognise these benefits and incorporate them in our lesson plans.

Good practice for all

The National Curriculum Council Circular No. 5 (NCC 1989) stated that good practice in relation to special educational needs is good practice for all. The keystone to this good practice, and indeed the effective learning that accompanies it, is 'differentiation', the process by which activities are matched to the competencies and context of the pupil. Associated with this is effective assessment, used to diagnose areas of difficulty. Activities need to be devised to overcome them and an interactive record of achievement, based on social and personal achievements, developed.

Special needs can best be met when a general concern for individual differences is uppermost in teachers' thinking. This is all very well, but how can this be achieved with 9T, a mixed ability science set? The KS 3 strategy states that although setting varies across schools, most organise Year 9 pupils in ability sets for their science lessons. It goes on to explain that planning tends to be easier if the attainment spread in class is not too wide, but recognises that even in an ability set there is still a range of attainment.

The most fundamental approach to meeting the needs of all pupils within the class is to ensure that the learning environment is a safe, non-threatening place where pupils feel motivated, can concentrate and feel comfortable in contributing to the lesson. At times this is easier said than done. Expectation of all pupils should be high, but within their ability and accessibility range.

Effective differentiation

Differentiation is achieved by identifying the needs of individuals and developing opportunities to guide, encourage and support learning through whatever resources, processes and tactics are available. For this to be effective, the teacher must get to know the pupils as well as the knowledge, experiences and abilities they bring with them to their lessons. Good record keeping and regular marking of pupils' work achieve this. Armed with this information, discerning teachers can fulfil their role of encouraging independent learning. This learning-centred approach follows the constructivist view of teaching and learning, building on or challenging pupils' everyday experiences and the conceptual models of understanding that develop from them. This follows intervention by the teacher that takes account of the range of ideas from the class. There can be a shift of emphasis from whole-class to individual-based learning, as pupils are encouraged to challenge and discuss their own models against the models presented by the teacher.

Once we know the range of ideas and capabilities of the pupils in our class it is the effective use of differentiation that will ensure that all pupils are working at their best and on the most appropriate activity for them. Begin the lesson with a starter activity that will involve and interest the whole class. This can be adapted (differentiated) to meet the ability range of the pupils and, with careful preparation, can be accessible to all pupils. This may be achieved through independent, group or whole-class working, using a range of differentiation strategies (see below). These can then be deployed in a similar way during the intervention section of the lesson (Chapter 7).

Differentiation by task

Differentiated tasks, on a common theme, pitched at various levels of ability, are available around the room, with the pupils being directed to the relevant ones. This approach ensures that the pupils are working within their means.

Differentiation by outcome

Here the task will be the same, but we expect different pupils to achieve differently. Such tasks will have to be 'open-ended', such as creative writing or experimental design. Some will complete it fairly superficially, while others make a great deal of it.

Differentiation by support

If all the pupils have the same task, and are expected to complete the activity by the end of the lesson, some will need more support from the teacher than others. While we cannot spend all our classroom time helping a minority of pupils, this approach is effective and the more able (or willing) pupils are happy to be given the independence and responsibility to get on by themselves.

Such support can lead to adjustments that make the task or the outcome different. Pupils' responses will provide important information about the suitability of the task, allowing us to adjust the task at that point, making it more challenging for some, and more accessible to others.

Naylor and Keogh (1998) suggest a full range of activities that can be employed to differentiate appropriately, including:

- adjust the level of scientific skills used;
- introduce a range of learning styles such as using structured work cards, designing an investigation to explore pupils' own ideas, using a computer simulation or textbook for research;
- provide a range of suitable resources;
- adjust the levels of oral and written skills required;
- adjust the levels of mathematical skills required;
- vary the amount and nature of teacher and assistant support;
- vary the degree of pupil independence (investigations serve as a good vehicle for this);
- use suitable questions, prepared in advance;
- vary the response required;
- vary the pace and sequence of the lesson;
- vary the method of recording and presentation.

These strategies could be employed at any stage in the lesson, as well as being incorporated in your planning. Mention needs to be made here of your use of support staff: always ensure that they are involved in your planning and the production of any worksheets. However, in order to determine the effectiveness of your efforts, ongoing assessment needs to be carried out.

Putting ideas into practice

The KS 3 strategy gives a wealth of scenarios, expanding upon the strategies outlined above:

- differentiation in whole-class oral and mental work;
- differentiation in written work and homework;
- able pupils and those who are gifted and talented;
- pupils who make less than expected progress;
- pupils who need help with English, including English as an additional language learners.

Lists, such as those above, only come to life with actual examples. What, for example, are *suitable resources*? Many SEN pupils find the written word the biggest barrier to learning. Anything we can do to provide additional clues for them will be useful for the rest of the class too. We focus here on two ideas: three-dimensional objects and models, and the use of colour clues for words.

Objects and models

It is simple to bring into your class a box of cornflakes, a bicycle pump, a banana, a coffee filter, samples of building materials (plastic guttering, a brick etc.). Holding something up as we talk about it is simple, and makes such a difference to pupils who are trying to make sense of what we are saying.

How often do we draw sectional diagrams on the board, or from the OHP, and expect our pupils to understand what they mean? The eye is usually drawn with the optic nerve (with the associated blind spot) coming off to one side: how many realise that this is a top view? If we show a model of the eye before the sectional diagram, everything becomes much clearer. This is true for most biological (and chemical) diagrams, which are drawn two-dimensionally, but many pupils never succeed in realising the three-dimensional shape these diagrams represent. See Box 25.1.

For plant and animal cells, why not get the pupils to make a 3-D model? For a plant we need a transparent rectangular plastic box, which we fill with jelly in which we suspend green bits (chloroplasts) and a round bit (nucleus). When the cell is cut through, children can interpret the two-dimensional diagrams much more easily. The animal cell needs to be cast in jelly and tipped out onto a plate – no chloroplasts this time.

BOX 25.1 Making three-dimensional models of cells

The three-dimensional picture can also be brought to life through acting. We gave two examples in Chapter 8. Box 25.2 presents another idea.

When sound bounces off a distant wall we hear an echo. Many pupils think of this as being the same as the way a ball bounces, but with sound it is the energy that moves, not the material. Get ten pupils to line up side by side to represent molecules in the air. Someone at one end gives a push (remember safety: calm, gentle, with no fooling about), which is transferred down the line – sound is transmitted, but the air stays in one place. If the pupil at the other end is near a wall they can bounce back off the wall and the sound wave is transmitted back along the line – an echo.

BOX 25.2 Modelling an echo

Colour

We mentioned the use of atomic models to replace word equations at KS 3, especially in Chapter 12. If these model atoms are coloured (oxygen, red; hydrogen, white; carbon, black; nitrogen, blue), we can use the same colours to write the word and symbol equations. This gives pupils an enormously helpful clue: where words in black writing would be a blur of meaningless letters, the colours suddenly bring the whole thing to life. Diagrams can be labelled in colour too, so that the word and the part match. In their writing pupils can use the same colours in their text. This would be an example of a text-labelling DART (see Chapter 9).

Are all the pupils learning?

Well before the end of the lesson, a constructive plenary needs to be carried out. The purpose of this is twofold: to indicate the level of knowledge and understanding achieved by the pupils, i.e. the degree of learning attained; and to inform your planning for the next lesson. You will need to gain as much information as possible from the pupils; this could be achieved either orally (try the 'tell each other' strategy here – Chapter 8) or by group presentations.

Using the support teacher

Many pupils on statements will have support teachers assigned to them for some of their lessons, and this often happens in science. We need to plan carefully to make maximum use of them. It is a waste of their time if the lessons they come to are full of teacher-led intervention activities. If we know which lessons they are to attend we can plan to have the maximum amount of group work. When there is no support teacher we might want to mix up groups so that pupils can support each other, but when the support teacher is present it makes sense to put a group together so that all benefit from the additional personal adult attention. The activity can be made challenging, knowing that differentiation will be by support, full-time, for the whole lesson. Careful planning, and a meeting with the support teacher, are essential if we are to make full use of this valuable resource. It is unlikely that support teachers will have a strong science background, so we may have to provide them with brief background teacher notes, as well as explaining the activity we want them to do with their group. Although the support teacher will be assigned to one child or possibly to specific children in your class, it is wholly legitimate to include additional pupils who might benefit from the support – their presence may enhance the quality of the group discussions.

Science for all: race and gender issues

British society is a multicultural one, which is often reflected in our schools. Pupils bring with them differences in cultural understanding relating to gender, class and ethnicity. Being members of a multi-ethnic society, many of these pupils may have special needs and also bring with them unique experiences we can draw on in our teaching. Hoyle (1995: 227) states: 'All aspects of the culture and ethnicity of pupils need to be recognised, valued and used if all our young people are truly to benefit from and have equality of access to education.' When teaching we need to remember that racism remains a powerful force in our society, affecting pupils' attitudes and the way they learn. The National Curriculum 2000 reflects concern for this and encourages teachers to draw on multicultural ideas, beliefs and successes when teaching science. It states that pupils should be helped to:

recognise how scientific discoveries and ideas have affected the way people think, feel, create, behave and live, and draw attention to how cultural differences can influence the extent to which scientific ideas are accepted, used and valued.

(DfEE 1999: 8)

Children's views of how science works and is carried out affect both the way they learn science and their attitude to scientific knowledge. This being the case, it is important to elicit these views and images of what scientific work might be. Driver *et al.* (1996) worked with 11–14-year-olds exploring their ideas about how scientific knowledge is acquired. They identified a set of seven images of scientists, most embodying some notion of how scientists go about getting to know the world. These ranged from the stereotypical cartoon image of a 'white-coated, wispy-haired, bespectacled male doing something reckless with a giant chemistry set', via the 'vivisectionist', to the 'all-knowing' scientist as portrayed in television documentaries. They concluded that these ideas were a mixture of classroom experience and images gained from the wider community, but seldom from contact with a genuine scientist. The scientist as a *white male* dominated all these images.

Teaching and learning approaches

To ensure equality of access we need to recognise that, contrary to common belief, science is not objective and value-free (see Chapter 1), but shrouded in controversy and influenced by politics and economics. We need only to look to the current debate on genetically modified foods for support of this view. We need to appreciate the influence of culture on science, to understand society's reluctance to accept scientific and technological advances. The story of Darwin and evolutionary theory reiterates this point. The context in which scientific development takes place is as important as the science itself. Once again this is reinforced in the National Curriculum, which states that

> Science provides the opportunity to promote social development, through helping pupils recognise how the formation of opinion and the justification of decisions can be informed by experimental evidence, and drawing attention to how different interpretations of scientific evidence can be used in discussing social issues.

(DfEE 1999: 8)

Associated with this is the content through which the science is afforded to the pupils. Hoyle (1995) cites a useful list of general principles for science education, promoting equal opportunities. We illustrate this list of what teachers should do with examples of ideas to use in school.

Incorporate a global perspective in teaching

Many people in the Third World live by subsistence farming, growing what they need and relying purely on solar power for their cooking (firewood), transport and ploughing (human and animal muscle power). This is a sustainable way of life that we explore in Ross *et al.* (2002: energy). We are encouraging a move towards a more sustainable transport policy in the UK through greater use of human power (cycling and walking, for example, in the 'safer routes to schools' movement). We need to applaud all these solar technologies, not look at them as 'underdeveloped'. However, sustainable development means sharing the advantages of technological development with all of humanity. We need to build on sustainable practices from all over the world. See Chapter 3 for further discussion.

Understand issues relating to justice and equality

Much of the land in the Third World is used for cash crop agriculture, providing us with cheap coffee and tea, bananas and pineapples, beef and groundnuts. If these crops were produced in the UK we would not allow the workers to live in the conditions they do. The moral issue is more about the way we, the consumers, are being profligate with the world's resources than about the sustainable conditions under which these cash crop farmers live. We must not teach science in isolation of these issues.

Elaborate science in its social, political and economic context

This is clearly apparent in a discussion exercise comparing the use of chewing sticks and toothbrushes (Leicestershire LEA 1985). Chewing sticks are fully replenishable (unlike the plastic toothbrush and toothpaste). They are also equally effective in keeping teeth clean. Chewing sticks are readily available and are used here in Britain. We need to see them (and many other sustainable practices, such as cycling) as being beneficial to the world.

Make apparent the distribution of and access to power

Technological advances are very often linked to the multinationals. Many of these large companies are paying more than lip-service to the concept of sustainable development and to the welfare of their employees in the Third World. Many 'free' resources for science teachers are available from these companies. We need to ensure that we provide our pupils with a balanced worldview if we use such materials.

Incorporate a historical and global perspective

Two historical examples that support a global perspective include the story of Ibn al'Haitham, an Egyptian Islamic scholar (c.965–1038) who rejected the belief that light was emitted from the eye, taking the view that light was emitted from self-luminous sources and then entered the eye. The Islamic school was very active at this time in developing many scientific ideas, linked to experiments. The concept of an element as an indestructible part of material was grasped, as the extract in Box 25.3 suggests. Many of these Islamic ideas were translated into Greek or Latin and incorporated into the ideas of the Renaissance in Christian Europe, which looked back to the classical era for inspiration, but from which our modern understanding of science developed.

Mercury and sulphur unite to form one single product, but it is wrong to assume this product to be entirely new and that mercury and sulphur changed completely. The truth is that both kept their natural characteristics and that all that happened was that parts of the two materials interacted and mixed, in such a way that it became impossible to differentiate them with accuracy. If we were to separate . . . the tiniest parts of the two categories by some special instrument, it would have been clear that each element kept its own theoretical characteristics. The result is that the chemical combination between the elements occurs by permanent linking without change in their characteristics.

BOX 25.3 Extract from the writings of Jabir Ibn Hayyan (738–813 CE) from Butt (1991)

The second story is about the invention of blood banks. An Afro-American doctor, Charles Drew (1904–50), was responsible for the development and administration of the blood-bank programme used on battlefields during the Second World War. Drew was subject to racism all his life, and the cruel hand of fate wielded its final blow when he was seriously injured in a car accident. He was in need of a blood transfusion but (the story goes) the hospital he was admitted to would not treat him because he was black. He died before reaching a hospital that would. Material developed by Leicestershire LEA (1985) includes three accounts of Drew's life, each providing about a third of the details. These accounts can be given to three pupils (in a group), who then have to compile the full details of his tragic life story by filling in a sheet, with the rule that pupils cannot show their story sheet to one another: they have to do it by talking.

These accounts hold a wealth of material for use in creative writing. Being highly controversial, they lend themselves to debate and discussion; but perhaps of more immediate value, they bring home to pupils the reality of life and the true nature of science.

Celebrate everyone involved in developments in science

Rosalind Franklin's and Maurice Wilkin's role in elucidating the nature of DNA is a case in point. Francis and Crick received the Nobel Prize for their work in the project, but we tend to forget that many other people dedicated their lives to the cause, with little recognition. Issues of gender can often be addressed here, when we consider female scientists as well as male. Remember Marie Curie and her role in developing our understanding of nuclear processes. And Madame Lavoisier was an equal (if not greater) partner in her husband's work on the nature of air.

Start from and value the experiences and knowledge of pupils

Reiss (1998) explains the use of separating and purifying mixtures in terms of a pluralistic approach to teaching. He recounts seeing a very successful lesson in which much time was dedicated to exploring domestic devices for separating and purifying mixtures, brought in by a group of Year 8 pupils. He explains how the exercise could be developed into a detailed discussion of why people need to separate substances: for example, 'Why do people want pure salt?', 'Where, in everyday life, do we use the idea that iron can be separated from aluminium through the action of magnets?' or 'When is it a nuisance that mixtures separate out?' (salad dressings, paints etc.).

Use flexible teaching and learning strategies

Everything we have said about a constructivist approach to learning (Chapter 6), and the need to incorporate 'word work', applies here.

Integrate practical approaches as and when appropriate

The danger here, as always, is that we rely too much on the resources available in our school science laboratories. These are an essential part of our repertoire but should only be used to isolate and examine things that are too complex in pupils' everyday experiences. We must continue to point out the importance of using the everyday world of our pupils as our primary resource.

Summary

In this chapter we have identified the need to maximise pupils' independence in the learning environment, and in so doing to involve them more directly in their own learning. With this in mind, differentiation becomes something that is not just for the less able, but also a means of challenging the most able.

To achieve 'science for all' we need to know our pupils, and we need to recognise their special educational needs from whatever aspect they may arise. We need to be able to differentiate our teaching and their learning accordingly. This chapter has explored a range of strategies to ensure that this can be achieved, with effective teaching and learning as the outcome. These strategies can loosely be summarised as follows:

- including cross-curricular links in your teaching, especially to world cultures;
- working closely with the SEN coordinator, and possibly team teaching with other specialist staff;
- creating partnerships with home, the local community and other relevant organisations;
- using global issues, including environmental and world development.

We need to make science relevant to everyday life and to enhance sustainable development in a peaceful world.

Learning outside the classroom

Effective links between education and industry are a crucial bridge between the world of work and the world of education. The growth of such links in the UK has been a major success story. They add value and improve business competitiveness by raising the aspirations and skills of the individuals involved – a view increasingly shared by education, business and government. In this chapter we trace the history of such developments, tracking the successes but also visiting the low points. We identify effective strategies and focus on specific resources, exploring at the same time the possibility of bias. We conclude with a comprehensive guide to how to ensure effective education liaison, with the mechanics of taking pupils off-site being a key focus, and look to the future in a drive towards industrial development that is sustainable.

The early days

The Technical and Vocational Education Initiative (TVEI) of the 1980s was instigated by the government to get industry involved with education. Local education authorities set up bodies to drive the initiatives forward and were given funds to help schools to achieve their wishes. This coincided with the start of the IT revolution and most schools seized the opportunity to stock up on computing equipment as well as to set money aside to generate links with industry.

Most teachers treated industry with suspicion and questions were asked concerning hidden agendas and ulterior motives. Anyone working for a controversial industry was suspected of trying to use this initiative as a means of improving the image of their industry and imparting their beliefs to unsuspecting pupils. Many teachers, although very suspicious of the reasons behind industry's involvement, saw these links as a means of getting their hands on an open chequebook. A great deal of money was spent, and wasted, on trying to satisfy wish lists of the many initiatives that were around.

There was a need to clarify the situation and to blow away the chaff. TVEI coordinators, members of industry and government bodies started to put together criteria for effective links. Industry recognised the need for a member of staff to become the liaison link between industry and education. This led to a better identification of what industry could do to help, at the same time reducing wasted money.

What is it that industry wants from education?

Part of any effective working relationship is the recognition that both partners have a role to play. In order for them to play that role effectively it must be tuned to their needs. These needs have to be identified before they can be achieved. When asked what they felt school pupils would be expected to offer to industry, on applying for a job, our trainee teachers came up with the following list of attributes:

- an all-round education;
- basic skills of literacy and numeracy;
- communication and ICT skills;
- social and academic skills;
- commitment;
- good time management;
- good health.

This list illustrates something that all good education systems aim to achieve, but in reality industry was unhappy with the education system at that time, which was producing a future workforce that lacked even the basic literacy and communication skills and was weak in science and technology. Apprenticeships and Youth Training Schemes (YTS) responded by adding core skills to their training programmes, forming part of the early learning competencies, which now feature in the GNVQ (see Chapter 23). Pupil numbers taking science and engineering were seen to be dropping and the workforce in these areas was becoming scarce. At this stage British industry was still fairly strong, with the shift to high commercial profitability, including downsizing, yet to start.

For a number of years industry–education links became quite effective. Industrialists went into schools, teachers spent time in industry and a wealth of good educational resources was developed. However, this was not to last. Following government decisions to privatise much of the public sector, industry had to look seriously at what it was doing with the money. The perceived benefits to the company of improved public awareness and future recruitment began to pale into insignificance.

The term downsizing became commonplace – this sounds better than 'making people redundant'. Core business became the main focus of business activities. Profit and competition may have been good for industry but they had a devastating effect on education links. As the workforce diminishes the peripheral activities are scrutinised and, if not reduced, are done away with altogether, regardless of the long-term effects on both parties. Some industries are still involved, but probably not as much as they once were. Many industries no longer have a liaison staff member in a permanent position. Some industries carried out detailed exercises to assess the benefits to them of education links, and at the stroke of a pen saved thousands if not millions of pounds not only in money terms but in manpower resources.

For many years, government has expected industry to maintain strong links with local education institutions by the many ways that still exist and the new ways that are bound to come in the future. In the early days there was government money to help but all too often the processes were highly bureaucratic and wasteful.

For a more effective learning environment in the future, it will become increasingly important for links with industry to strengthen again. At its best it is one of the most successful means of bringing reality into the classroom. If a pupil can see and understand the reasons for learning a particular subject then the learning process becomes more effective.

What does education want from industry?

Our trainee teachers were asked to summarise their views on what education wants from industry. They said that it:

- enhances the curriculum;
- contributes to economic and industrial understanding;
- supports career awareness;
- provides financial support and 'gifts'.

The ideas presented are self-evidently laudable. Delivering the curriculum through 'real-life' examples and experiences underpins the National Curriculum 2000 Science Orders. The industrial perspective has much to offer regarding the application of science and technology. This has influenced curriculum development over the years and continues to do so (see Science for the 21st Century, discussed in Chapters 19 (p. 141) and 27 (pp. 208–9)), bringing a more holistic view of the world beyond the classroom. This in turn raises awareness of social and environmental issues among tomorrow's decision-makers and consumers, with the long-term aim of developing a sustainable lifestyle.

All these are commendable and realistic benefits, but how can they be achieved?

Strategies for links

When trainee teachers were asked to list a range of initiatives they had either experienced themselves or heard of, the outcome was quite impressive:

- work experience and work shadowing;
- talks at school by representatives from local firms;
- sponsorship;
- staff and curriculum development;
- representatives on school governing bodies;
- school visits to companies;
- Young Enterprise Schemes;
- mini research projects for post-16;
- industry days;
- careers advice;
- training;
- resources and 'freebies'.

In the sections that follow we deal with two aspects from this list: resources and research.

Resources

A myriad of resources has been produced by industry, business and other organisations. These resources have a chequered history. Organisations learnt the hard way and, at times, wasted millions of pounds. They saturated schools with literature that was collected by enthusiastic staff or sent unso-licited by mail but later assumed the role of doorstop or 'shelf support'; other resources have disappeared into the depths of the staff room never to see the light of day again. The problem was that they were neither pitched at an appropriate level for the pupils nor related to the schools' curriculum. Although well presented, usually in a glossy format, they lacked the important hallmark of teacher input. Organisations began to rethink their approach. They recognised the need for highly tuned, relevant resource material, produced by a suitable team of teachers. Several also appreciated the value of INSET sessions in terms of promoting and using the resource. Teachers were invited to attend a day or half-day session sponsored by the company concerned or possibly in association with the Local Education Business Partnership. This is an organisation established to create effective links between both worlds – it often contributes to supply cover, so is worth knowing about.

Most curriculum materials are now produced with the involvement of a dedicated team of teach-ers whose role is to assist in producing a meaningful context for teaching and learning. For example, British Energy has developed an elaborate power station location resource, called the *Energy Game*, which involves pupils in exploring the controversial issues associated with satisfying the ever-increasing demand for electrical energy. With several clearly defined objectives, the game introduces pupils to the generation of electrical energy and associated energy sources. Consideration has to be given to the environmental, social and economic impacts of generation from a variety of energy sources, while respecting the views of others. The plethora of information available requires pupils to practise and develop research skills as well as develop collaborative teamwork. On completion of their decision-making exercise, pupils present their findings to their peers.

Throughout the 'game' children develop personal abilities and attitudes, such as confidence, perseverance and initiative, which will need to be nurtured and enhanced to take them into other aspects of their learning.

Coping with values and bias in resources

Despite the advances in resource writing, one has to expect a certain amount of company bias coming through. After all, they have probably put thousands of pounds into the production of the material and will expect some recognition and spin-off. By being vigilant to this and observing the following guidelines, the resource can be used effectively:

- Realise that nobody is completely free of bias. We all need to recognise our own bias.
- Identify the aspects of the material that you consider most credible.
- Ask yourself which information looks most suspect. How could you check it?
- Consider what important information has been left out.
- Debate the perspective of the person(s) who wrote the resource.
- If possible, obtain similar information from a complementary organisation.

SATIS

A section on industrial links would not be complete without mention of the Science and Technology in Society (SATIS) material published by the ASE in the 1980s and reprinted in the late 1990s. The original series consisted of seven books, each containing ten units. The units were designed to be used in conjunction with conventional science courses, especially at KS 4. Each unit is self-contained and linked to the major science topics, as well as exploring important social and technological applications and issues. For example, SATIS 7 explores issues pertaining to electricity in the home, problems with gas supply, artificial limbs and biotechnology. Each unit has clearly defined aims, background information relating to the issues, suggested activities and further study. Although the early series is becoming outdated, the approach used and much of the information given are still relevant and well worth including in your lessons.

Pupil Research Initiative (PRI)

The PRI (www.shu.ac.uk/schools/sci/pri) was established in 1996/7 and has gained considerable momentum. Its main aims are to:

- raise pupil motivation and achievement in science;
- improve the teaching and learning of science, particularly investigative and ICT skills;
- increase the interaction between schools and the science and engineering research community.

PRI has developed three main areas through which these aims can be achieved:

- Production of curriculum materials and activities that are linked to the National Curriculum but adopt a research theme associated with the research councils involved in the initiative.
- Promotion of events to celebrate the science achievements of pupils in the form of regional school science fairs.
- Mobilisation of the science and engineering research community to support science education. A researcher in residence scheme has been established that places a PhD student in a school science department, working alongside the pupils, supporting investigative work. This scheme in particular has gained considerable interest.

Establishing links

In this chapter we have traced the history of industry education liaison in Britain. Nowadays, with greater emphasis on the application of science and technology, the need to reach out to the 'real world' for experience, advice and assistance is as important as ever. This whole approach is central to the new applied science GCSE and the vocational aspects of Science for the 21st Century, where such topics as brewing and baking feature heavily in the curriculum content. We must ensure, however, that the links we create are effective and productive. The following pointers should be considered before such links are established:

- identify your needs and those of the pupils;
- establish initial contact with the organisation in plenty of time;
- maintain one point of contact;
- ensure mutual familiarity with both environments, which will necessitate a preliminary visit on the part of one or the other;
- evaluate the exercise in terms of the original needs;
- give feedback to both parties;
- if the liaison worked, maintain a long-term link.

Important pivotal conferences for both industry and education are the national and regional meetings of the ASE and the Education Show. Industries that have produced materials for use in schools exhibit at the ASE Annual Meeting held in January of each year at a British university and at the annual Education Show held in March at the National Exhibition Centre in Birmingham.

Preparing for off-site visits

Any form of off-site visit or activity necessitates thorough planning, with special attention paid to health and safety issues. This can be time consuming but is vital to ensure that a safe, legal and educationally beneficial experience is obtained by all concerned. A general risk assessment will need to be carried out prior to the visit, with a more specific one being carried out once at the site. Companies will often have their own generic one to help you. Often preparation for the visit begins a year in advance, when the initial booking is made with the organisation concerned. This will coincide with the preliminary visit by a member of the teaching staff. A couple of months before the visit a letter will need to be sent to parents to gain permission for the pupils to attend. If the visit is residential details concerning special diets and any medical conditions will need to be identified. Money will be collected in at this time and you will need to be familiar with the 'voluntary contribution' system operated by most schools. A week or so before the visit a general meeting with the pupils will be necessary to inform them of final arrangements, special clothing and reiteration of aims and expectations. Most schools have a strategy informing parents about 'pick-up' arrangements if delays in travel occur. From your point of view, an up-to-date list of names and contact telephone numbers is vital – so too is a mobile phone. During the visit it is the responsibility of you and other members of staff to ensure the well-being of the pupils. Familiarise yourself with the legalities of this through the DfEE website and other organisations, such as the Youth Hostel Association and the Field Study Councils.

It is often the health and safety aspects, together with curriculum demands and potential behaviour problems, that put teachers off taking pupils out of school, yet the educational benefits have been demonstrated on numerous occasions. Careful planning and preparation go a long way to ensuring that this is the case.

Summary

This chapter has re-emphasised the need to relate learning in science to everyday life. Although young pupils are less familiar with industrial techniques, they need to know where their artefacts came from and how they were produced. They need to question the sustainability, in global terms, of the continuity of supply of our consumer goods and recognise the impact this is having on the global scene. Links with industry are therefore essential for the next generation to move towards a more sustainable future. If this liaison is carried out in a safe and well planned manner, it can make a significant contribution to the whole education of the pupil.

CHAPTER

27

Becoming a professional teacher

This chapter re-examines the nature of science and the picture children have of science and scientists. We review the historical events that allowed science to become a compulsory part of the National Curriculum. We look at the reasons why it should remain so by placing emphasis on the public understanding and social responsibility of science. We will see the important part science teachers have played over the past 150 years, either on their own or through what became the Association for Science Education, in enabling science to reach the place it has in the National Curriculum. We then look ahead to developments we would like to see.

What is science?

Our opening chapter constructed a model of how science worked (Figure 1.1a and b) and made the important distinction between technology and science. It was possible for early humans to develop stone tools, wooden spears, clay pots and thatch that didn't leak, without understanding the science behind these technologies. However, ideas would be forming in their minds that enabled them to see the potential of stone, wood, clay and straw for their new purposes. These ideas would be strengthened through the successful use of the technology, and in turn provide inspiration regarding how to make improvements.

Thus, from humanity's earliest beginnings, the ideas of science and the products of technology have developed side by side. When we began to try to make sense of the heavenly bodies, to explain the annual cycles and to tell stories of our origins, the ideas took on an independent existence – a cultural value. However, the ideas, to be classified as scientific, must be able to be tested using our senses, and that distinguishes the creativity of science from that of art and of myth. We established that science does not progress by *induction* to find *laws*, as Francis Bacon in the sixteenth century and many scientists through to the twentieth century thought. Science deals not with the search for absolute truth but with the creation of models in our minds that attempt to make sense of our world.

Popper's conjectures and refutations

The *two conceptions* view of science by Karl Popper (1959) gives a more realistic picture. Stimulated by things we notice, we have an *idea* about what might be going on: Popper's *conjectures*. This must be followed by careful, controlled testing, where we check if the idea works, or attempt to prove ourselves wrong: Popper's *refutations*. This logical process of *falsification* was important to Popper, who wanted to distinguish science from the pseudo-science of political or economic ideas. For every scientific idea, there had to be a way in which it could be disproved or falsified. If it stood up to this test we would be able to use it more widely, and it would become part of our scientific understanding (though it might fail at any later time). In our current science National Curriculum Sci1, scientific enquiry, features these two parts of science: ideas and evidence, the creative side; and investigations, the logical side.

Kuhn's normal and revolutionary science

Scientists, however, do not spend their time falsifying their own hypotheses. On the contrary, they try to persuade others to believe in them and to use them to interpret and predict outcomes of their experiments. Thomas Kuhn's concepts of *normal* and *revolutionary* science are a more realistic view of what really happens (Kuhn 1970). *Normally* scientists work within a particular set of scientific ideas (which Kuhn called a *paradigm*). Over time anomalies build up, and questions remain unanswered – it takes more than one unexplained result (refutation) to make the scientists change their minds. For example, Newton remained an alchemist all his life, despite a number of important chemical results that were obtained by his seventeenth-century contemporaries that began to show that transmutation of elements was impossible. Eventually there has to be a *revolution*, and the new ideas displace the old.

Read this commentary about whether fuels contain energy, then answer the question below.

Everyone knows that we use fuels as a source of energy – for our bodies and for driving our technology. In Chapter 12, however, we suggested that this energy is not *in* the food or fuels. We explained that those textbooks and cereal packets (just about all of them) that say food *contains* energy that is transferred when they are used are wrong. We argued, instead, that energy is stored in the *fuel–oxygen system*. Methane contains no energy, coal contains no energy and, except for the tiny anaerobic energy transfer when glucose rearranges its bonds during anaerobic respiration, there is no fuel-energy in glucose either.

Children who have not been exposed to the idea that energy from combustion is stored *in* the fuels find it easy to see the *fuel–oxygen system* as a store of energy. It makes understanding photosynthesis and trophic levels much more straightforward. It allows them to keep a separate account of *energy* (stored in stretched or broken bonds, released when strong bonds are remade) and of *matter* (atoms bond in different ways, but are never lost or made).

Science teachers and graduates, steeped in years of 'knowing' that fuels 'contain' energy, find it very hard to see systems in this way. Many refuse to change their minds, preferring the old, comfortable, accepted paradigm.

This puts forward a 'revolutionary' view about 'energy in fuels/food'. Having now read and thought about an explanation involving fuel–oxygen systems:

- Do you reject our view?
- Do you accept it, but think it too difficult to use with your pupils?
- Or do you acknowledge a paradigm shift (or already accept this view) and intend to (or do) share it with your pupils?

BOX 27.1 Modern day paradigm shifts?

Revolutions are difficult to effect

Chinn and Brewer (1998) studied learners' responses to anomalous data (i.e. data that conflict with their existing ideas). They asked students to read an account of one of two alternative theories for a particular phenomenon (for example, why the dinosaurs died out). They then presented the students with data that conflicted with the original biased views. They found that the students were more likely to hold on to their original beliefs than to modify their ideas and adopt the alternative theory – it was the theory they heard first that they held on to. In science teaching, the naive theory held by the student can be shown to be incorrect through presented evidence. Nevertheless, we must be wary of assuming that simple cognitive conflict is all that is required to effect conceptual change in students. Box 27.1 provides a modern example of how difficult it is to revolutionise our scientific beliefs.

Paradigm shifts are inconvenient: they turn your world over and they force you to rethink your world. Many science teachers are happy to take the middle way of Box 27.1. 'I've always said there is energy in food, and it makes it easier for my pupils.'

Children's ideas about science and scientists

We may be happy to accept this view of how science works, and the model in Chapter 1 may be helpful to us as science teachers in trying to share this view with children. However, children come to our science lessons with their views about science and scientists already partially formed. Many have a vision of 'white men in white coats', often bearded and bespectacled (see also p. 191). These scientists, in the eyes of children, undertake experiments and observation, which then lead to the 'discovery' of theories. But why should scientists bother to do experiments if they already 'know' what is going to happen? Driver *et al.* (1996) show that it is not until the GCSE years that pupils begin to see science in ways other than this 'discovery' view. How can we, as science teachers, show children that the discovery comes *before* the experiment? You need a *guess* in order to set up the *check*.

The social and cultural contexts of science

It would be hard to ask for science to be a compulsory part of our National Curriculum if it was only as we describe above. Then it could only be justified as a useful study for those making a career in science or technology and as having some cultural value for those with a love of learning. However, science, through technology, has a huge impact on society, which has grown apace ever since the industrial and technological revolutions got under way. We have now reached a situation where our technology is causing global environmental change at an unsustainable rate; people need to understand science to enable them to play their part in democratic life. We return to this theme at the end of the chapter, but a bit of history comes first.

How did science become a part of the National Curriculum?

By the start of the nineteenth century in England there were schools for the wealthy and universities at Oxford and Cambridge (Scotland had three well established universities as well) but little teaching of science. Developments in science itself had taken place mainly through amateur efforts of the leisured classes since the Renaissance. Cambridge began awarding science degrees in the 1850s and before that students were able to study natural philosophy as part of their ordination degree. The Victorian era saw the foundation of new universities in London and Durham, and 'red-brick' cities such as Birmingham and Manchester. Elementary schools for the working classes were set up by the churches, with the government providing grant aid. It was then that two clergymen, Richard Dawes and John Henslow, inspired by scientific philosophy at Cambridge, started the teaching of science in their respective parish schools. In two rather different ways they laid the foundations for the appearance of science in our schools today.

Dawes's object lessons in elementary schools

Richard Dawes moved to his parish, near Winchester, in 1836, and built a model school (Layton 1973). Although the well-to-do paid more, once inside the school instruction took no account of social standing or fees paid. But the comprehensive ideal was not complete: girls had to do needlework, while the boys studied science. Science lessons were *object lessons*: pupils could observe for themselves the objects of common daily life to inspire them with an intelligent curiosity (see Figure 27.1).

The Kettle: an object lesson

An old kettle, blackened at the bottom to absorb the radiation from the fire, and shiny on top to prevent radiation loss, has a metal body for good conduction of heat to the water and a handle made of poorly conducting wood to prevent you burning your hand.

FIGURE 27.1 An idea taken from *Victorians at School* (Ironbridge Gorge Museum Trust, undated).

Dawes's *Suggestive Hints towards Improved Secular Instruction*, published in 1847, provided teachers countrywide with a common-sense explanation of things used in everyday life. The newly formed government education department agreed to pay of the cost of the apparatus list published in *Hints* for any school qualified to use it. Helped by the Government Inspector of Education, Dawes's ideas spread, so that by 1857 about 8 per cent of elementary schools (3500 total) had the apparatus sets at about £20 each, supported by the government grant, and the newly formed teacher training colleges were including his ideas in their curriculum.

By 1861 it all came to an end. The grant stopped, science was taken out of the teacher training curriculum and the revised code – payment by results – meant that schools and teachers were judged by their results in the three Rs. Schools resorted to rote learning and cramming pupils for the tests. Dawes's ideas were largely forgotten by 1870, when legislation for universal primary education was enacted.

Science as process: Henslow's systematic botany

As a child, Henslow had a keen interest in natural history, which he pursued at Cambridge. When he moved to his parish in Hitcham in 1837 he continued his summer botany lecturing duties at

Cambridge. His parish school opened in 1841 and there he developed his idea of using botany as a way of training the mind. In 1852 he started his 'systematic botany' lessons, involving the classification of plants on the basis of their structure. Pupils were trained in observation and rational thought. Henslow's approach to science education emphasised the scientific method rather than the subject matter: the process rather than the content. Unlike Dawes's, his ideas did not spread in elementary schools but were taken up instead by the public schools (fee-paying and 13–18 age range), where they were safe from the ravages of 'payment by results' (Layton 1973). A direct link can be made between Henslow's emphasis on scientific processes and the Nuffield Science revolution of the 1960s, where the emphasis was on science as a process of induction of laws, but with some recognition of conflicting theories through the art of hypothesising.

Factual science teaching

Apart from a few schools using Henslow's ideas, mainstream secondary science in the first half of the twentieth century became very content based, with lots of rote learning of laws and facts. Science teaching in school was geared to passing the university entrance examinations which developed into the School Certificate and more recently O- and A-levels.

The Nuffield Science movement in the 1960s was a direct challenge to this factual approach to science teaching, reviving Henslow's ideas from a century earlier. Pupils were to become 'scientists for a day', and the tedious learning of facts for exams was to be replaced by opportunities to do practical investigations and to think about the process of being scientific. The 1970s saw the rise of *process science*, especially in the primary school, where some teachers were beginning to extend nature study into something broader. Secondary science projects followed (e.g. *Warwick Process Science* and *Science in Process* from the former Inner London Education Authority). If the old method overemphasised facts, this 'new' approach overemphasised process, and it was the wrong process too.

Research scientists acquire a scientific understanding of their world through their own inspiration, but we cannot expect children to have similar inspirations. Pupils' existing ideas remained unchallenged by these new process-based courses, and scientifically accepted ideas were not overtly being taught. Pupils were expected to 'discover' things for themselves by doing experiments. Few ever did, and teachers took to telling the pupils what they were supposed to have 'discovered'. We must not, however, lessen the importance of these early attempts to bring the nature of the scientific process into the school curriculum. The final section in this historical review brings us to the present, and to the teaching model we developed in Chapter 6: the constructivist approach.

An entitlement to science for all

We accept the double award science at GCSE, and its equivalent triple science, as the statutory right of almost all pupils in England and Wales, but it was not always so. Initiatives came mostly from science teachers themselves, through their professional association. The Association for Science Education (ASE) began life as the Association of Public School Science Masters in 1911. It was quickly joined by the women's association and they both took in teachers from the state schools to become the 'Association of Women Science Teachers' and the 'Science Masters' Association'. The ASE was formed in the 1960s when the men's and women's associations joined. The *School Science Review*, which began in 1919, was a joint publication almost from the start. Several policy statements for school science (1916, 1936, 1943, 1957 and 1961) were jointly published. The policy on general science (1936) was the first to campaign for broad balanced science. Originally Nuffield Science was to be integrated, but we had to wait for the Schools Council Integrated Science Project before broad balanced science for O-level pupils was available. Nuffield Combined Science (for ages 11–13) and Nuffield Secondary Science (for the CSE pupils who were now legally required to remain at school until aged 16) provided a broad approach for the rest.

The development of the National Curriculum (1987) was heralded by the Assessment of Performance Unit (APU) project. The APU conducted tests nationally during the early 1980s, but only with a sample of pupils in a sample of schools, allowing them to look at how standards vary with type of school and location, and over time. This prevented the identification of individual schools or teachers, which might have upset the cooperation that existed between them.

The first APU science tests were in 1980, and defined science into five process categories covering aspects of being scientific and only one concept category (testing children's understanding of scientific ideas). *Brenda and Friends* (West 1984; reviewed in Ross 1998) is a very exciting document that sketches out a *minimum entitlement* in science for every child in the form of a series of stories. Each curriculum topic has a different child, 16 in all. See Box 27.2 for an extract from Abdul as he looks back on his school science experience of particles and the nature of science.

Abdul: particulate nature of matter

His new science teacher understood Abdul's problem with particles and to his amazement he discovered that she had had difficulty with particulate theory too. She explained that scientists couldn't see particles . . . but accepted particulate explanations because of their usefulness, and because they are not disproved by any of their observations . . . Because Abdul's teacher appreciated his ideas she was able to set him a number of experiments to do to check out his thinking. He carefully observed two gases – one coloured – mixing together . . .

BOX 27.2 Extract from *Brenda and Friends* (West 1984)

The government policy statement for science, *Science 5–16: a Statement of Policy*, in 1985, was the first in which science was recommended, as official government policy, to be a part of everyone's school experience. It also recommended that all branches of science be studied from five to 16. No longer were we to have physicists with no biology, and biologists with no physics.

Rosalind Driver (who died in 1997 shortly after becoming Professor of Science Education at King's – a great loss to the profession) directed one of the APU teams from Leeds. It was from an analysis of scientifically incorrect answers to the concept category questions that the Children's Learning in Science (CLIS) project was born, and we began to see how strongly held children's naive ideas were. Many of the questions we use today to probe children's ideas trace their origin to the APU questions (see, for example, *tub-tree* in Figure 14.1, p. 11). Projects researching children's ideas sprang up worldwide, led by work in New Zealand (Osborne and Freyburg 1985). Since then much work on primary pupils' concepts has been done, resulting in the Science Process and Concept Evaluation project (Watt and Russell 1990) and the Nuffield Primary Science materials (1993). The constructivist approach to learning, which we emphasise in this book, became influential as a result of this work.

The Science National Curriculum for England (and Wales)

The National Curriculum had four dimensions on first publication in 1990 (process, concepts, communication and context). *Process* became Attainment Target 1 (AT 1), with an emphasis on observation and systematic testing, *concepts* became ATs 2–16 (and now AT 2, 3 and 4), *communication* 'went across the curriculum' and *context* went originally into AT 17, which was called 'The nature of science'. The three *concept* attainment targets we now have (Sc2 biology, Sc3 chemistry and Sc4 physics) are similar to the original draft for the concepts, which were then deliberately split to provide a more topic-based integrated approach. In the current version (DfEE 1999) the nature of science (the old AT 17) has been brought into the programme of study 'Scientific enquiry', enabling it to be assessed in AT 1. Hull (1995) provides a fascinating review of this turbulent history of science in the National Curriculum.

The public understanding of science

Our science schemes of work tend to follow the sequence of ideas from a scientist's perspective. This suggests that to understand, for example, photosynthesis properly we must first introduce cells, gaseous diffusion, transpiration, the nature of carbon dioxide, chlorophyll and so on. This may not be the best way from a child's point of view. This book has argued that we need to start from the pupils' own ideas, and begin by suggesting that plants grow by using materials not only from soil but also from the air and that this growth is fuelled by energy from sunlight. This overarching picture can be refined as necessary. If we are to produce a public that understands science we need them first of all to be able to say 'green plants obtain carbon, their stuff of life, from the air'. Without this basic idea about how life works and how carbon is cycled, many environmental issues, such as greenhouse gas emission, make little sense.

We need to ask what science will remain with our pupils once they leave school. Will everything be forgotten as they trade in their knowledge for a GCSE certificate (as we showed in Figure 7.2, p. 57)? Or will they, instead, retain usable knowledge of how the world works, enabling them to understand some of the pressures we are placing on ourselves and the environment? A national curriculum written in unrelated topics is helpful if you teach it in that way, and it does provide a sort of checklist. However, when we build our schemes of work, the statements of minimum entitlement in *Brenda and Friends* (see Box 27.2) are far more useful in enabling us to relate the topics to the everyday lives of our pupils.

Justification for the inclusion of science into the school curriculum

Some topics in our science curriculum owe their presence more to accidents of history than to anything else, though we could justify any part of our existing curriculum from a *cultural* point of view. If the ideas form part of our scientific heritage, humanity as a whole has a right to share this knowledge. We can justify including the cultural achievements of humanity from other disciplines of knowledge on the same basis: there is little distinction between studying the evolution of humans two million years ago (studied in science) and studying the rise of the Maya civilisation in Central America 2000 years ago (studied in history). Similarly, the second law of thermodynamics and atomic theory are just as much creations of human inspirations as the plays of Shakespeare and the music of Mozart, and children should be aware of these achievements.

There are, however, more immediate reasons to teach science, which 21st Century Science, discussed below, has grasped. Perhaps the most basic is that it has a *utility* value. If you understand the science behind everyday activities, you are more likely to undertake them safely. Once we understand the germ theory of disease, we are happy to follow basic hygiene rules, such as washing hands before eating, cleaning a cut and storing cooked and raw meat separately. If they are followed only as rules, without the science, they are much less likely to be followed sensibly or at all.

Between these two extremes is what some have called the *democratic* justification for teaching science (Ratcliffe 1998). Some big ideas in science have no controllable effect on our lives. The idea of stars as element factories, for instance, is fascinating, and we are dominated by our nearest star, the sun, but there is nothing we can do about it, except to enjoy the knowledge – a cultural pursuit. However there are some ideas that we need to understand if our lives on Planet Earth are to be sustainable. Decisions are being made that affect our lives, and we need to understand the science to help to make choices ourselves.

At the Rio Earth Summit in 1992 a common agenda for the twenty-first century, 'Agenda 21', was agreed to by 179 governments (Lakin 2000). One commitment was to reduce carbon dioxide emissions. This can only be achieved by burning less fossil fuel, meaning that less 'useful' energy will be available. Either we make do with less or we develop ways to make our current processes more efficient. In a democratic state it is important that the public understands the reasons behind new legislation. We need to realise that the materials we have access to have to be cycled, just as materials are cycled in natural systems. We cannot continue to mine raw materials and dump them on land, in water and into the air, because the raw materials will become depleted, and the dumps will cause pollution. They also need to understand that this cycling needs to be fuelled. Natural systems rely mostly on sunlight, which drives both life and climate, but we have escaped from this reliance on solar power through our use of fossil fuels.

Many have said that the study of science is too difficult for this democratic justification to be valid. They claim that a little learning – for example, about genetic engineering or nuclear power – simply makes people frightened. A number of questions spring to mind:

- Since not even the scientists can ever understand fully, why do we bother at all with the general public?
- How can the public ever hope to understand 'enough' of these conceptual areas to help them to make democratic decisions?
- In any case, is such an understanding really necessary before any real action on environmental issues can be taken by a democratic society?
- Since the scientists cannot agree, why should the general public bother?

We must not fall into the trap that says that science is too difficult to understand, so the public has to rely on 'experts'. In this case the public has no choice but to build up emotional responses to issues. The science can be obscure, full of difficult words and complications, but it doesn't have to be that way. Everyone can obtain a sufficient scientific understanding to make judgements on what the 'experts' say, as long as we teach science in the meaningful context of real issues, and begin from the ideas that the learners bring with them. A population ignorant of science will have a majority who don't care about the environment, and a minority whose only weapon is emotion, and who are dismissed by the majority as eco-freaks. A population that is ignorant about the nature of the scientific process will not appreciate the need for argument to continue among 'experts'. Science can only give us a 'best guess' and other considerations, e.g. moral philosophy, have their part to play – but we ignore the science at our peril. It is for this reason that the development of 21st Century Science is so exciting.

21st Century Science: science for scientific literacy

Traditional GCSE qualifications are based largely on the needs of those who are to go on to A-level and undergraduate science courses, but we need a science curriculum that offers greater flexibility and genuine choice to cope with the diversity of students' interests and aspirations. Only a minority become professional scientists. But all of us, as citizens, need to be able to cope with the science that shapes our lives. We are on the receiving end of scientific ideas and technical information in many different roles, such as householder, parent, patient, voter or juror. The development of 21st Century Science redresses the balance. This programme, being trialled during 2003–5, offers three different GSCE science courses for different purposes. We mentioned the course in Chapter 19, but provide more details here. The descriptions here are taken from the 21st Century Science web site: http://www.21stcenturyscience.org/home/.

Everyone studies the core science course, which leads to one GCSE grade. Central to the core science course is an understanding of the major science explanations and of the key ideas about science. These are the things that we want students to take with them from the course and 'carry with them' into their adult lives. All young people, whatever their future, need a science education to prepare them to make sense of science, while appreciating what science has to say about themselves, their environment and the universe. 21st Century Science features many of the major theories of science presented in a way that will encourage young people to appreciate their significance. Students will explore the key science explanations which help us to make sense of our lives.

However, in order to respond to scientific information presented in the media and everyday situations, it is important to understand how this information is obtained, how reliable it is, what its limitations are and how it is used. The core course also explores these aspects of science so as to prepare young people to deal with issues such as childhood vaccinations, GM food scares and mobile phone safety as they arise.

Of course, some young people aspire to be scientists or to work in fields where a knowledge of science is essential. Educating the next generation of scientific practitioners is also crucial, so we need both science for citizens and science for scientists. Along with the core, students can study a choice of one of two additional science courses:

- Additional science (applied), when taken together with core science, will provide a sound basis for progressing to a range of technical, pre-vocational and vocational courses involving science.
- Additional science (general), when taken together with core science, will prepare students for progression to study AS- and A-levels in the sciences.

This pilot course does not comply with the current National Curriculum for England and Wales (DfEE 1999) for KS 4, so changes will be needed if it is to be adopted nationally.

Summary

In this final chapter, as in the book as a whole, we have examined the nature of science, how it has become a part of our curriculum and why it should stay there. From these insights comes the imperative to teach by starting with the learners' existing ideas, and setting the teaching in an everyday context. To be a professional science teacher requires that you have high expectations of all pupils. These high expectations are necessary if our pupils are to be able to leave school with a scientific understanding of their world that enables them to work for a sustainable future.

References

ASE (2001) *Topics in Safety*, 3rd edn. Hatfield: ASE.

Ausubel, D. P., Novak, J. D. and Hanesian, H. (1978) *Educational Psychology: A Cognitive View*, 2nd edn. New York: Holt Rinehart and Winston.

Borrows, P. (1998) Safety in science education, in M. Ratcliffe (ed.), *ASE Guide to Secondary Science Education*. Hatfield: ASE.

Butt, N. (1991) *Science and Muslim Societies*. London: Grey Seal.

Callaghan, P. (1997) Staying alive – a circulation game, *School Science Review*, **78**(285), 100–1.

Chin, C. (2003) Students' approaches to learning science: responding to learners' needs, *School Science Review*, **85**(310), 97–105.

Chinn, C. A. and Brewer, W. F. (1998) An empirical test of a taxonomy of responses to anomalous data in science, *Journal of Research in Science Teaching*, **35**, 623–54.

CLEAPSS (1997) *Laboratory Handbook*. Uxbridge: CLEAPSS School Service.

Davies, F. and Greene, T. (1984) *Reading for Learning in the Sciences*. London: Oliver and Boyd.

Denby, D. (2003) Using modern technologies in 14–19 science, *School Science Review*, **85**(310), 41–6.

DfEE (1996) *Safety in Science Education*. London: HMSO.

DfEE (1999) *The National Curriculum for England*. London: HMSO.

DfES (2002) *Qualifying to Teach*. London: DfES.

DfES (2003) *Key Messages: Pedagogy and Practice*. Key Stage 3 National Strategy. London: DfES.

Driver, R., Leach, J., Millar, R. and Scott, P. (1996) *Young People's Images of Science*. Buckingham: Open University Press.

Driver, R. (1983) *The Pupil as a Scientist*. Milton Keynes: Open University Press.

Driver, R., Guesne, E. and Tiberghien, A. (eds) (1985) *Children's Ideas in Science*. Milton Keynes: Open University Press.

Driver, R., Squires, A., Rushworth, P. and Wood-Robinson, V. (1994) *Making Sense of Secondary Science: Research into Children's Ideas*. London: Routledge.

Frost, R. (1999) *Data Logging in Practice*. London: IT in Science.

Gadd, K. (2000) Post-16 notes, *Education in Science*, **187**, 23.

Gilbert, J. K., Watts, D. M. and Osborne, R. J. (1985) Eliciting student views using an interview-about-instances technique, in L.H.T. West and A.L. Pines (eds), *Cognitive Structure and Conceptual Change*. Orlando, FL: Academic Press.

Goldsworthy, A. and Feasey, R. (1999) *Making Sense of Primary Science Investigations*, 2nd edn. Hatfield: ASE.

Goldsworthy, A., Watson, R. and Wood-Robinson, V. (1999) *Getting to Grips with Graphs: From Bar Charts to Lines of Best Fit*. Hatfield: ASE.

Guesne, E. (1985) Light, in R. Driver, E. Guesne and A. Tiberghien (eds), *Children's Ideas in Science*. Milton Keynes: Open University Press.

Gunstone, R. and Watts, M. (1985) Force and motion, in R. Driver, E. Guesne and A. Tiberghien (eds), *Children's Ideas in Science*, Milton Keynes: Open University Press.

Holding, B. (1987) Investigation of schoolchildren's understanding of the process of dissolving with special reference to the conservation of matter and the development of atomistic ideas, Unpublished PhD thesis, University of Leeds School of Education.

Hoyle, P. (1995) Race equality and science teaching, in R. Hull (ed.), *ASE Science Teachers' Handbook*. Cheltenham: Stanley Thornes.

HSE (1997) *Health and Safety Executive 1996/7*. London: HSE.

Hull, R. (ed.) (1995) *ASE Science Teachers' Handbook*. Cheltenham: Stanley Thornes.

Hunt, A. and Millar, R. (2000) *AS Science for Public Understanding*. Oxford: Heinemann.

Keogh, B. and Naylor, S. (1996) *Thinking about Science* (set of posters). Sandbach: Milgate House Publishers.

Kerr, D., Lines, A., Blenkinsop, S. and Schagen, I. (2001) *Citizenship and Education at Age 14: A Summary of the International Findings and Preliminary Results for England*. Windsor: NFER.

Kuhn, T. S. (1970) *The Structure of Scientific Revolutions*, 2nd edn. London: University of Chicago Press.

Lakin, E. (2000) Stardust, takeover bids and biodiversity, in M. Littledyke, K. A. Ross and E. Lakin (eds), *Science Knowledge and the Environment*. London: David Fulton Publishers.

Layton, D. (1973) *Science for the People*. London: George Allen & Unwin.

Leicestershire LEA (1985) *Science Education for a Multicultural Society*. Leicester: Leicestershire Education Authority.

Littledyke, M. (1998) Constructivist ideas about learning, in M. Littledyke and L. Huxford (eds), *Teaching the Primary Curriculum for Constructive Learning*. London: David Fulton.

MacKay, D. (2003) Forthcoming changes to the 14–19 science curriculum, *School Science Review*, **85**(310), 65–8.

Medawar, P. B. (1969) Two conceptions of science, in *The Art of the Soluble*. London: Penguin Books.

Millar, R. (1996) Towards a science curriculum for public understanding, *School Science Review*, **77**(280), 7–18.

Millar, R. and Osborne, J. (eds) (1998) *Beyond 2000*. London: King's College.

Naylor, S. and Keogh, B. (1998) Differentiation, in M. Ratcliffe (ed.) *ASE Guide to Secondary Science Education*. Cheltenham: Stanley Thornes.

NCC (1989) *Circular No. 5: Implementing the National Curriculum. Participation by Pupils with Special Educational Needs*. London: NCC.

Newell, A. and Ross, K. (1996) Children's conception of thermal conduction – or the story of a woollen hat, *School Science Review*, **78**(282), 33–8.

Newton, L. R. and Rogers, L. (2001) *Teaching Science with ICT*. London: Continuum.

Nicholls, J. and Turner, T. (1998) Differentiation and special educational needs, in T. Turner and W. Dimarco (eds), *Learning to Teach Science in the Secondary School*. London: Routledge.

Nuffield Primary Science (1993) *Nuffield Primary Science: Science Processes and Concept Exploration (SPACE)*. London: Collins Educational.

Nussbaum, J. (1985) The Earth as a cosmic body, in R. Driver, E. Guesne and A. Tiberghien (eds), *Children's Ideas in Science*. Milton Keynes: Open University Press.

Osborne, R. and Freyberg, P. (1985) *Learning in Science*. Oxford: Heinemann.

Osbourne, J. and Ratcliffe, M. (2002) Developing effective methods of assessing ideas and evidence, *School Science Review*, **83**(305), 113.

Piaget, J. (1929) *The Child's Conception of the World*. London: Routledge & Kegan Paul.

Popper, K. R. (1959) *The Logic of Scientific Discovery*. London: Hutchinson.

Postlethwaite, K. (1993) *Differentiated Science Teaching: Responding to Individual Differences and to Special Educational Needs*. Milton Keynes: Open University Press.

QCA (2001) *Citizenship: A Scheme of Work for Key Stage 3*. London: QCA.

Ratcliffe, M. (1998) The purposes of science education, in M. Ratcliffe (ed.), *ASE Guide to Secondary Science Education*. Cheltenham: Stanley Thornes.

Reiss, M. J. (1998) Science for all, in M. Ratcliffe (ed.), *ASE Guide to Secondary Science Education*. Cheltenham: Stanley Thornes.

Ross, K. A. (1989) A cross-cultural study of people's understanding of the functioning of fuels and burning, Unpublished PhD thesis, University of Bristol.

Ross, K. A. (ed.) (1990) Can children learn science?, Mimeo, Cheltenham and Gloucester College of Higher Education.

Ross, K. A. (1991) Burning: a constructive not a destructive process, *School Science Review*, **72**(251), 45.

Ross, K. A. (1997) Many substances but only five structures, *School Science Review*, **78**(284), 79–87.

Ross, K. A. (1998) Science: Brenda grapples with the properties of a mern, in M. Littledyke and L. Huxford (eds), *Teaching the Primary Curriculum for Constructive Learning*. London: David Fulton.

Ross, K. A. (2000a) Matter and life – the cycling of materials, in M. Littledyke, K. A. Ross and E. Lakin (eds), *Science Knowledge and the Environment*. London: David Fulton Publishers.

Ross, K. A. (2000b) Constructing a scientific understanding of our environment, in M. Littledyke, K. A. Ross and E. Lakin (eds), *Science Knowledge and the Environment*. London: David Fulton Publishers.

Ross, K. A. (2000c) Energy and fuel, in M. Littledyke, K. A. Ross and E. Lakin (eds), *Science Knowledge and the Environment*. London: David Fulton Publishers.

Ross, K. A., Lakin, E., Littledyke, M. and Burch, G. (2002) *Science Issues and the National Curriculum* (CD-ROM). Cheltenham: University of Gloucestershire (www.glos.ac.uk/science-issues).

Ross, K.A. and Sutton, C. R. (1982) Concept profiles and the cultural context, *European Journal of Science Education*, **4**(3), 311–23.

SSERC (1997) *Hazardous Chemicals Manual*. Edinburgh: SSERC.

Stavey, R. and Berkovitz, B. (1980) Cognitive conflict as the basis for teaching cognitive aspects of the concept of temperature, *Science Education*, **64**(5), 679–92.

Sutton, C. (1992) *Words, Science and Learning*. Milton Keynes: Open University Press.

Taber, K. S. (2002) A core concept in teaching chemistry, *School Science Review*, **84**(306), 105–10.

Turner, T. and DiMarco, W. (1998) *Learning to Teach Science in the Secondary School*. London: Routledge.

Twenty-first Century Science Team (2003) 21st Century Science – a new flexible model for GCSE science, *School Science Review*, **85**(310), 27.

Watt, D. and Russell, T. (1990) *Primary SPACE Reports*. Liverpool: Liverpool University Press.

West, L. H. T. and Pines, A. L. (eds) (1985) *Cognitive Structure and Conceptual Change*. Orlando, FL: Academic Press.

West, R. (ed.) (1984) *Towards the Specification of Minimum Entitlement: Brenda and Friends*. London: Schools Council Publications.

Williams, J. D. (2002) Ideas and evidence in science: the portrayal of scientists in GCSE textbooks, *School Science Review*, **84**(307), 89.

Index

Note: linked page refs are indicated with / (e.g. 41/44)

Printed in the United Kingdom
by Lightning Source UK Ltd.
126277UK00008B/91-92/A